CB $ 4.95

FROM EXPERIENCE

a basic rhetoric and reader

a
self-instructional
writing course

FROM EXPERIENCE

a basic rhetoric and reader

MONTE M. HART
BENSON R. SCHULMAN

Los Angeles Pierce College

WM. C. BROWN COMPANY PUBLISHERS

To Sandra Schulman
    for editorial criticism, encouragement, and forbearance . . .

To Mary Hart
    for encouragement and more forbearance . . .

To Laura, Mark, Marlyssa, Randy, and Stephanie
    for providing much sound, fury, and cheerfulness . . .

To Charles Cobb, Professor of English at Los Angeles Pierce College,
    whose advice was most helpful . . .

To our many students
    who participated in the years of trial and error . . .

CONTENTS

PREFACE

We are convinced that there are better ways of learning to write than are conventionally used. This book is the product of that conviction, and some years of experimentation, based upon the premise that written expression proceeds best from the individual's desire and *need* to record his own experiences and ideas.

The text is designed to be flexible; that is, instructor and student are encouraged to select from the contents that which seems most appropriate to the individual need of the learner. On the other hand, the book may be followed systematically to its conclusion.

Motivation for Reluctant Students

The text is constructed to meet the problems of the many college students who have not as yet learned to enjoy writing. Therefore, the experience and process of written expression are introduced in an Orientation section in order to build motivation, and initial assignments are based upon the student's own personal experiences. Thereafter, the student is led (through gradually expanding experiences—from the strictly personal to objective analysis of ideas and literary works) to lose his fear of writing and to *wish* to express himself because he has a *purpose* for doing so.

Self-Instructional Approach

The course is meant to be largely self-instructional, leaving the instructor free to work with students individually.

Delineation of Objectives and Criteria

The text shows the use of objectives and criteria. Objectives are specified generally in Part I, Chapter 1, of Orientation, and specifically for all writing samples. Within each writing sample, furthermore, criteria are weighted for contents, but the *suggested* criteria for English mechanics are left to the instructor's discretion as to weighting.

Contents of Instruction

Instruction in rhetoric is divided into two categories, narration and exposition. Narration, which is introduced first, offers the student an effective style for writing about his own experiences and explains this form of rhetoric in an easily understood manner. Since experience is essentially chronological (a sequence of events), the initial use of narration, which stresses active verbs, lends power to the student's ability to express himself about his own background.

Exposition, which includes the conventional categories of argumentation, rational organization, definition, and others, is introduced after the student has had experience in narration. The treatment of exposition, furthermore, stresses the related nature of the forms of expository writing to give the student insight into the purpose of rhetorical structure as a medium of self-expression.

Individualization of Instruction

The materials of the course may be individualized at the instructor's option. That is, not all students need be required to complete all of the same writing samples. In fact, this approach may be the most effective instructional technique for motivating students, for rarely is an English class sufficiently homogeneous to warrant identical treatment for all. Thus, a student who shows special promise early in the course may be encouraged to "go through" the self-instructional lessons at an accelerated speed and to complete only the selected writing samples prescribed by the instructor. On the other hand, the student who learns more slowly may be allowed to follow a more moderate plan to build his skills.

Many materials from the text may be assigned by the instructor according to personal preference. Otherwise, he may prescribe many chapters, in any order he chooses, according to individual student need. Such materials, for example, include paragraphing, which may be prescribed whenever needed; outlining; and the various chapters on organizing the essay. To facilitate individualization, the evaluation sheets provided for writing samples already contain prescriptive assignments from the textbook to deal with many types of student errors. The instructor need only encircle the printed prescriptions to assign them as necessary.

Suggested Approach to Instruction in English Mechanics

Although selected materials concerning sentence structure, pronouns, verbs, and punctuation are presented because they are important to the rhetorical content of the text, a complete treatment of mechanics is not included. The authors suggest the supplementary use of a mechanics text or handbook so that the teacher may prescribe *individual study for students on the basis of their errors.* We have found that even reluctant students can see purpose in such study and, thus, are more inclined to learn.

Use of Assignment-Evaluation Forms

Each of the evaluation forms provided for writing samples is placed *in duplicate* in an addendum at the end of the text as well as within each chapter. These forms are for the convenience of the instructor who may, if he wishes, ask students to remove and submit duplicate forms with writing samples. Thus, when grading papers, the instructor may conveniently make an original and carbon copy of his evaluation, returning one to the student with his graded paper and retaining one for his own records. Collected evaluation forms show a detailed record of student progress throughout the semester.

A Final Comment

The materials in this text have been validated by instructors from three different colleges. Collectively, these individuals have reported on the positive results of delineation of objectives and criteria and the advantages of teaching reluctant students on the basis of the students' own experiences. The instructors have also reported on how easily the materials are adaptable to individual instructor preference and student need.

Finally, the instructors have made a few suggestions which are repeated here. First, all students show increased motivation if they are exposed to Part I of the text which is designed to build interest and dissipate fear. Second, Parts II and III, which deal with narration and exposition, may be followed either systematically or according to instructor preference; both approaches, apparently, work well. Third, the degree to which the instructor individualizes the course according to student need correlates positively with student success.

Thanks are extended to those who participated in developing the present form of the text: James Simmons and Dorothy Millhouse of Los Angeles City College, Los Angeles, California; Donna Croucher of Maple Woods Community College, Kansas City, Missouri; and to our colleagues and students at Los Angeles Pierce College and elsewhere who offered much helpful criticism and encouragement.

Monte M. Hart
Benson R. Schulman

ACKNOWLEDGMENTS

Literary Selections

"The Unspeakable Words," from *99 Fables by William March*, edited by William T. Going. Copyright © 1960, The University of Alabama Press.

"MacArthur Park" by Jimmy Webb, Copyright 1968, Canopy Music Inc. Used with permission of the publisher.

From *Teacher: Anne Sullivan Macy* by Helen Keller. Copyright © 1955 by Helen Keller. Reprinted by permission of Doubleday & Company, Inc.

From "Style in Science" by John Rader Platt. Used with permission of the author. Published in *Harper's Magazine*, October, 1956.

"Father and Son" by Art Seidenbaum, Copyright 1970, *Los Angeles Times*. Reprinted by permission.

From "The Jungle Sluggard" in *Jungle Days*, by William Beebe. Permission of G.P. Putnam's Sons (1925).

"It's Hard for Collegians to Live up to Roles" by Art Buchwald. Copyright June 16, 1968, by permission of Art Buchwald.

Excerpt from "A Clean, Well-Lighted Place" (Copyright 1933 Charles Scribner's Sons; renewal copyright © 1961 Ernest Hemingway) is reprinted by permission of Charles Scribner's Sons from *Winner Take Nothing*, pages 18-20, by Ernest Hemingway.

"University Days," Copyright © 1933, 1961, James Thurber. From *My Life and Hard Times*, published by Harper & Row. Originally printed in *The New Yorker*. By permission.

"The Unicorn in The Garden," Copyright © 1940, James Thurber. Copyright © 1968, Helen Thurber. From *Fables for Our Time*, published by Harper & Row. Originally printed in *The New Yorker*. By permission.

Walter Lippmann, "Edison: Inventor of Invention" from *Interpretations*. Copyright 1936 by The Macmillan Company, renewed 1964 by Walter Lippmann.

"Crime and Barbaric Punishment" reprinted by permission of The World Publishing Company from *For 2¢ Plain* by Harry Golden. Copyright © 1959, 1958, 1957, 1956, 1955, 1952, 1948, 1945, 1943 by Harry Golden.

"Dog" by Lawrence Ferlinghetti from *A Coney Island of The Mind*. Copyright © 1958 by Lawrence Ferlinghetti. Reprinted by permission of New Directions Publishing Corporation.

From "Private World of the Man with a Book," by Harold Taylor, January 7, 1961, *Saturday Review*. Copyright 1961, Saturday Review, Inc., by permission.

"Truth Is A Red Herring," by Arthur Hoppe. Copyright © April 30, 1965, Chronicle Publishing Company, by permission of author.

"Wallace" by Richard Rovere. Reprinted by permission; Copyright © 1950, The New Yorker Magazine, Inc.

"The Principles of Poor Writing," Merrill, P.W., *Scientific Monthly*, Vol. 64, pp. 72-74, January, 1947, by permission.

From *The Sensitives* by Louis Charbonneau. Copyright © 1968 by Bantam Books, Inc. Copyright © 1968 by Deane Romano, by permission.

"Do Insects Think?" by Robert Benchley from *The Benchley Roundup*, A Selection by Nathaniel Benchley. Copyright, 1922 by Harper & Row, Publishers, Inc., by permission of publisher.

"Weather Records" by Robert Benchley from *The Benchley Roundup*, A Selection by Nathaniel Benchley. Copyright, 1938 by Robert C. Benchley By permission of Harper & Row, Publishers, Inc.

From p. 49 in *The True Believer* by Eric Hoffer. (Harper & Row, 1951). Reprinted by permission of Harper & Row, Publishers, Inc.

"Over-Generalizing: Fallacy Number One, Secundum Quid" from *Guides to Straight Thinking* by Stuart Chase. Copyright, 1954 by The Reader's Digest Association. Copyright © 1956 by Stuart Chase. Reprinted by permission of Harper & Row, Publishers, Inc.

From *Ishi in Two Worlds* by Theodora Kroeber, page 5, paragraph 2, University of California Press, 1961. Originally published by the University of California Press; reprinted by permission of The Regents of the University of California.

"Nobel Peace Prize Acceptance Speech" by Martin Luther King, Jr. Reprinted by permission of Joan Daves. Copyright © 1964 by the Nobel Foundation.

From *Zorba The Greek* by Nikos Kazantzakis. Copyright © 1952 by Simon and Schuster, Inc. Reprinted by permission of the publisher.

From "Birches" from *The Poetry of Robert Frost* edited by Edward Connery Lathem. Copyright 1916, © 1969 by Holt, Rinehart and Winston, Inc. Copyright 1944 by Robert Frost. Reprinted by permission of Holt, Rinehart and Winston, Inc.

"August 2002: Night Meeting" from *The Martian Chronicles* by Ray Bradbury. Copyright 1946, 1948, 1949, 1950, 1958 by Ray Bradbury. Reprinted by permission of the Harold Matson Company, Inc.

"February 2002: The Locusts" from *The Martian Chronicles* by Ray Bradbury. Copyright 1946, 1948, 1949, 1950, 1958 by Ray Bradbury. Reprinted by permission of the Harold Matson Company, Inc.

"Mother to Son" by Langston Hughes. Copyright 1926 by Alfred A. Knopf, Inc., and renewed 1954 by Langston Hughes. Reprinted from *Selected Poems*, by Langston Hughes, by permission of the publisher.

"The Girls in Their Summer Dresses," Copyright 1939 and renewed 1967 by Irwin Shaw. Reprinted from *Selected Short Stories of Irwin Shaw;* by permission of Random House, Inc.

From *The Little Prince* by Antoine de Saint-Exupery, copyright 1943, by Harcourt Brace Jovanovich, Inc., and reprinted with their permission.

From *"Where Did You Go?" "Out" "What Did You Do?" "Nothing"* by Robert Paul Smith. Drawings by James J. Spanfeller. Reprinted by permission of W.W. Norton & Company, Inc. Copyright © 1957 by Robert Paul Smith.

"Carbon Monoxide Poisoning" from *An Introduction to The Study of Experimental Medicine* by Claude Bernard. By permission of Abelard-Schuman Limited.

"Introduction" by Isaac Asimov. Copyright © 1964 by Isaac Asimov. From the book *Adding A Dimension* by Isaac Asimov. Reprinted by permission of Doubleday & Company, Inc.

"Bandit" from *Goldfinger* by Ian Fleming. Copyright 1959, by permission of The Macmillan Company.

From *Another Country* by James Baldwin. Copyright © 1960, 1962 by James Baldwin. Used by permission of the publisher, The Dial Press.

"Young Man Axelbrod" by Sinclair Lewis from *Selected Short Stories* of Sinclair Lewis, 1917; by permission of R.L. Baltimore, Jr.

The Answer by Philip Wylie. Copyright, 1955 by The Curtis Publishing Company. Reprinted by permission of Holt, Rinehart and Winston, Inc.

Paintings, Photographs and Sketches

Photographic collage of faces, Take A Look around You, by a student photographer, John T. Rourke, by permission.

"The Ragpicker" by Edouard Manet; by permission of The Norton Simon Foundation, Los Angeles.

"Premiere" by Stuart Davis; by permission of Los Angeles County Museum of Art; Art Museum Council Fund.

"The Lovers" by Fred C. Money, Jr.; by permission of the owner.

"La Mer" by Max Ernst; from Mr. and Mrs. William Preston Harrison Collection; by permission of Los Angeles County Museum of Art.

A Detail from Studies of Expression for Battle of Anghiari by Leonardo da Vinci; original in Budapest Museum of Fine Arts (public domain).

"The Story of Meek" by Roger Johnson; by permission of the owner.

"Berry's World" by Jim Berry; reprinted by permission of Newspaper Enterprises Association, Inc.

Original sketches by Linda Schain, by permission.

Introduction

Figure 1. What forms of written expression did his people leave?

Purposes and Contents

This book was written for you, the student. It focuses upon your needs and emphasizes your growth in composition and reading skills through acquiring greater appreciation and understanding of the use of language as a function of *your own purposes*. The approach of this book is built upon the premise that you will learn if you are interested in what you do, if you see personal relevance in what you do, and if you are convinced that you are being treated as an individual and not merely as one member of a group.

Individualization of Instruction

The method of this book is individualized, which means, generally, that you are asked to study those things which you do not know and are not asked to study what you do not need. Other characteristics include the following:

1. Your needs are diagnosed through your own performance.
2. You are assigned work, based upon your own performance.
3. You are encouraged to move through the book at your own speed.
4. You are given the opportunity to work independently, in small groups, or as part of the entire class.
5. You are not penalized with low grades for poor initial performance, but are encouraged to study and revise your work until you and the instructor are satisfied.
6. Your own experiences, interests, purposes, and creativity are the basis of most of your composition.
7. You are encouraged to manage your own time and work habits.

Purpose of the Book

The purpose of the instruction provided in this book is to stimulate your growth in composition skills and to promote your ability to read with greater appreciation and comprehension. Finally, your growth in managing your own time and in improving your work habits is as important as any body of subject matter you might learn. Your composition assignments and your reading and discussion of literature are individualized as much as possible with the frank desire of building within you a "hunger" to learn for your own benefit. Your own purpose is to be as selfish as possible: *to acquire the skills and knowledge that will serve you best.* In order to fulfill your purposes as efficiently as possible, you are especially encouraged to seek your instructor's help and to participate in evaluating your progress as well as in planning future assignments.

Contents of the Book

1. Orientation, including objectives.
2. Lessons in composition with early emphasis upon narrative, and later, emphasis upon expository writing, with stress upon your experience, creativity, and interests.
3. Literary selections which are integrated with the lessons in composition to serve as models and to introduce writers whose work you may enjoy.
4. Assignment-Evaluation sheets for each writing assignment in the course to specify the contents and the precise criteria upon which contents are graded.
5. Student writing samples of the major expository assignments in the course.

Special Features of the Book

Composition lessons are arranged in order of difficulty but it is possible that you may not need to complete all lessons if your progress is rapid enough. Your instructor may permit you to omit some material if your skill and initiative warrant this exception, or you may, instead, be encouraged to accelerate the completion of your work.

You should seek help from your instructor if you need it, but lessons are designed to be self-instructional so that you can acquire needed skills independently. You should accept as much personal responsibility for your own growth as possible.

Objectives and Criteria

You will meet the objectives and criteria for composition by performing assignments that you and the instructor select. Your performance will show the following:

1. You can use appropriate English vocabulary, with emphasis upon the standard language of educated people.
2. You can organize your ideas clearly and effectively.
3. You can write both narrative and expository compositions to show experience and express ideas.
4. You can stress specific words and concrete ideas as opposed to generalities and abstract terms.
5. You can follow the directions for the contents of each assignment.

You are expected *through your performances* to show competence in composition and literature in the following areas of study:

I. Composition Style and Form

    A. Narrative Composition

        1. Sentence style

        2. Techniques

           a. Narrative hook (introduction)

           b. Imagism (specific detail)

           c. Recording sense impressions

               (1) Interesting use of words

               (2) Comparison through metaphor and simile

               (3) Use of contrast

               (4) Onomatopoeia

        3. Significance (theme)

        4. Narrative assignments

           a. Moments of experience

           b. Narrative-mood sequence

    B. Expository Composition

        1. Sentence style

        2. Purposes of exposition

           a. Definition

           b. Description of an object or a process

           c. Analysis

           d. Argumentation

        3. Techniques of exposition

           a. Specific details and sense impressions

           b. Concrete versus abstract words

           c. Concrete example

         4. Paragraph structure

           a. Introduction

           b. Development

           c. Coherence

           d. Termination

        5. Essay organization

           a. Introduction

           b. Development

               (1) Chronological

               (2) Rational or logical (to persuade)

               (3) Topical

           c. Termination

        6. Outlining

        7. Expository assignments

           a. Describing a group and the process of acquiring information about the group

           b. Definition of one's purpose in education

           c. Summary of an essay

           d. Identify theme and support by reference to work

           e. Present a critical opinion of a work

           f. Report on a novel

II. Comprehension and Structure of Literature

    A. Identifying Author's Purpose

    B. Interpreting Theme

C. Understanding Character Development in Narration

D. Understanding Plot Development in Narration

E. Understanding Method of Development in Exposition

F. Acquiring Insight into Effectiveness
   1. Sentence structure
      a. Economy
      b. Simplicity
      c. Precision
      d. Variety
   2. Use of words
      a. Appropriateness
      b. Precision
      c. Vividness
      d. Figures of speech

G. Applying Literature to Your Own Life
   1. Acquisition of new ideas
   2. Use as a stimulus to improve style of writing
   3. Use as a source of personal pleasure

How to Perform Your Lessons

You should follow a routine procedure to prepare your lessons thoroughly.

1. Read the chapters in the text carefully, following all instructions and completing the exercises. All exercises are followed by the correct answers so that you may check yourself.
2. Complete all assigned correlated readings for each lesson, including answering all questions and studying vocabulary words which follow the readings. The lessons, reading questions, and vocabulary may be discussed in class, small groups, and/or individual meetings.
3. Prepare all composition assignments according to the ASSIGNMENT-EVALUATION SHEETS, checking carefully that you have met criteria.
4. Study the examples of narration within the lessons which contain narrative writing assignments, and examine the sample student essays before performing expository assignments.
5. Always write rough drafts of your work, followed by as many rewrites as necessary, to be certain you have done your best.

A Few Final Words

Every effort has been made to stimulate your interest in the work you perform. For example, most of your composition assignments are based directly upon your own experiences on the theory that you can write best about the things you know most. Second, the reading materials have been especially selected to appeal to your interest, to help you gain insight into your composition assignments, and to help you grow in your ability to comprehend and appreciate literature.

Finally, *you* are the most important "feature" of this course of study. The materials were created for you, but they are wasted unless you make the effort to profit from them, unless you perform your assignments honestly, and unless you write and rewrite your compositions until they are the best work you can do. Ultimately, your education is in your hands!

Figure 2. Take a look around you. Reprinted by permission of John T. Rourke.

How Does a Writer Write?

Take a look around you. Notice the people in this class. Go ahead! Look at them; then resume reading.

Were you interested? Did you feel strange? If you did feel strange, perhaps you should consider that your success in this class could depend upon the way you and the other members of the class affect each other, as well as your attitude toward the subject and your efforts. Often, the way a class "jells" is an important factor in the process of education, and every class develops its own personality. What will be the personality of this group? Who are these people? What are their backgrounds, their sum of experiences? What can you learn from them? What can they learn from you? How well can you work together? How will you compete with each other? How can you cooperate?

There are many bits of information (data) you need before you can really begin to know this group. For example, names, ages, and samples of interests could be a good start. Suppose you assume that you are going to interview one of your neighbors in this class for the purpose of becoming acquainted. Prepare a list of questions you would like answered.

Take seven minutes, no more, to make up this list of questions you would use to interview one person. Try to use the kind of data that is interesting. Write your questions below.

1. Name?

2. Age?

3.

4.

5.

6.

7.

8.

Questions continued

9.

10.

11.

12.

13.

14.

15.

16.

Now that you have compiled a list of questions to obtain information about one member of this class, follow these steps:

1. Turn to your neighbor on your right or left and introduce yourself.
2. Compare your list of questions with his list.
3. Cooperate with your neighbor in preparing one final list of questions, based upon his list and yours.
4. Use the combined list of questions to interview your neighbor and permit him to interview you.
5. Record your neighbor's answers and allow him to record yours.
6. Complete the process within fifteen minutes.

You may record your answers below:

If you have conducted your interviews well, you should be reasonably informed about your neighbor. Can you pass this information on to others? While you are giving this information, can you be interesting? Let us see. *Try* to introduce your neighbors to each other in as interesting a manner as possible. Follow these steps:

1. Each pair of people will stand in turn, and each of the partners will introduce the person he interviewed.
2. Start with the first row on the left, facing the front of the room.
3. Follow this procedure until everyone in the class has been introduced.
4. Listen carefully and take notes about the interesting things you see or hear about the people speaking, those being introduced, or the procedure itself. Take accurate notes; you may need them.
5. Before starting the procedure, each of us should consult his interview notes to make final preparations. We'll begin our introductions in three minutes.

Now that you have finished introducing each other, let's talk about the experience. To get some idea of the things we might discuss, look at the questions below; however, we are not limited to them.

1. Were you uneasy?
2. What was the most difficult or challenging aspect of what we did?
3. Did you notice any voices in particular?
4. Did you notice any bits of information in particular?
5. How do you feel about the group now that you have been exposed to so much information about it?
6. How do you feel about the procedure we have followed? Would you recommend any changes?
7. Do you realize that you have just completed your first composition for this class, but instead of writing it, you did it orally?
8. Do you realize that you have just completed a small "piece of research"?

Understanding What We Did

Let's review the experience we just had and the steps we followed. We met, we were given a job to do, and we were told how to do the job. We collected information; we organized it; and, finally, each one of us delivered a verbal composition. In essence, we performed a small piece of research and reported the data resulting from that research.

Can you restate our procedure in *formal* terms? There were five steps. Supply the missing formal term in each of the five statements which follow. *Check answers on the following page.*

1. We were given a job to do. This became our_____.

2. We were told how to do the job. This was our_____.

3. Each of us interviewed one person. This was our_____.

4. We arranged the interview data _____.

5. We reported our information _____.

ANSWERS: 1. purpose; 2. organization of research; 3. research—collection of data; 4. organization of data; 5. writing

Do you now see that the things we say or write, even for school, come out of our experiences? What was the impact of our class experience on you? Did you react differently to various elements of the proceedings? Were you shy, pleased, nervous, stimulated, interested, or irritated? Can you record the experience and your feelings about it to give a reader an accurate picture?

> **Writing Sample Number One:** Follow the directions on the Assignment-Evaluation sheet on the next page.

WRITING SAMPLE 1—EVALUATION

Write a unified composition which gives your reaction to your experiences in learning about your English class. Deal with the ideas listed in "required contents."

Length: approximately 125 words

Required in Contents	Full	Earned	For Study
1. What were your feelings about this class before the interviews and speeches began?	34		
2. What is your attitude toward class now that you know its members better?	33		
3. What are your feelings about the procedures used to introduce the members of the class to each other?	33		
TOTAL	100		

Instructor's Comments: (Note—proofread your work carefully or you may be given a study assignment in mechanics for the errors you make.)

ENGLISH MECHANICS: Instructor Assigns Values for Criteria

Content Areas	Full	Earned	For Study
ORGANIZATION: Introduction	_____		Chapter 13
Chronological Organization	_____		Chapter 15
Topical Organization	_____		Chapter 16
Rational Organization	_____		Chapter 17
Smooth Development	_____		Chapter 14
Termination	_____		Chapter 18
PARAGRAPHING: Introduction			Page 163
Development (unity)	_____		Page 165
Development (coherence)			Page 168
SENTENCES: completeness; variety; economy; use of modifiers; pronouns; agreement; use of verbs, phrases, clauses	_____		
USE OF LANGUAGE: Level of usage Idiomatic usage Vividness	_____		Chapter 8
PUNCTUATION AND CAPITALIZATION and related graphics: Quotation marks	_____		Chapter 7
SPELLING:			
TOTAL	100		

Mechanics not in this text are assigned in supplementary text.

Figure 3. What is the artist trying to show us? "The Ragpicker" by Manet. Permission from The Norton Simon Foundation, Los Angeles.

To Tell or to Show:
The Writer's Purpose

Read "Young Man Axelbrod" by Sinclair Lewis which follows. As you read the story for the first time, "listen" for the total effect, but try, especially, to understand the character of Knute Axelbrod.

YOUNG MAN AXELBROD

The cottonwood is a tree of a slovenly and plebeian habit. Its woolly wisps turn gray the lawns and engender neighborhood hostilities about our town. Yet it is a mighty tree, a refuge and an inspiration; the sun flickers in its towering foliage, whence the tattoo of locusts enlivens our dusty summer afternoons. From the wheat country out to the sagebrush plains between the buttes and the Yellowstone it is the cottonwood that keeps a little grateful shade for sweating homesteaders.

In Joralemon we called Knute Axelbrod "Old Cottonwood." As a matter of fact, the name was derived not so much from the quality of the man as from the wide grove about his gaunt white house and red barn. He made a comely row of trees on each side of the country road, so that a humble, daily sort of man, driving beneath them in his lumber wagon might fancy himself lord of a private avenue. And at sixty-five Knute was like one of his own cottonwoods, his roots deep in the soil, his trunk weathered by rain and blizzard and baking August noons, his crown spread to the wide horizon of day and the enormous sky of a prairie night.

This immigrant was an American even in speech. Save for a weakness about his j's and w's, he spoke the twangy Yankee English of the land. He was the more American because, in his native Scandinavia, he had dreamed of America as a land of light. Always, through disillusion and weariness, he beheld America as the nursery for justice, for broad, fair towns, and eager talk; and always he kept a young soul that dared to desire beauty.

As a lad Knute Axelbrod had wished to be a famous scholar, to learn the ease of foreign tongues, the romance of history, to unfold in the graciousness of the wise books. When he first came to America he worked in a sawmill all day and studied all evening. He mastered enough book learning to teach district school for two terms; then when he was only eighteen, a great-hearted pity for faded Lena Wesselius moved him to marry her. Gay enough, doubtless, was their hike by prairie schooner to new farm lands, but Knute was promptly caught in a net of poverty and family. From eighteen to fifty-eight he was always snatching children away from death or the farm away from mortgages.

He had to be content—and generously content he was—with the second-hand glory of his children's success and, for himself, with pilfered hours of reading—that reading of big, thick, dismal volumes of history and economics which the lone, mature learner chooses. Without ever losing his desire for strange cities and the dignity of towers, he stuck to his farm. He acquired a half-section, free from debt, fertile, well-stocked, adorned with a cement silo, a chicken-run, a new windmill. He became comfortable, secure, and then he was ready, it seemed, to die; for at sixty-three his work was done, and he was unneeded and alone.

His wife was dead. His sons had scattered afar, one a dentist in Fargo, another a farmer in the Golden Valley. He had turned over his farm to his daughter and son-in-law. They had begged him to live with them, but Knute refused.

"No," he said, "you must learn to stand on your own feet. I will not give you the farm. You pay me four hundred dollars a year rent, and I live on that and vatch you from my hill."

On a rise beside the lone cottonwood which he loved best of all his trees Knute built a tar-paper shack, and here he "bached it": cooked his meals, made his bed—sometimes, sat in the sun, read many books from the Joralemon library, and began to feel that he was free of the yoke of citizenship which he had borne all his life.

For hours at a time he sat on a backless kitchen chair before the shack, a wide-shouldered man, white-bearded, motionless; a seer despite his grotesquely baggy trousers, his collarless shirt. He looked across the miles of stubble to the steeple of the Jack-rabbit Forks church and meditated upon the uses of life. At first he could not break the rigidity of habit. He rose at five, found work in cleaning his cabin and cultivating his garden, had dinner exactly at twelve, and went to bed by afterglow. But little by little he discovered that he could be irregular without being arrested. He stayed abed till seven or even eight. He got a large, deliberate tortoise-shell cat, and played games with it; let it lap milk upon the table, called it the Princess, and confided to it that he had a "sneaking idee" that men were fools to work so hard. Around this coatless old man, his stained waistcoat flapping about a huge torso, in a shanty of rumpled bed and pine table covered with sheets of food-daubed newspapers, hovered all the passionate aspiration of youth and the dreams of ancient beauty.

He began to take long walks by night. In his necessitous life, night had ever been a period of heavy slumber in close rooms. Now he discovered the mystery of the dark; saw the prairies wide flung and misty beneath the moon, heard the voices of grasses and cottonwoods and drowsy birds. He tramped for miles. His boots were dew-soaked, but he did not heed. He stopped upon hillocks, shyly threw wide his arms, and stood worshipping the naked, slumbering land.

These excursions he tried to keep secret, but they were bruited abroad. Neighbors, good, decent fellows with no nonsense about walking in dew at night, when they were returning late from town, drunk, lashing their horses, and flinging whisky bottles from their racing democrat wagons, saw him, and they spread the tiding that Old Cottonwood was "getting nutty since he give up his farm to that son-in-law of his and retired. Seen the old codger wandering around at midnight. Wish I had his chance to sleep. Wouldn't catch me out in the night air."

Any rural community from Todd Center to Seringapatam is resentful of any person who varies from its standard, and is morbidly fascinated by any hint of madness. The countryside began to spy on Knute Axelbrod, to ask him questions, and to stare from the road at his shack. He was sensitively aware of it, and inclined to be surly to inquisitive acquaintances. Doubtless that was the beginning of his great pilgrimage.

As a part of the general wild license of his new life—really, he once roared at that startled cat, the Princess: "By gollies! I ain't going to brush my teeth tonight. All my life I've brushed 'em, and alvays vanted to skip a time vunce"—Knute took considerable pleasure in degenerating in his taste in scholarship. He wilfully declined to finish *The Conquest of Mexico*, and began to read light novels borrowed from the Joralemon library. So he rediscovered the lands of dancing and light wines, which all his life he had desired. Some economics and history he did read, but every evening he would stretch out in his buffalo-horn chair, his feet on the cot and the Princess in his lap, and invade Zenda or fall in love with Trilby.

Among the novels, he chanced upon a highly optimistic story of Yale in which a worthy young man "earned his way through" college, stroked the crew, won Phi Beta Kappa, and had the most entertaining, yet moral, conversations on or adjacent to "the dear old fence."

As a result of this chronicle, at about three o'clock one morning when Knute Axelbrod was sixty-four years of age, he decided that he would go to college! All his life he had wanted to. Why not do it?

When he awoke in the morning he was not so sure about it as when he had gone to sleep. He saw himself as ridiculous, a ponderous, oldish man among clean-limbed youths, like a dusty cottonwood among silver birches. But for months he wrestled and played with that idea of a great pilgrimage to the Mount of Muses; for he really supposed college to be that sort of place. He believed that all college students, except for the wealthy idlers, burned to acquire learning. He pictured Harvard and Yale and Princeton as ancient groves set with marble temples, before which large groups of Grecian youths talked gently about astronomy and good government. In his picture they never cut classes or ate.

With a longing for music and books and graciousness such as the most ambitious boy could never comprehend, this thick-faced prairie farmer dedicated himself to beauty, and defied the unconquerable power of approaching old age. He sent for college catalogues and schoolbooks, and diligently began to prepare himself for college.

He found Latin irregular verbs and the whimsicalities of algebra fiendish. They had nothing to do with actual life as he had lived it. But he mastered them; he studied twelve hours a day, as once he had plodded through eighteen hours a day in the hayfield. With history and English literature he had comparatively little trouble; already he knew much of them from his recreative reading. From German neighbors he had picked up enough Plattdeutsch to make German easy. The trick of study began to come back to him from his small schoolteaching of forty-five years before. He began to believe that he could really put it through. He kept assuring himself that in college, with rare and sympathetic instructors to help him, there would not be this baffling search, this nervous strain.

But the unreality of the things he studied did disillusion him, and he tired of his new game. He kept it up chiefly because all his life he had kept up onerous labor without any taste for it. Toward the autumn of the second year of his eccentric life he no longer believed that he would ever go to college.

Then a busy little grocer stopped him on the street in Joralemon and quizzed him about his studies, to the delight of the informal club which always loafs at the corner of the hotel.

Knute was silent, but dangerously angry. He remembered just in time how he had once laid wrathful hands upon a hired man, and somehow the man's collarbone had been broken. He turned away and walked home, seven miles, still boiling. He picked up the Princess, and, with her mewing on his shoulder, tramped out again to enjoy the sunset.

He stopped at a reedy slough. He gazed at a hopping plover without seeing it. He plucked at his beard. Suddenly he cried:

"I am going to college. It opens next week. I t'ink that I can pass the examinations."

Two days later he had moved the Princess and his sticks of furniture to his son-in-law's house, had bought a new slouch hat, a celluloid collar, and a solemn suit of black, had wrestled with God in prayer through all of a star-clad night, and had taken the train for Minneapolis, on the way to New Haven.

While he stared out of the car window Knute was warning himself that the millionaires' sons would make fun of him. Perhaps they would haze him. He bade himself avoid all these sons of Belial and cleave to his own people, those who "earned their way through."

At Chicago he was afraid with a great fear of the lightning flashes that the swift crowds made on his retina, the batteries of ranked motorcars that charged at him. He prayed, and ran for his train to New York. He came at last to New Haven.

Not with gibing rudeness, but with politely quizzical eyebrows Yale received him, led him through entrance examinations, which after sweaty plowing with the pen, he barely passed, and found for him a roommate. The roommate was a large-browed, soft white grub named Ray Gribble, who had been teaching school in New England, and seemed chiefly to desire college training so that he might make more money as a teacher. Ray Gribble was a hustler; he instantly got work tutoring the awkward son of a steel man, and for board he waited on table.

He was Knute's chief acquaintance. Knute tried to fool himself into thinking that he liked the grub, but Ray couldn't keep his damp hands off the old man's soul. He had the skill of a professional exhorter of young men in finding out Knute's motives, and when he discovered that Knute had a hidden desire to dabble in gay, polite literature, Ray said in a shocked way:

"Strikes me a man like you, that's getting old, ought to be thinking more about saving your soul than about all these frills. You leave this poetry and stuff to these foreigners and artists, and you stick to Latin and math and the Bible. I tell you, I've taught school, and I've learned by experience."

With Ray Gribble, Knute lived grubbily, an existence of torn comforters and a smelly lamp, of lexicons and logarithm tables. No leisurely loafing by fireplaces was theirs. They roomed in West Divinity, where gather the theologues, the lesser sort of law students, a whimsical genius or two, and a horde of unplaced freshmen and "scrub seniors."

Knute was shockingly disappointed, but he stuck to his room because outside of it he was afraid. He was a grotesque figure, and he knew it, a white-polled giant squeezed into a small seat in a classroom, listening to instructors younger than his own sons. Once he tried to sit on the fence. No one but "ringers" sat on the fence any more, and at the sight of him trying to look athletic and young, two upperclassmen snickered, and he sneaked away.

He came to hate Ray Gribble and his voluble companions of the submerged tenth of the class, the hewers of tutorial wood. It is doubtless safer to mock the flag than to question that best-established tradition of our democracy—that those who "earn their way through" college are necessarily stronger, braver, and more assured of success than the weaklings who talk by the fire. Every college story presents such a moral. But tremblingly the historian submits that Knute discovered that waiting on table did not make lads more heroic than did football or happy loafing. Fine fellows, cheerful and fearless, were many of the boys who "earned their way," and able to talk to richer classmates without fawning; but just as many of them assumed an abject respectability as the most convenient pose. They were pickers-up of unconsidered trifles; they toadied to the classmates whom they tutored; they wriggled before the faculty committee on scholarships; they looked pious at Dwight Hall prayer meetings to make an impression on the serious-minded; and they drank one glass of beer at Jake's to show the light-minded that they meant nothing offensive by their piety. In revenge for cringing to the insolent athletes whom they tutored, they would, when safe among their own kind, yammer about the "lack of democracy in colleges today." Not that they were so indiscreet as to do anything about it. They lacked the stuff of really rebellious souls. Knute listened to them and marveled. They sounded like young hired men talking behind his barn at harvest time.

This submerged tenth hated the dilettantes of the class even more than they hated the bloods. Against one Gilbert Washburn, a rich esthete with more manner than any freshman ought to have, they raged righteously. They spoke of seriousness and industry till Knute, who might once have desired to know lads like Washburn, felt ashamed of himself as a wicked, wasteful old man.

With the friends of his roommate began Knute's series of disillusions. Humbly though he sought, he found no inspiration and no comradeship. He was the freak of the class, and aside from the submerged tenth, his classmates were afraid of being "queered" by being seen with him.

As he was still powerful, one who could take up a barrel of pork on his knees, he tried to find friendship among the athletes. He sat at Yale Field, watching the football tryouts, and tried to get acquainted with the candidates. They stared at him and answered his questions grudgingly— beefy youths who in their simple-hearted way showed that they considered him plain crazy.

The place itself began to lose the haze of magic through which he had first seen it. Earth is earth, whether one sees it in Camelot or Joralemon or on the Yale campus—or possibly even in the Harvard yard! The buildings ceased to be temples to Knute; they became structures of brick or stone, filled with young men who lounged at windows and watched him amusedly as he tried to slip by.

The Gargantuan hall of Commons became a tri-daily horror because at the table where he dined were two youths, who, having uncommonly penetrating minds, discerned that Knute had a beard, and courageously told the world about it. One of them, named Atchison, was a superior person, very industrious and scholarly, glib in mathematics and manners. He despised Knute's lack of definite purpose in coming to college. The other was a play boy, a wit and a stealer of street signs, who had a wonderful sense for a subtle jest; and his references to Knute's beard shook the table with jocund mirth three times a day. So these youths of gentle birth drove the shambling, wistful old man away from Commons, and thereafter he ate at the lunch counter at the Black Cat.

Lacking the stimulus of friendship, it was the harder for Knute to keep up the strain of studying the long assignments. What had been a week's pleasure reading in his shack was now thrown at him as a day's task. But he would not have minded the toil if he could have found one as young as himself. They were all so dreadfully old, the money-earners, the serious laborers at athletics, the instructors who worried over their life work of putting marks in class-record books.

Then, on a sore, bruised day, Knute did meet one who was young.

Knute had heard that the professor who was the idol of the college had berated the too-earnest lads in his Browning class, and insisted that they read *Alice in Wonderland.* Knute floundered dustily about in a second-hand bookshop till he found an *Alice,* and he brought it home to read over his lunch of a hot-dog sandwich. Something in the grave absurdity of the book appealed to him, and he was chuckling over it when Ray Gribble came into the room and glanced at the reader.

"Huh!" said Mr. Gribble.

"That's a fine, funny book," said Knute.

"Huh! *Alice in Wonderland!* I've heard of it. Silly nonsense. Why don't you read something really fine, like Shakespeare or *Paradise Lost* ?"

"Vell—" said Knute, but that was all he could find to say.

With Ray Gribble's glassy eye on him, he could no longer roll and roar with the book. He wondered if indeed he ought not to be reading Milton's pompous anthropological misconceptions. He went unhappily out to an early history class, ably conducted by Blevins, Ph.D.

Knute admired Blevins, Ph.D. He was so tubbed and eye-glassed and terribly right. But most of Blevins' lambs did not like Blevins. They said he was a "crank." They read newspapers in his class and covertly kicked one another.

In the smug, plastered classroom, his arm leaning heavily on the broad tablet-arm of his chair, Knute tried not to miss one of Blevins' sardonic proofs that the correct date of the second marriage of Themistocles was two years and seven days later than the date assigned by that illiterate ass, Frutari of Padua. Knute admired young Blevins' performance, and he felt virtuous in application to these hard, unnonsensical facts.

He became aware that certain lewd fellows of the lesser sort were playing poker just behind him. His prairie-trained ear caught whispers of "Two to dole," and "Raise you two beans." Knute revolved, and frowned upon these mockers of sound learning. As he turned back he was aware that the offenders were chuckling, and continuing their game. He saw Blevins as merely a boy. He was sorry for him. He would do the boy a good turn.

When the class was over he hung about Blevins' desk till the other students had clattered out. He rumbled:

"Say, Professor, you're a fine fellow. I do something for you. If any of the boys makes themselves a nuisance, you yust call on me, and I spank the son of a guns."

Blevins, Ph.D., spake in a manner of culture and nastiness:

"Thanks so much, Axelbrod, but I don't fancy that will ever be necessary. I am supposed to be a reasonably good disciplinarian. Good day. Oh, one moment. There's something I've been wishing to speak to you about. I do wish you wouldn't try quite so hard to show off whenever I call on you during quizzes. You answer at such needless length, and you smile as though there were something highly amusing about me. I'm quite willing to have you regard me as a humorous figure, privately, but there are certain classroom conventions, you know, certain little conventions."

"Why, Professor!" wailed Knute. "I never make fun of you! I didn't know I smile. If I do, I guess it's yust because I am so glad when my stupid old head gets the lesson good."

"Well, well, that's very gratifying, I'm sure. And if you will be a little more careful—"

Blevins, Ph.D., smiled a toothy, frozen smile, and trotted off to the Graduates' Club, to be witty about old Knute and his way of saying "yust," while in the deserted classroom Knute sat chill, an old man and doomed. Through the windows came the light of Indian summer; clean, boyish cries rose from the campus. But the lover of autumn smoothed his baggy sleeve, stared at the blackboard, and there saw only the gray of October stubble about his distant shack. As he pictured the college watching him, secretly making fun of him and his smile, he was now faint and ashamed, now bull-angry. He was lonely for his cat, his fine chair of buffalo horns, the sunny doorstep of his shack, and the understanding land. He had been in college for about one month.

Before he left the classroom he stepped behind the instructor's desk and looked at an imaginary class.

"I might have stood there as a prof if I could have come earlier," he said softly to himself.

Calmed by the liquid autumn gold that flowed through the streets, he walked out Whitney Avenue toward the butte-like hill of East Rock. He observed the caress of the light upon the scarped rock, heard the delicate music of leaves, breathed in air pregnant with tales of old New England. He exulted:

"I could write poetry now if I yust—if I yust could write poetry!"

He climbed to the top of East Rock, whence he could see the Yale buildings like the towers of Oxford, Long Island Sound, and the white glare of Long Island itself beyond the water. He marveled that Knute Axelbrod of the cottonwood country was looking across an arm of the Atlantic to New York State.

He noticed a freshman on a bench at the edge of the rock, and he became irritated. The freshman was Gilbert Washburn, the snob, the dilettante, of whom Ray Gribble had once said: "That guy is the disgrace of the class. He doesn't go out for anything, high stand or Dwight Hall or anything else. Thinks he's so doggone much better than the rest of the fellows that he doesn't associate with anybody. Thinks he's literary, they say, and yet he doesn't even heel the 'lit' like the regular literary fellows! Got no time for loafing, mooning snob like that."

As Knute stared at the unaware Gil, whose profile was fine in outline against the sky, he was terrifically public-spirited and disapproving and that sort of moral thing. Though Gil was much too well-dressed, he seemed moodily discontented.

"What he needs is to work in a thrashing-crew and sleep in the hay," grumbled Knute almost in the virtuous manner of Gribble. "Then he vould know when he vas vell off, and not like he had the earache. Pff!"

Gil Washburn rose, trailed toward Knute, glanced at him, hesitated, sat down on Knute's bench.

"Great view!" he said. His smile was eager.

That smile symbolized to Knute all the art of life he had come to college to find. He tumbled out of his moral attitude with ludicrous haste, and every wrinkle of his weathered face creased deep as he answered:

"Yes; I t'ink the Acropolis must be like this here."

"Say, look here, Axelbrod; I've been thinking about you."

"Yas?"

"We ought to know each other. We two are the class scandal. We came here to dream, and these busy little goats like Atchison and Giblets, or whatever your roommate's name is, think we're fools not to go out for marks. You may not agree with me, but I've decided that you and I are precisely alike."

"What makes you t'ink I come here to dream?" bristled Knute.

"Oh, I used to sit near you at Commons and hear you try to quell jolly old Atchison whenever he got busy discussing the reasons for coming to college. That old, motheaten topic! I wonder if Cain and Abel didn't discuss it at the Eden Agricultural College. You know, Abel the mark-grabber, very pious and high stand, and Cain wanting to read poetry."

"Yes," said Knute, "and I guess Prof Adam say, 'Cain, don't you read this poetry; it von't help you in algebry'."

"Of course. Say, wonder if you'd like to look at this volume of Musset I was sentimental enough to lug up here today. Picked it up when I was abroad last year."

From his pocket Gil drew such a book as Knute had never seen before, a slender volume, in a strange language, bound in hand-tooled, crushed levant, an effeminate bibelot over which the prairie farmer gasped with luxurious pleasure. The book almost vanished in his big hands. With a timid forefinger he stroked the levant, ran through the leaves.

"I can't read it, but that's the kind of book I alvays t'ought there must be some like it," he sighed.

"Let me read you a little. It's French poetry."

Gil read aloud. He made of the alien verses a music which satisfied Knute's sixty-five years of longing for he had never known what.

"That's—that's fine," he said.

"Listen!" cried Gil. "Ysaye is playing up at Hartford tonight. Let's go hear him. We'll trolley up, make it in plenty of time. Tried to get some of the fellows to come, but they thought I was a nut."

What an Ysaye was, Knute Axelbrod had no notion, but "Sure!" he boomed.

When they got to Hartford they found that between them they had just enough money to get dinner, hear Ysaye from gallery seats, and return only as far as Meriden.

At Meriden, Gil suggested:

"Let's walk back to New Haven, then. Can you make it?"

Knute had no knowledge as to whether it was four miles or forty back to the campus, but "Sure!" he said. For the last few months he had been noticing that, despite his bulk, he had to be careful, but tonight he could have flown.

In the music of Ysaye, the first real musician he had ever heard Knute had found all the incredible things of which he had slowly been reading in William Morris and *Idylls of the King.* Tall knights he had beheld, and slim princesses in white samite, the misty gates of forlorn towns, and the glory of the chivalry that never was.

They did walk, roaring down the road beneath the October moon, stopping to steal apples and to exclaim over silvered fanedog. It was Gil who talked, and Knute who listened, for the most part; but Knute was lured into tales of the pioneer days, of blizzards, of harvesting, and of the first flame of the green wheat. Regarding the Atchisons and Gribbles of the class, both of them were youthfully bitter and supercilious. They were wandering minstrels, Gilbert the troubadour with his man-at-arms.

They reached the campus at about five in the morning.

Fumbling for words that would express his feeling, Knute stammered:

"Vell; it vas fine. I go to bed now and I dream about—"

"Bed? Rats! Never believe in winding up a party when it's going strong. Too few good parties. Besides, it's only the shank of the evening. Besides, we're hungry. Besides—oh besides! Wait here a second. I'm going up to my room to get some money, and we'll have some eats. Wait! Please do!"

Knute would have waited all night. He had lived sixty-five years and traveled fifteen hundred miles and endured Ray Gribble to find Gil Washburn.

Policemen wondered to see the celluloid-collared old man and the expensive-looking boy rolling arm in arm down Chapel Street in search of a restaurant suitable to poets. They were all closed.

"The Ghetto will be awake by now," said Gil. "We'll go buy some eats and take 'em up to my room. I've got some tea there."

Knute shouldered through dark streets beside him as naturally as though he had always been a nighthawk, with an aversion to anything as rustic as beds. Down on Oak Street, a place of low shops, smoky lights, and alley mouths, they found the slum already astir. Gil contrived to purchase boxed biscuits, cream cheese, chicken loaf, a bottle of cream. While Gil was chaffering, Knute stared out into the street milkily lighted by wavering gas and the first feebleness of coming day; he gazed upon Kosher signs and advertisements in Russian letters, shawled women and bearded rabbis; and as he looked he gathered contentment which he could never lose. He had traveled abroad tonight.

The room of Gil Washburn was all the useless, pleasant things Knute wanted it to be. There was more of Gil's Paris days in it than of his freshmanhood: cloisonné on the mantelpiece, Persian rugs, a silver tea service, etchings, and books. Knute Axelbrod of the tar-paper shack and piggy farmyards gazed in satisfaction. Vast-bearded, sunk in an easy-chair, he clucked amiably while Gil lighted a fire and spread a wicker table.

Over supper they spoke of great men and heroic ideals. It was good talk, and not unspiced with lively references to Gribble and Atchison and Blevins, all asleep now in their correct beds. Gil read snatches of Stevenson and Anatole France; then at last he read his own poetry.

It does not matter whether that poetry was good or bad. To Knute it was a miracle to find one who actually wrote it.

The talk grew slow and they began to yawn. Knute was sensitive to the lowered key of their Indian-summer madness, and he hastily rose. As he said good-by he felt as though he had but to sleep a little while and return to this unending night of romance.

But he came out of the dormitory upon day. It was six-thirty in the morning, with a still, hard light upon red-brick walls.

"I can go to his room plenty times now; I find my friend," Knute said. He held tight the volume of Musset, which Gil had begged him to take.

As he started to walk the few steps to West Divinity, Knute felt very tired. By daylight the adventure seemed more and more incredible.

As he entered the dormitory he sighed heavily:

"Age and youth, I guess they can't team together long." As he mounted the stairs he said: "If I saw the boy again, he vould get tired of me. I tell him all I got to say." And as he opened his door, he added: "This is what I come to college for—this one night; I live for it sixty-five years. I go avay before I spoil it."

He wrote a note to Gil, and began to pack his telescope. He did not even wake Ray Gribble, sonorously sleeping in the stale air.

At five that afternoon, on the day coach of a westbound train, an old man sat smiling. A lasting content was in his eyes, and in his hands a small book in French, though the curious fact is that this man could not read French.

Understanding the Basic Elements of a Story

Before proceeding further, you may find a brief review of the elements of the story helpful. Basically, stories show the common elements of setting, plot, and characterization. In addition, in a meaningful story, one in which the author attempts to make an important statement about life, the reader is usually able to find a theme.

Setting is the time and place where a story occurs. In "Young Man Axelbrod," the early setting is farm country, somewhere in the Midwest, and the time is the past. Later in the story, the action moves to New England, to Yale College. Sometimes, if it is important, the author may even include details of weather or other information about the place.

Plot is the series or sequence of events, sometimes called the storyline. In "Young Man Axelbrod," we see Knute Axelbrod living the life of a farmer, doing the things farmers do. We also see Knute studying and planning for future changes in his life. Then, we see him become a student in a new place. In essence, the things that happen, the *acts* of characters *which occur in a sequence of time*—one after the other—comprise the plot of the story.

Characterization is the author's way of giving life to the living creatures in his story. If characters are well-drawn, we come to know them as we would know real people, including personality, temperament, even appearance. If characters are not well-drawn, then we scarcely know them, the same as we would know a real person in a crowd if we had seen him only briefly. Do we become well-acquainted with Knute?

Theme, unlike setting, plot, and characterization, is not a definite, structural part of a story. It is the "big idea" or moral that the writer wants the reader to get from his entire experience with the story. In "Young Man Axelbrod," could Sinclair Lewis have expressed the theme that life has worth only so long as a human being has a goal or a purpose for living? What do you think?

Knute Axelbrod's Purpose

You can profit most from "Young Man Axelbrod" by understanding the *purposes* Knute Axelbrod had for obtaining a college education. All of his life he had regretted not having had the opportunity to go to college, but when he found he could, he was willing to endure much pain to make this goal possible. For example, he studied subjects unrelated to his life to prepare for entrance examinations. After entering Yale, he endured the immaturity of his much younger fellow students and withstood the unsympathetic treatment of some of his professors. All of these things he accepted without complaint.

Finally, for one night, Axelbrod "lived" his dream of an education: he was able to feed his soul through his short experience with Gil Washburn. In a sense, Axelbrod fulfilled his purpose. Will you, likewise, formulate and fulfill a *personal* purpose in this class? By understanding Axelbrod's purpose, you may either understand your own purpose or you may be stimulated to develop one.

Two Questions for Your Consideration

1. So far, this class has been structured to introduce you and your fellow students to each other through a clearly delineated process. Also, composition and literature have been presented as important elements of content for you to experience and to understand. In what way have the first meetings of the class influenced your attitudes toward participation?

   ANSWER: _____

   _____

   _____

   _____

   _____

   _____

2. If the old man's purpose in "Young Man Axelbrod" characterizes the spirit of this course of study, what will you have to do to follow his lead?

   ANSWER: _____

   _____

   _____

   _____

   _____

   _____

Understanding the Importance of Purpose in Writing

You began this course by preparing and delivering a verbal composition about one of your classmates, after which you wrote a brief composition about your experience in doing so. Next, you read a short story by a famous writer. Each of the compositions, including the speech you delivered, the paragraph you wrote, and the short story by Sinclair Lewis, was composed by its author to serve a particular purpose.

Each author, you or Sinclair Lewis, either understood his subject to begin with or performed research to find out about it before composing his thoughts.

Furthermore, when you performed research, you followed certain steps:

1. You developed (or were given) a procedure for gathering data and you followed it.
2. You organized your data according to a plan related to your purpose.
3. You composed your data into some particular form related to your purpose.

In these or any other steps to writing (or speaking), one particular consideration comes first: *an author must have a purpose before he can do anything else.* An author's purpose controls not only the process of gathering and arranging information, but it also affects his *style* or technique of writing and the *form* in which he writes.

Two Styles: Narration and Exposition

Thus far, we have looked at two different *styles* of writing, exposition and narration. The first was exposition, and you used it *to tell* about a member of the class in your speech, after which you wrote about the entire class and your experience in gathering data. Expository writing, then, is that *style* of writing (or speaking) in which the author's purpose is *to tell* the reader what the author has discovered or believes about a particular subject. In your case, the subject was your class and your experience in learning about your class. You used the expository style to reveal your findings and to express your opinions directly.

The second *style* of writing was the narrative in the story, "Young Man Axelbrod" by Sinclair Lewis. Lewis' purpose was to reveal human character and motivation by *showing* it in action. Lewis did not tell us what he thought; instead, he placed his characters in various situations, in imitation of life, and allowed these characters to act out their reactions to these situations. Lewis, then, *showed* us human experience by *re-creating* it as well as he could. We saw his characters do and say things much as we might see real people do and say things.

Lewis' *style* was essentially *narrative* and his *form* was a short story. In a *narrative style*, things happen in some order of time, one situation or behavior leading to another, until the experience the author is showing comes to an end. A short story is a *form* of writing in which *narrative style* is commonly used.

Whether an author uses *expository* or *narrative style* or the *form* of an essay (your speech and your first written paper were both essays) or a short story, depends upon his *purpose.* Generally, if an author wishes *to tell* you what he thinks or what he has learned, he'll use an *expository style* because he wishes to be direct. If he wishes you to experience life, on the other hand, he'll *show* it to you through narration, giving you the details of experience and stimulating you to decide for yourself what is the meaning (significance) of this experience. In short, through exposition, the author *tells* and is direct; through narration, the author *shows* and is less direct. Finally, both exposition and narration are a function of the author's *purpose*. More about the stylistic differences between telling and showing is presented in the next lesson; for now, answer the following questions to review the material you have just covered.

ANSWER THE FOLLOWING QUESTIONS. CHECK ANSWERS AT END.

1. Before writing or speaking you must formulate a _____ .

2. If you formulate a clear_____ , then the steps you must follow to complete a piece of writing are often easier to select.

3. Generally, in an essay, your_____ is *to tell* the reader something.

4. An essay, written or spoken, and a short story fulfill the identical purpose._____(True *or* False)

5. In exposition, you_____(Tell *or* Show) something.

6. In narration, you_____(Tell *or* Show) something.

7. In narration, you_____(Re-create *or* Tell about) experience.

8. When reading an essay in which you expect to have the author tell you what he thinks, is your point of view or purpose the same as that of the author?_____(Yes *or* No)

9. In a narrative, does the author want you to live through the experiences he re-creates for you?_____ (Yes *or* No)

10. Expository style involves_____(Showing *or* Telling).

11. Narrative style involves_____(Showing *or* Telling).

12. Your verbal composition in class was an example of_____ (Narration *or* Exposition).

13. Lewis' short story was an example of_____ (Narration *or* Exposition).

14. The author of an essay (verbal or written) tries to communicate his ideas about experience, not the active experience itself._____(True *or* False)

15. The author of a short story encourages you, the reader, to live through the experiences he shows._____(True *or* False)

16. The author of an essay encourages you, the reader, to accept what he says as true; but he doesn't give you the opportunity to live through the experience itself, from which his idea came._____(True *or* False)

17. Narration is a style of writing._____(True *or* False)

18. Exposition is a style of writing._____(True *or* False)

19. An essay is a form of writing._____(True *or* False)

20. A short story is a form of writing._____(True *or* False)

(Check your answers to questions 1 through 20.
Then go on to additional questions about the
story, "Young Man Axelbrod.")

ANSWERS: 1., 2., 3. purpose; 4. false; 5. tell; 6. show; 7. re-create; 8. no; 9. yes; 10. telling; 11. showing; 12. exposition; 13. narration; 14. true; 15. true; 16. true; 17. true; 18. true; 19. true; 20. true

QUESTIONS ABOUT "YOUNG MAN AXELBROD"

Understanding of Structure

1. Which element of structure is strongest in "Young Man Axelbrod," setting, plot, or characterization? Explain.
2. Why is it correct to say that Lewis did not tell you everything about the people and events in this story, but tried *to show* you instead?

Test Your Comprehension

1. This story tells the importance of a man's purpose in life and how it can be frustrated. All of the following interfered with Axelbrod's purpose. Prove that each is true.
   a. The difficulties of an immigrant
   b. Marriage and its responsibilities
   c. Poor communication between youth and age
   d. Conflict between a person's ideal view of life and the reality he eventually meets
2. What was Axelbrod's purpose in life? Did he fulfill it?
3. Did Axelbrod show similar personal qualities in his life as a farmer and as a student?
4. Do you share Axelbrod's purpose in life? Explain.

Vocabulary for Study

eccentric	plebian	gargantuan
ponderous	engender	berated
convention	pilfered	supercilious
grotesque	sonorous	voluble

Writing Sample Number Two: Follow the directions on the Assignment-Evaluation sheet *after* you read A FEW WORDS OF CAUTION which follows.

A Few Words of Caution

Acceptable writing is generally the result of good work habits. Some habits which have been helpful to students and other writers include:

1. Following directions concerning the contents of any piece of writing.
2. Formulating a clear purpose for writing.
3. Performing whatever research is necessary in order to gather information.
4. Arranging research data carefully in usable form through an outline, a rough draft(s), or any other practical means.
5. Writing as many rough drafts as necessary to fulfill an assignment in content and correctness of English mechanics.
6. Submitting a final draft only after careful proofreading.

WRITING SAMPLE 2—EVALUATION

Write a statement of your personal goals for this course. Relate your ideas to those you discovered in "Young Man Axelbrod."

Length: approximately 125 words

Required in Contents	Full	Earned	For Study
1. Based upon the objectives in the Orientation to this course, can you state goals you hope to accomplish?	34		
2. Can you relate your goals to the *importance* of having goals which you found in "Young Man Axelbrod"?	33		
3. Can you make your contents clear to a general reader, one who is not familiar with this lesson?	33		
PROOFREAD YOUR WORK CAREFULLY!	0		

TOTAL   100

Instructor's Comments:

ENGLISH MECHANICS: Instructor Assigns Values for Criteria

Content Areas	Full	Earned	For Study
ORGANIZATION: Introduction Chronological Organization Topical Organization Rational Organization Smooth Development Termination	_____ _____ _____ _____ _____ _____		Chapter 13 Chapter 15 Chapter 16 Chapter 17 Chapter 14 Chapter 18
PARAGRAPHING: Introduction Development (unity) Development (coherence)	_____ _____		Page 163 Page 165 Page 168
SENTENCES: completeness; variety; economy; use of modifiers; pronouns; agreement; use of verbs, phrases, clauses	_____		
USE OF LANGUAGE: Level of usage Idiomatic usage Vividness	_____		Chapter 8
PUNCTUATION AND CAPITALIZATION and related graphics: Quotation marks	_____		Chapter 7
SPELLING			

TOTAL   100

Mechanics not in this text are assigned in supplementary text.

Elements of Narration

Figure 4. Art and Language: To tell or to show. Stuart Davis "Premiere"; permission from Los Angeles County Museum of Art.

To Tell or to Show:
Two Kinds of Sentences

Earlier, you reviewed material about the importance of the writer's purpose in writing. You learned that *purpose* affects both the style and the form a writer uses. For example, if a writer is interested mainly in describing his subject, he is likely to use an expository style *to tell* his reader about the subject. You used this style in the oral and written expository essay to tell about your reaction to the class and to state the goals you hope to achieve.

On the other hand, if the author's desire is *to show* his subject in action, in a lifelike manner, he is likely to use a narrative style. Sinclair Lewis used this style in the form of a short story, "Young Man Axelbrod."

Just as an author selects a style and form to fulfill his purpose, so does he choose the sentences he uses. Basically, there are two sentence types. One is more effective if the author wishes *to tell;* the other, if he wishes *to show.* Before we proceed to consider these two types in detail, however, let us be certain about what a sentence is. Let us look at the following word groups:

EXAMPLES

1. John is angry at his friend.
2. John angry friend.
3. John makes his friend angry.

ANSWER QUESTIONS ABOUT THE THREE WORD GROUPS

1. What is the word "John" in all three groups?
   a. A word that describes
   b. A word that names

2. What is "friend" in all three word groups?
   a. A word that describes
   b. A word that names

3. What is "angry" in all three word groups?
   a. A word that describes
   b. A word that names

4. In which word group are you sure "John" is angry?

   (1, 2, 3) _____

5. In which word group are you sure "friend" is angry?

   (1, 2, 3) _____

6. In which word group are you *not* sure which person, "John" or "friend," is angry?

   (1, 2, 3) _____

7. Why aren't you sure which person is angry in one of the word groups?
   a. The word order is different.
   b. John is doing something in one group but not in the other.
   c. A word is missing in one of the word groups.

8. What sort of word is missing from one of the word groups?
   a. A word that describes
   b. A word that names
   c. A word that neither describes nor names

9. The word that is missing from one of the word groups helps us know that:
   a. John is being something.
   b. John is doing something.
   c. John is *either* being *or* doing something.

10. The sort of word that is missing is:
    a. A word that names (a NOUN)
    b. A word that describes (an ADJECTIVE)
    c. A word that identifies being or doing (a VERB)

11. A word that identifies being or doing is:
    a. A verb
    b. A noun
    c. An adjective

12. The word that is missing from word group number two (John angry friend) is:
    a. A verb
    b. A noun
    c. An adjective

13. The word that is missing from word group number two (John angry friend) had an effect that:
    a. Made the meaning unclear
    b. Made word group two an incomplete idea
    c. Both a and b

ANSWERS: 1. b; 2. b; 3. a; 4. one; 5. three; 6. two; 7. c; 8. c; 9. c; 10. c; 11. a; 12. a; 13. c

Review: Identifying the Sentence

Word groups one and three ("John is angry at his friend" and "John makes his friend angry") have words that name, NOUNS; words that describe, ADJECTIVES; and words that show either being or doing, VERBS. Both word groups are called sentences. On the other hand, word group two ("John angry friend") lacks a verb and is not a sentence. May we say, then, that a word group which lacks a verb is not a sentence? Finally, may we conclude that a word group which lacks a verb is not a sentence and does not communicate a clear meaning?

Now, let us return to the two original examples of sentences again, but this time, let us examine them in a different way.

EXAMPLES

1. John is angry at his friend.
2. John makes his friend angry.

In one of these sentences, "John" is merely described; in the other, he is doing something or acting. Sentences in which the subject is not doing anything but is merely being described are called *descriptive sentences;* those in which the subject is acting are called *active sentences.* In a descriptive sentence, moreover, the writer's purpose is *to tell* about the subject; but in an active sentence, he wishes *to show* what the subject is doing. Finally, the difference between the *active sentence* and the *descriptive sentence* lies in the verb.

In one of our sample sentences we had "John is angry at his friend." Could we have written "John equals (=) angry."? Would the (=) have served as well as "is" to describe John's emotional state? Clearly, the answer to both questions is "yes." Let us write two more sentences similar to our first example.

EXAMPLES

John seems ill.
John becomes captain.

In these sentences, could we have said, instead, "John equals (=) ill" or "John equals (=) captain"? Again, the answer to both questions is "yes," for in each sentence we see only a *description* of John. Let us form a conclusion: In a *descriptive sentence*, the VERB acts like an (=) to *link* the subject (John) to a word that describes him (ill), or names him (captain) in a new way. Thus, the VERB in a *descriptive* sentence is called a LINKING VERB. Furthermore, in a descriptive sentence containing a linking verb, the writer's purpose is *to tell about* the subject's condition, be it physical, mental, emotional, or whatever, but *not* to show the subject doing anything. As a contrast, let us look now at the example we gave earlier which we called an *active sentence.*

EXAMPLE

John makes his friend angry.

In this sentence, we see that John *is acting upon* (makes) his friend. Our purpose is *to show* John doing something. Let us look at some more sentences with similar verbs.

EXAMPLES

John eats bread.
John peeled a banana.
John ran away.

In each of these sentences, John *acts*, does something; or *acted*, did something. Thus, each sentence is an *active sentence* containing an *active verb* (eats, peeled, ran). Let us form a conclusion: In an *active sentence*, the verb is active and allows the writer *to show* his subject doing something.

QUESTIONS FOR REVIEW

14. Two types of sentences are_____and _____.

15. An active sentence contains an_____verb.

16. A descriptive sentence contains a _____ verb.

17. A linking verb is like an_____ sign.

18. A descriptive sentence
    a. Shows the subject acting
    b. Tells about the subject

19. An active sentence
    a. Shows the subject acting
    b. Tells about the subject

20. The writer uses an active sentence
    a. To tell about the subject
    b. To show the subject doing something

21. The writer uses a descriptive sentence
    a. To tell about the subject
    b. To show the subject doing something

22. A linking verb is used
    a. To show
    b. To tell

23. An active verb is used
    a. To show
    b. To tell

ANSWERS: 14. active and descriptive; 15. active; 16. linking; 17. =; 18. b; 19. a; 20. b; 21. a; 22. b; 23. a

Now, let us put our knowledge of active and descriptive sentences to a further test. Examine the following sentences. Mark the active sentences with an "a" and the descriptive sentences with a "d."

24. Our teacher asks questions._____

25. Sharon is a nice name._____

26. He caught the ball._____

27. The wind bent the tree. _____

28. I am a tree._____

29. He blew his nose. _____

30. We are friends._____

31. We sang a song._____

32. The dog is a friendly animal._____

33. He walked the dog. _____

ANSWERS: 24. a; 25. d; 26. a; 27. a; 28. d; 29. a; 30. d; 31. a; 32. d; 33. a

Relating Sentence Types to Exposition and Narration

Earlier in this chapter you read that a writer's purpose determines whether he uses exposition or narration. Exposition, you read, is used mainly to tell about a subject; narration, to show a subject in action. You also read that a writer chooses sentences to fulfill his purpose and that the two basic sentence types are active and descriptive.

Now, here is some good news: essentially, there are no other sentence types. The writer, however, may still exercise his ingenuity by utilizing these two types in a variety of ways. For example, he may change the time (blow vs. blew) in which his showing or telling occurred or he may include various words which describe in the same sentence.

EXAMPLES

1. John was a tall man with strong arms.
2. John slowly peels and eats a succulent banana.

The verbs in these two examples above are essentially the same types as in previous examples of active and linking verbs. In sentence 2, the author *shows* the reader the action he observed; in sentence 1, he *tells* his interpretation of John's physical state. However, these sentences differ from earlier examples through the inclusion of descriptive words (tall, strong, slowly, succulent) to give the reader more information than he would have without them. Note, also, the use of the verb to show time (is vs. was).

Now, how are we going to focus upon use of these sentence types? For our purposes, we shall give them new labels:

Active-Narrative Sentence

From now on, we shall call a sentence with its main verb active (peels, peeled, makes, ran), active-narrative. Such sentences are particularly useful when the writer's purpose is *to show* his subject in action, in imitation of life.

Descriptive-Expository Sentence

From now on, we shall call a sentence with its main verb linking (is, was, seems, became), descriptive-expository. Such sentences are particularly useful when the writer's purpose is *to tell* about a subject.

Finally, in any given piece of writing, the author may mix both sentence types *to show* the reader what he experienced or observed, or *to tell* the reader about experience, giving his interpretation of it. Writers do not usually limit themselves to only one sentence type.

We shall deal later in this text with the special emphasis of the active-narrative sentence in narration and the descriptive-expository sentence in exposition. For now, examine the following sentences. Indicate whether each is active-narrative *(to show)* or descriptive-expository (to tell). Mark sentences which *show* A-N, and sentences which *tell* D-E.

QUESTIONS FOR REVIEW

34. We loaded hay on the wagon._____

35. A cat is a graceful animal._____

36. I am here._____

37. We were late for class._____

38. We worked to learn._____

39. In anger, he threw the baseball bat._____

40. John bashfully asked a question._____

41. Tim was a good dancer._____

42. This is a test._____

43. It is time to eat._____

COMPLETE THE FOLLOWING STATEMENTS

44. An active-narrative sentence contains an _____ verb.

45. A descriptive-expository sentence contains a _____ verb.

46. The writer interprets his experience, describing his subject, through a

_____ sentence.

47. The writer shows experience through an _____ sentence.

48. In an active-narrative sentence, the writer's purpose is _____ .

49. In a descriptive-expository sentence, the writer's purpose is _____ .

50. Writers use active-narrative sentences primarily for narration and descriptive-expository sentences primarily for exposition. _____ (True or False)

ANSWERS: 34, 38, 39, 40 are A-N; 35, 36, 37, 41, 42, 43 are D-E; 44. active; 45. linking; 46. descriptive-expository; 47. active-narrative; 48. to show; 49. to tell; 50. true

Other Linking Verbs Used to Tell

Thus far we have identified three verbs as linking verbs: is (was), seems (seemed), becomes (became). We said that these verbs function like an (=) sign and link their subjects with descriptions of them or with words that name the subjects in a new way. Do you remember these examples?

EXAMPLES

1. John is angry at his friend.
2. John seems ill.
3. John becomes captain.

There are, however, relatively few exclusively linking verbs, but there are several more that may serve both as linking and as active verbs; whether these words are being used one way or the other is determined by the meaning and the logic of the sentence in which they appear. Let us look at a few examples.

EXAMPLES

Mary looks good.

Is Mary doing something (looking) or is the writer merely describing her appearance?

The music sounds beautiful.

Is the music acting or is the writer describing the quality of the sound?

The coffee tastes bitter.

Is the coffee actually tasting or is the writer describing the quality of the flavor?

The meat smells terrible.

Is the meat acting or is the writer describing the quality of the odor?

John feels ill.

Is John acting (feeling, as one might feel with his hands) or is the writer describing the state of John's health?

Sam appears happy.

Is Sam acting or is the writer describing Sam's emotional state?

In each of the examples above, the sentence is descriptive-expository and the writer's purpose is *to tell* about the subject of the sentence. Thus each of the verbs is used as a linking verb. However, for the sake of contrast, let us pair these samples with others in which the same verbs are used as active verbs.

EXAMPLES

Mary looks good.
Mary looks at James.

The music sounds beautiful.
The sailor sounds (measures) the ocean depths.

The coffee tastes bitter.
Bill tastes the coffee.

The meat smells terrible.
I smell the meat.

John feels ill.
John feels the cloth.

Sam appears happy.
Sam appears nightly on the stage.

Can you see, now, that some verbs are both linking and active? Would it be helpful, furthermore, if you had a test of whether a verb is active or linking? Here is one you can use: insert the phrase "in the state of being" *after the verb* in any sentence in which you suspect that the verb is linking. If the verb is linking, you will not change the meaning of the sentence. Let us look at two examples:

EXAMPLES

Mary looks good.
Mary looks *in the state of being* good.
The music sounds beautiful.
The music sounds *in the state of being* beautiful.

Since we have already identified the verbs "looks" and "sounds" as both linking and active, let us test them with the same phrase when they are used as active verbs. Let us see if they make any sense at all when *in the state of being* is inserted.

EXAMPLES

Mary looks at James.
Mary looks *in the state of being* at James.
The sailor sounds the ocean depths.
The sailor sounds *in the state of being* the ocean depths.

These examples are silly; "in the state of being" doesn't fit.

Forms of Linking Verbs

As you read earlier, there are relatively few verbs which are used to link subjects with descriptions of the subjects. A listing of the principal forms of many of these verbs follows. You would do well to memorize them.

Subjects	Verbs			
I	am	seem	become	feel
you	are	seem	become	feel
he, she, it	is	seems	becomes	feels
he, she, it	was	seemed	became	felt
we, you, they	were	seemed	became	felt
(am, is, was)*	being	seeming	becoming	feeling
(have, has)*	been	seemed	become	felt
I	taste	look	sound	smell
you	taste	look	sound	smell
he, she, it	tastes	looks	sounds	smells
he, she, it	tasted	looked	sounded	smelled
we, you, they	tasted	looked	sounded	smelled
(am, is, was)*	tasting	looking	sounding	smelling
(have, has)*	tasted	looked	sounded	smelled

*These forms are used as auxiliary verbs in compound tenses. For example, "I am becoming tired."

Learn the linking verbs. All other verb uses are active! Learn, furthermore, to look at the verb as it functions in the sentence. If the verb links one thing with another, it is a *linking verb*. If the verb shows one thing acting, physically or mentally, it is an *active verb*.

QUESTIONS FOR REVIEW

Examine the following sentences. Identify whether the verb in each sentence is linking or active. Remember to ask yourself whether the writer is *telling* us his interpretation or *showing* us the action of the subject. Mark each sentence with an L for linking and an A for active.

51. John loves to bake bread._____

52. We bought gasoline in Bakersfield._____

53. The fan belt cut the water hose._____

54. Chalk is pressed sea shells._____

55. The class wrote papers._____

56. Marlene made her grand entrance._____

57. Marlene appeared shaken._____

58. He took two aspirins._____

59. The well seemed dry._____

60. The Russian River appears green._____

ANSWERS: 51, 52, 53, 55, 56 and 58 are active; 54, 57, 59 and 60 are linking

A Final Review

The two sentence types, descriptive-expository and narrative-active, are dependent upon verb usage. A descriptive-expository sentence is built upon a linking verb; an active-narrative sentence, upon an active verb.

There are very few exclusively linking verbs (is, seems, becomes) and there are some verbs which are both linking and active (appear, feel, taste, sound). The vast majority of verbs, however, is active.

Sentence and verb types are used by the writer to fulfill his purpose, *to tell* or *to show*. When a writer wishes *to tell*, he uses a descriptive-expository sentence with a linking verb. When he wishes *to show,* he uses an active-narrative sentence with an active verb.

Only when we examine a sentence from the writer's point of view can we talk intelligently about its structure. Only when we consider the writer's purpose, can we fully appreciate his sentence structure.

QUESTIONS FOR REVIEW

Look at the following sentences and indicate which are narrative (active-narrative) and which are expository (descriptive-expository). Mark each with N (narrative) or D (descriptive).

61. He threw a curve. _____

62. She sneaked across the room. _____

63. He lied but he smiled. _____

64. Helen likes to talk. _____

65. John surfs. _____

66. Nonfat milk tastes chalky. _____

67. Elmer looked at the Milky Way. _____

68. Riding the bus, he felt nervous. _____

69. Coffee tastes good in the morning. _____

70. I love to sleep. _____

71. The dog barked at our cat. _____

72. The group of students became a class. _____

73. We have been here before. _____

74. English just seems hard. _____

75. Are we being tested? _____

76. We felt relieved after the first session. _____

77. We tried to broaden our minds. _____

78. My coffee tasted bitter this morning. _____

79. Sometimes, new ideas are painful._____

80. This has been an exercise. _____

ANSWERS: 61, 62, 63, 64, 65, 67, 70, 71 and 77 are narrative; 66, 68, 69, 72, 73, 74, 75, 76, 78, 79 and 80 are expository

"Now," as William Carlos Williams wrote, "You have the ground sense necessary." Read the following paragraphs. Your first purpose when reading is to experience the total effect in order to understand the writers' purposes for putting the words on paper. Then, read the paragraphs a second time. Your second purpose is to examine the sentences closely to determine which kind of sentence each writer used predominantly. If you decide that a writer has used mainly expository (descriptive-expository) sentences, then his paragraph is *expository*, no matter what the form. If a writer has used mainly narrative (active-narrative) sentences, then his sample is *narrative*.

TEACHER
Helen Keller

One of Teacher's first steps was to teach me (Helen Keller) how to play. I had not laughed since I became deaf. One day, she came into the room laughing merrily. She put my hand on her bright, mobile face and spelled "laugh." Then she tickled me into a burst of mirth that gladdened the hearts of the family. Next she guided me through the motions of romping—swinging, tumbling, hopping, skipping—suiting the spelled word to each act. In a few days I was another child, pursuing new discoveries through the witchery of Teacher's finger-spelling.

81. How many sentences are there in this paragraph?_____

82. What type are the first and last sentences?_____

83. What type are the remaining sentences?_____

84. Is this passage of writing primarily expository or narrative?_____

85. Was the writer's primary purpose to show or to tell?_____

ANSWERS: 81. seven; 82. expository; 83. narrative; 84. narrative; 85. to show

JOHN

The distant tower bells rolled out their delicate toll. The peals, like bright wounded birds, struggled up-wind against March breezes heavy with the sounds of the city. Like confused starlings, the bell notes collided down the canyonlike walls of apartment buildings to fall dying among the branches of the park trees. John stopped on the park path. He cocked an ear toward the tower and closed his eyes, his forehead wrinkled in concentration. Slowly, he smiled and nodded his head in time to the timpani. He hurried off along the path, his gawky arms and legs swinging in unison with the faint bells.

86. Are there any expository sentences in this paragraph?_____

87. Copy down any five active verbs you can find. _____

88. In what types of sentences did you find the five active verbs you listed? _____

89. Is this passage expository or narrative?_____

90. Was the writer's primary purpose to show or to tell?_____

ANSWERS: 86. no; 87. rolled, struggled, collided, stopped, cocked, and others; 88. narrative; 89. narrative; 90. to show

BANDIT

Ian Fleming

What an extraordinary difference there was between a body full of person and a body that was empty! Now there is someone, now there is no more. This had been a Mexican with a name and an address, an employment card and perhaps a driving license. Then something had gone out of him, out of the envelope of flesh and cheap clothes, and had left him an empty paper bag waiting for the dust-cart. And the difference, the thing that had gone out of the stinking Mexican bandit, was greater than all Mexico.

91. How many sentences are there in this paragraph? _____

92. What type of sentence is number four?_____

93. What types are the remaining sentences?_____

94. Is the passage primarily narrative or descriptive?_____

95. Was the writer's primary purpose to tell or to show?_____

ANSWERS: 91. five; 92. narrative; 93. descriptive; 94. descriptive; 95. to tell

FINAL EXERCISE

Write ten sentences, five which are expository (descriptive-expository) and five which are narrative (active-narrative). In each sentence, *underline* the verb and place parentheses ( ) around the subject of the verb. Then label the sentence E (expository) or N (narrative).

Label

1. _____   _____

2. _____   _____

3. _____   _____

4. _____   _____

5. _____   _____

6. _____   _____

7. _____   _____

8. _____   _____

9. _____   _____

10. _____   _____

Continue on for Reading Assignments

THE UNSPEAKABLE WORDS

William March

There were words in the Brett language considered so corrupting in their effect on others that if anyone wrote them or was heard to speak them aloud, he was fined and thrown into prison. The King of the Bretts was of the opinion that the words were of no importance one way or the other, and besides, everybody in the country knew them anyway; but his advisers disagreed, and at last, to determine who was right, a committee was appointed to examine the people separately.

At length everyone in the kingdom had been examined, and found to know the words quite well, without the slightest damage to themselves. There was then left only one little girl, a five-year-old who lived in the mountains with her deaf and dumb parents. The committee hoped that this little girl, at least, had never heard the corrupting words, and on the morning they visited her, they said solemnly: "Do you know the meaning of poost, gist, duss, feng?"

The little girl admitted that she did not, and then, smiling happily, she said, "Oh, you must mean feek, kusk, dalu, and liben!"

Those who don't know the words must make them up for themselves.

Appreciation of Style

1. Analyze this selection. Are most of the verbs active or descriptive (linking)?
2. Does the author *tell* you what he thinks or does he *show* you?
3. If you think this is a narrative, which is the strongest element, setting, plot, characterization or theme?

Test Your Comprehension

1. Why did the King of the Bretts disagree with his advisors?
2. What was the truth (theme) in the words of the little girl when she answered the committee?
3. What *are* "unspeakable words"? Explain.

Vocabulary for Study

solemnly   determine   corrupting

THE UNICORN IN THE GARDEN
James Thurber

Once upon a sunny morning a man who sat in a breakfast nook looked up from his scrambled eggs to see a white unicorn with a gold horn quietly cropping the roses in the garden. The man went to the bedroom where his wife was still asleep and woke her. "There's a unicorn in the garden," he said. "Eating roses." She opened one unfriendly eye and looked at him. "The unicorn is a mythical beast," she said, and turned her back on him. The man walked slowly downstairs and out into the garden. The unicorn was still there; he was now browsing among the tulips. "Here, unicorn," said the man, and he pulled up a lily and gave it to him. The unicorn ate it gravely. With a high heart, because there was a unicorn in his garden, the man went upstairs and roused his wife again. "The unicorn," he said, "ate a lily." His wife sat up in bed and looked at him, coldly. "You are a booby," she said, "and I am going to have you put in the booby-hatch." The man, who had never liked the words "booby" and "booby-hatch," and who liked them even less on a shining morning when there was a unicorn in the garden, thought for a moment. "We'll see about that," he said. He walked over to the door. "He has a golden horn in the middle of his forehead," he told her. Then he went back to the garden to watch the unicorn; but the unicorn had gone away. The man sat down among the roses and went to sleep.

As soon as the husband had gone out of the house, the wife got up and dressed as fast as she could. She was very excited and there was a gloat in her eye. She telephoned the police and she telephoned a psychiatrist; she told them to hurry to her house and bring a straitjacket. When the police and the psychiatrist arrived they sat down in chairs and looked at her, with great interest. "My husband," she said, "saw a unicorn this morning." The police looked at the psychiatrist and the psychiatrist looked at the police. "He told me it ate a lily," she said. The psychiatrist looked at the police and the police looked at the psychiatrist. "He told me it had a golden horn in the middle of its forehead," she said. At a solemn signal from the psychiatrist, the police leaped from their chairs and seized the wife. They had a hard time subduing her, for she put up a terrific struggle, but they finally subdued her. Just as they got her into the straitjacket, the husband came back into the house.

"Did you tell your wife you saw a unicorn?" asked the police. "Of course not," said the husband. "The unicorn is a mythical beast." "That's all I wanted to know," said the psychiatrist. "Take her away. I'm sorry, sir, but your wife is as crazy as a jay bird." So they took her away, cursing and screaming, and shut her up in an institution. The husband lived happily ever after.

Moral: Don't count your boobies until they are hatched.

Appreciation of Style

1. In this narrative, the character of the wife is effectively shown. *How* does the author *show* her character?
2. *Prove* that this selection is a narrative.

Figure 5. Unicorn. By Schain.

Test Your Comprehension

1. How does the wife feel about her husband?
2. Which of the two, husband or wife, is the villain of the fable?
3. Did the unicorn ever really appear in the garden?
4. What is the serious meaning (theme) of the fable?

Vocabulary for Study

mythical   browsing   solemn   gloat

Re-creating Experience
Through Narration

Thus far, you have learned about writing styles, exposition and narration; and sentence types, descriptive-expository and active-narrative. These styles and sentence types, which you learned, are used by the author to fulfill his purpose, *to tell* or *to show* his reader what he wishes to communicate. Now, you will have the opportunity to put these lessons into practice through writing of your own.

If you write in the spirit of the lessons you have studied thus far, you will be very deliberate in what you do. For example, you will select your words, sentences, and style carefully to fulfill your purpose which, in this case, is to re-create experiences from your own life so that a reader may share them with you. Your concerns are: "What effect will my words and sentences have on my reader's mind? Will the impact of the writing help the reader to 'live' the events as I did?"

Follow the steps outlined below very carefully, for they are designed to provide you with a method of selecting and recording the ideas you decide to share with a reader.

Step One: Remembering Experience

Try to remember some of the experiences you have had which stand out clearly in your mind. Do they resemble these?

1. A fight during the first day of kindergarten.
2. A nasty odor in a room which resulted from a mixture of sulphur and film negative thrown through a window.
3. The unpleasantness of being fired from a job.
4. A nightmare which resulted from a horror movie.
5. The thrill of a first kiss.
6. The pleasure of tasting a favorite food for the first time.

Now, make your own brief list of memorable experiences. Try to recall five or more, limiting yourself to brief events, occurrences which began and ended quickly, almost in a moment.

1. _____

2. _____

3. _____

4. _____

5. _____

Step Two: Sharing Your Memories with the Group

When you have stopped writing, select one of your five experiences to share by reading aloud to the group. While the experiences are being read by others, listen carefully, and if you hear one that reminds you of an event in your own life which you had forgotten earlier, add it to your list.

Step Three: Recording Your Experience on Paper

Now that you have shared one of your experiences and have heard some reported by your fellow students, your next step is to select one of your memories to report in writing. Pick one that will lend itself to narration, an event that was very brief—only a single moment. (A trip across the United States or a *day* at the beach are not single moments.)

Before you begin, however, remember that your purpose is to write in *narrative* style, *to show* the experience as realistically as possible. This means that you will emphasize active-narrative sentences with active verbs. It also means that, as much as possible, you will show the subject(s) of your sentences acting, alive, as if the event you are describing is happening right now. Finally, do not concern yourself with time: you may use any verb tenses (past, present, future) you wish or any point of view (I, you, he, she, it, we, they) you prefer.

Recall the event in your mind's eye, seeing the things you saw, feeling the emotions you felt. When you have the experience clearly in mind, write it down quickly—do not worry about grammar, spelling, or the other things that normally trouble writers—in order to "catch" it before you forget.

Step Four: Sharing Your Writing with the Group

Are you willing to volunteer to read the rough draft of your moment of experience to the group? Doing so will give you invaluable exposure if you make use of the friendly criticisms you receive. Whether you read your account or not, listen carefully to those of your fellow students. Pay particular attention to these matters: Are the selections restricted to *moments* of experience? Are emphases upon *narra-*

tion? Are the experiences vividly presented so that you are able to visualize them clearly? Did the writers *show* you or tell you?

Step Five: Studying the Narrative Checklist

Now that you have had the opportunity to learn of some of the interesting experiences of others, are you impressed? Do you see that each of us can be a "gold mine" as a *source* of material for writing? Finally, are you better prepared now to revise your own writing than you were before you heard and discussed the work of others? Proceed to review the Narrative Checklist which follows *before* you revise. See how well your narrative compares with the elements of narration which are explained in the list.

NARRATIVE CHECKLIST

I. Narrative Hook: The narrative hook is the writer's introduction to a narrative; it is designed to "catch" the reader's attention. There is a variety of hooks commonly used.

  A. Contrast: The author establishes a black-white or sweet-sour mood or tone through the use of contrasting ideas.

    EXAMPLE: He is a very untidy person, but he has such a fine mind that I love him.

    The tortoise, one of the slowest of creatures, won the race against the hare, one of the fastest of creatures.

  B. Five-Way Sentence: This is an introduction full of detail, tightly packed, in which a *character* is *doing* a particular thing, in a particular *way*, at a particular *time*, in a particular *place*. All of the elements are important to what follows the five-way sentence.

    EXAMPLE: Mark Hastings lounged against the overturned rowboat, digging with his feet in the cooling sand, as his eyes anxiously scanned the breaking waves dark against the sunset.

    Flying through her apartment door, Emily Jones angrily threw her purse at the sofa and collapsed into her favorite evening chair in front of the television.

  C. Dramatic Statement: This introduction shows or implies violence of action, the kind that leads to bodily harm.

    EXAMPLE: Mark's fist ripped against his opponent's cheek, sending him crashing to the earth.

    John retreated toward the car as the Doberman, stiff-legged, ears pointed forward, silently stalked toward him from the porch.

  D. Believe-It-or-Not: This type of introduction is hard to believe, but it must not mislead the reader into expecting details which the writer doesn't supply as he develops his story.

    EXAMPLE: Paul Bunyan's blue-eyed Ox, Babe, cried one day; and when he had finished, he had created the Mississippi River.

    Of the millions of men in the world, Millicent had married the one man most incompatible.

REVIEW OF NARRATIVE HOOKS

Examine the opening sentences from the three paragraphs in the previous lesson, "Teacher," "John," and "Bandit." Identify the type of narrative hook each is.

1. From "Teacher": "One of Teacher's first steps was to teach me (Helen Keller) how to play."

2. From "John": "The distant tower bells rolled out their delicate toll."

3. From "Bandit": "What an extraordinary difference there was between a body full of person and a body that was empty."

ANSWERS: 1. believe-it-or-not; 2. contrast; 3. contrast

II. Imagism: Imagism in narration is simply the writer's way of developing his story by selecting just the "right" detail to picture the action he wishes *to show*. Often, his biggest job is deciding what *not* to show because too many details or the wrong details can slow down the action of a narrative.

EXAMPLE: As we excitedly pulled into the cluttered dirt yard of our cousin's country hotel, we saw cousin John running down the wooden porch to dive into the storm cellar, desperately yanking the massive doors closed after him. We pointedly ignored the storm cellar as we climbed from the car to meet cousins Teddy and Rutherford who were calling out their welcomes. For the moment, we forgot John as we were swept up by the happy reunion.

ANALYSIS: In this brief paragraph, does the writer supply details about the weather, the geographical location, the size of the hotel, or the curiosity of the visitors about John's behavior? On the other hand, he does give the actual events as they happened and there is no distracting use of detail.

III. Emotional Revelation: The writer knows that when he reveals his own or a character's emotions, the reader may experience and respond to those emotions. He may express emotion through a character or by addressing a reader directly in expository fashion. In the sample which follows, note how Sinclair Lewis shows Axelbrod's emotional reaction toward his rejection by a professor at Yale after Axelbrod innocently offers his help to the professor who has been having trouble with some of his students. Could Lewis, himself, be commenting indirectly on how callous people can be to each other?

EXAMPLE: "Say, Professor, you're a fine fellow. I do something for you. If any of the boys make themselves a nuisance, you yust call on me, and I spank the son of a guns."
Blevins, Ph.D., spoke in a manner of culture and nastiness:
"Thanks so much, Axelbrod, but I don't fancy that will ever be necessary. I am supposed to be a reasonably good disciplinarian. Good day. Oh, one moment. There's something I've been wishing to speak to you about. I do wish you wouldn't try quite so hard to show off whenever I call on you during quizzes. You answer at such needless length, and you smile as though there were something highly amusing about me. I'm

quite willing to have you regard me as a humorous figure, privately, but there are certain classroom conventions, you know, certain little conventions."

"Why, Professor!" wailed Knute. "I never make fun of you! I didn't know I smile. If I do, I guess it's yust because I am so glad when my stupid old head gets the lesson good."

"Well, well, that's very gratifying, I'm sure. And if you will be a little more careful—"

Blevins, Ph.D., smiled a toothy, frozen smile, and trotted off to the Graduates' Club, to be witty about old Knute and his way of saying "yust," while in the deserted classroom Knute sat chill, an old man and doomed. Through the windows came the light of Indian summer; clean, boyish cries rose from the campus. But the lover of autumn smoothed his baggy sleeve, stared at the blackboard, and there saw only the gray of October stubble about his distant shack. As he pictured the college watching him, secretly making fun of him and his smile, he was now faint and ashamed, now bull-angry. He was lonely for his cat, his fine chair of buffalo horns, the sunny door-step of his shack, and the understanding land. He had been in college for about one month.

IV. Significance: The writer achieves significance, the *meaning* or *lesson* in narration, by showing experience in a deliberate way. Generally, in a narration, the reader must make his own judgment about the meaning of experience; but in exposition the author tells the reader the author's own interpretation of the experience.

Consider the meaning we may draw from Axelbrod's experience above. He had offered himself, in friendship, in the only way he knew how and was brutally shattered by his reception. What might this teach us about human relationships? Consider, furthermore, how *directly* Ian Fleming comments on how, oftentimes, life, the most precious possession we have, is regarded so cheaply. Fleming uses the fleshly remains of a "stinking Mexican bandit" to tell about this in the expository selection from *Goldfinger* which you read in Chapter 4.

Step Six: Rewriting Your Moment of Experience

Now that you have studied the Narrative Checklist, revise your first draft of the moment of experience. Make whatever changes are necessary to include the elements which are described in the list. For now, don't worry about the rewrite "sounding" mechanical.

Step Seven: Obtaining Objective Reaction

After you finish your revision of the first draft, give it to someone to read. Try to find out the following things:

1. Does it have an interesting total effect?
2. Is it narrative in style?
3. Does it have narrative elements including the hook, imagism, emotional revelation, and significance?
4. Did the reader feel and "live" the experience?

Take notes on your reader's reaction as preparation for revising.

Step Eight: Another Revision

Revise your moment of experience again, incorporating all of the ideas you have acquired. However, don't worry too much about English mechanics. Concentrate, instead, on perfecting the contents and style. After you finish your rewrite, file it away for review later, after you have completed the correlated reading below. This reading is an example of a "moment of experience" which the chief character in the story encountered. As you will discover when you read the entire story later, this "moment" has a great deal to do with the outcome of the entire story.

Correlated Reading: An excerpt from

THE PIECE OF STRING
Guy de Maupassant

Maître Hauchecorne, of Bréauté, had just arrived at Goderville, and was taking his way towards the square, when he perceived on the ground a little piece of string. Maître Hauchecorne, economical, like all true Normans, reflected that everything was worth picking up which could be of any use; and he stooped down—but painfully, because he suffered from rheumatism. He took the bit of thin cord from the ground, and was carefully preparing to roll it up when he saw Maître Malandain, the harness-maker, on his door-step, looking at him. They had once had a quarrel about a halter, and they had remained angry, bearing malice on both sides. Maître Hauchecorne was overcome with a sort of shame at being seen by his enemy looking in the dirt so for a bit of string. He quickly hid his find beneath his blouse; then in the pocket of his breeches; then pretended to be still looking for something on the ground which he did not discover; and at last went off towards the market-place, with his head bent forward, and a body almost doubled in two by rheumatic pains.

After reading this selection, can you see what a narration which shows a very limited experience is like: a few actions following in sequence, nothing more. In this case, the author provides some "flashback information," but even this is not necessary, if the experience will stand alone. If you need further proof, try acting out the sequence shown; you will discover that only a few moments are necessary to complete it.

Step Nine:

Read the selection, "The Steadfast Tin Soldier," which follows. Prepare answers to the questions which follow the selection.

THE STEADFAST TIN SOLDIER
Hans Christian Andersen

There were once five and twenty tin soldiers who were all brothers, for they were all born of one old tin spoon. They all shouldered arms and stood eyes front; red and blue was their beautiful uniform. The very first thing they heard in this world when the lid was taken off the box they lay in, was the words "Tin soldiers!" It was a little boy who shouted it, and clapped his hands: he had been given them because it was his birthday; and now he set them up on the table. Each soldier was exactly like his neighbor; there was only one who was a little different.

He had one leg. He had been the last to be cast, and there was not enough tin left. Still, he stood just as steady on his one leg as the rest on their two, and he it is to whom we have to pay attention.

On the table where they were set up stood many other toys, but the one which caught the eye most was a lovely paper castle. Through the little windows you could see right into the rooms. In front of it, little trees stood round a tiny looking-glass; which was meant to look like a lake. Swans made of wax swam on it and looked at their reflections. The whole thing was very pretty, but the prettiest of all was a little lady who stood in the open door of the castle: she too was cut out of paper, but she had a skirt of the finest possible muslin, and a little painted blue stripe crossing her shoulder like a scarf: in the middle of it was a bright spangle as big as the whole of her face. The little lady had her arms stretched out, for she was a dancer, and one of her legs was lifted so high that the Tin Soldier could not see it, and thought that she had only one leg like him.

"That would be the wife for me," he thought, "but she's very genteel. She lives in a castle, and I have only a box, and there's five and twenty of us to go in it—it's no place for her. Still, I must try to get introduced."

Then he laid himself down at his full length behind a snuff box which was on the table. From there he could look straight at the elegant little lady, who continued to stand on one leg without losing her balance.

In the evening, all the other Tin Soldiers were put into their box, and the people of the house went to bed. Then the toys began to play: they played at paying calls, at fighting battles, and getting up balls. The Tin Soldiers rattled in their box, for they wanted to join in, but they couldn't get the lid off. The nutcracker turned head over heels, the slate pencil made a great to-do on the slate. Such a fuss there was that the canary woke up and began to talk—in verse, too!

The only two who did not leave their places were the Tin Soldier and the little dancer: she stood stock-still on tip-toe, with her arms spread out; and he was just as steady on his one leg. He did not take his eyes off her for a second.

Then the clock struck twelve, and "crack," up sprang the lid of the snuff box. But there was no snuff in it, no, but a little black troll—it was just a trick.

"Tin Soldier," said the troll, "will you keep your eyes to yourself?"

But the Tin Soldier pretended not to hear.

"All right, wait till to-morrow," said the troll.

Well, when to-morrow came and the children got up, the Tin Soldier was put on the window-sill, and whether it was the troll's doing or the draught, all at once the window flew open and the soldier fell down on his head from the third storey. It was a fearful fall. His leg pointed straight up, and there he stayed on his cap, with his bayonet stuck between two paving-stones.

The nurserymaid and the little boy ran down at once to look for him, but though they as nearly as possible trod on him, they could not see him. If the Tin Soldier had only shouted "Here I am," they would have found him easily enough, but he thought it was not proper to call out loud, seeing he was in uniform.

Next it began to rain. The drops came faster, one after another; it became a regular downpour. When it was over, two street-boys came along. "Look here," said one of them, "there's a tin soldier. He shall go for a voyage."

So they made a boat out of newspaper, put the Tin Soldier in it, and off he sailed, down the gutter; the two boys ran along with him and clapped their hands. Mercy on us! What billows raged in that gutter, and what a stream was there! There had, indeed, been a torrent of rain. The paper boat tossed up and down and sometimes whirled round and round so that the Tin Soldier became dizzy; but he was as steady as ever, turned not a hair, looked straight in front of him, and kept shouldering arms.

All at once the boat darted under a broad culvert. It was as dark there as if he had been still in his box. "Where can I be going to now?" thought he. "Aye, this is the troll's doing. Ah, dear, if that little lady was here in the boat, it might be twice as dark for all I cared!" Just then came up a big water-rat who lived under the culvert.

"Got a pass? Out with your pass?" But the Tin Soldier said nothing, and held his rifle tighter than ever. The boat rushed on, and the rat after it. Ugh! How it gnashed its teeth and called out to the chips and straws: "Stop him! stop him! he hasn't paid the toll! he hasn't shown his pass!"

But the stream ran stronger and stronger. Already the Tin Soldier could see daylight, ahead where the culvert ended; but at the same time he heard a rushing sound that was enough to appal the bravest heart. Think of it! at the end of the culvert the gutter ran straight into a huge canal. For him it was as dreadful as for us to go down a great waterfall in a boat.

By this time he was so near it that he could not stop: on went the boat, and the poor Tin Soldier held himself as stiff as he could—no one should say of him that he winked an eye.

The boat turned round three or four times, and filled with water to the gunwale: it was bound to sink. The Tin Soldier was up to his neck in water. Deeper and deeper sank the boat. Softer and softer grew the paper. The water closed over the Soldier's head, and he thought of the pretty little dancer whom he should never see again, and in his ears rang the words: "Onward, onward, warrior, Death waits for thee!"

Then the paper parted in sunder, and the Tin Soldier fell though—and in the same instant was swallowed by a fish. Goodness, how dark it was in there!—darker even than in the culvert, and besides, the space was so cramped. But the Tin Soldier was steady as ever and lay all his length with shouldered arms. The fish darted hither and thither and executed the most alarming movements. Finally it became quite quiet, then a ray of light seemed to break through. The light shone out full, and somebody called out: A TIN SOLDIER!

The fact was, the fish had been caught, brought to market, sold and taken into the kitchen where a maid cut it open with a big knife. She took the Soldier by the body in her finger and thumb and carried him into the parlour, where everybody wanted to see the remarkable man who had travelled about in the inside of a fish. But the Tin Soldier was not in the least above himself.

They set him up on the table, and there—well! it is funny how things do come about in the world—the Tin Soldier was in the self-same room he had been in before: he saw the very same children, and the toys were on the table—the lovely castle with the pretty little dancer, who was still standing on one leg, with the other lifted high up. She too was steadfast. The Tin Soldier was touched, and could have wept tears of tin, but it would not have been becoming. He looked at her and she looked at him, but neither of them said a word. At that moment one of the little boys picked up the Soldier and threw him right into the stove. He had no explanation to give: of course, it was the troll in the snuff box who was responsible.

The Tin Soldier stood there, all lit up, and felt a heat that was overpowering, but whether it came from the real fire, or from love, he did not know. The colours had all come off him: nobody could say whether that had happened on his journey or was the result of sorrow. He looked at the little lady, and she looked at him; and he felt he was melting, but still he stood steady with shouldered arms. Then a door opened, the wind caught the dancer, and she flew like a sylph into the stove to the Tin Soldier, blazed up into a flame and was gone.

The Tin Soldier melted down into a lump, and when next day the maid took out the ashes, she found him in the shape of a little tin heart. Of the dancer, only the spangle was left, and that was burnt as black as a coal.

Appreciation of Style

1. Identify the following elements of narration by making specific reference to the story.
   a. Narrative Hook: What type is it?
   b. Imagism: Select three examples of effective use of detail.

   c. Emotional Revelation: What emotions of the soldier are shown to reveal his character?

   d. Significance: What is the theme which the author communicates to us?

2. Andersen uses two *symbols*, a heart and a spangle, to reinforce his theme at the end of the story. Give the meaning of these symbols and show how they relate to the theme.

3. Which *element* of narration is most important in this story? Explain.

Test Your Comprehension

1. In a sense, the author's use of "steadfast" to describe his chief character is intended as a message. What is the message?

2. Contrast the characters of the soldier and the dancer. What meaning can one get from this contrast?

Vocabulary for Study

     troll   sylph   steadfast

Writing Sample Number Three: Follow the directions on the Assignment-Evaluation sheet on the next page.

WRITING SAMPLE 3—EVALUATION

Write to re-create a moment of experience in narrative style.
Length: approximately 200 words

Required in Contents	Full	Earned	For Study
1. Use narrative hook as introduction to awaken reader's interest	25		
2. Use imagism (carefully chosen detail) to build a mental picture of the experience	25		
3. Provide emotional revelation to show how the character or "I" felt during the experience	25		
4. Make the significance (meaning) of the experience clear to the reader by showing what it meant to you (the character or the "I")	25		
PROOFREAD YOUR WORK CAREFULLY!	0		
TOTAL	100		

Instructor's Comments:

ENGLISH MECHANICS: Instructor Assigns Values for Criteria

Content Areas	Full	Earned	For Study
ORGANIZATION: Introduction	———		Chapter 13
Chronological Organization	———		Chapter 15
Topical Organization	———		Chapter 16
Rational Organization	———		Chapter 17
Smooth Development	———		Chapter 14
Termination	———		Chapter 18
PARAGRAPHING: Introduction			Page 163
Development (unity)	———		Page 165
Development (coherence)	———		Page 168
SENTENCES: completeness; variety; economy; use of modifiers; pronouns; agreement; use of verbs, phrases, clauses	———		
USE OF LANGUAGE: Level of usage / Idiomatic usage / Vividness	———		Chapter 8
PUNCTUATION AND CAPITALIZATION and related graphics: Quotation marks	———		Chapter 7
SPELLING			
TOTAL	100		

Mechanics not in this text are assigned in supplementary text.

The Writer's Point of View

In any style of writing, it is important that the writer select a point of view from which to express his ideas. He may do so through characters which he creates or by showing clearly that the ideas come from himself alone. Ultimately, of course, all of the ideas in any writing do come directly from the author, but the way in which he expresses them increases or decreases the extent to which the reader becomes involved.

Definition of Point of View

Technically, point of view is the eye or vantage point from which the writer expresses the action or ideas, and it may vary considerably. The various "eyes" which we shall examine include first person, first person minor, second person, third person, objective, omniscient, and stream of consciousness.

First Person Point of View

First person point of view may involve the writer in a very personal way. When he uses "I," "me," or "we," he means literally either himself (I) or himself *and* someone else (we), or he wishes the reader to accept him as one of the characters. Examine the following excerpt from the autobiographical essay "Wallace"* by Richard Rovere.

As a schoolboy, my relations with teachers were almost always tense and hostile. I disliked my studies and did very badly in them. There are, I have heard, inept students who bring out the best in teachers, who challenge their skill and move them to sympathy and affection. I seemed to bring out the worst in them. I think my personality had more to do with this than my poor classroom work. Anyway, something about me was deeply offensive to the pedagogic temperament.

Often it took a teacher no more than a few minutes to conceive a raging dislike for me. I recall an instructor in elementary French who shied a textbook at my head the very first day I attended his class. We had never laid eyes on each other until fifteen or twenty minutes before he

---

*From *The New Yorker*, February 4, 1950.

assaulted me. I no longer remember what, if anything, provoked him to violence. It is possible that I said something that was either insolent or intolerably stupid. I guess I often did. It is also possible that I said nothing at all. Even my silence, my humility, my acquiescence, could annoy my teachers. The very sight of me, the mere awareness of my existence on earth, could be unendurably irritating to them.

QUESTIONS

1. To whom do all of the pronouns, "I" refer?_____

2. To whom does the pronoun "We," which is underlined in paragraph two, refer?_____

_____

3. The author uses the pronoun_____in his writing to show strong personal involvement.

ANSWERS: 1. Richard Rovere; 2. Rovere and his teacher; 3. I

First Person Minor Point of View

As in first person point of view, first person *minor* involves the author personally. However, in first person, the author (I) is the chief character; in *first person minor*, the author (I) is a *minor* character and someone or something else is more important (major). The author's intent is to focus on someone else. In the following, is the author or Zorba emphasized?

ZORBA THE GREEK
Nikos Kazantzakis

The ropes were creaking on the masts, the coastlines were dancing, and the women on board had become yellower than a lemon. They had laid down their weapons—paint, bodices, hairpins, combs. Their lips had paled, their nails were turning blue. The old magpie scolds were losing their borrowed plumes—ribbons, false eyebrows and beauty spots, brassieres—and to see them on the point of vomiting, you felt disgust and a great compassion.

Zorba was also turning yellow and green. His sparkling eyes were dulled. It was only towards the evening that his eyes brightened again. He pointed out two dolphins, leaping through the water alongside the ship.

"Dolphins!" he exclaimed joyously.

I noticed for the first time that almost half of the index finger on his left hand was missing. I started and felt sick.

"What happened to your finger, Zorba?" I cried.

"Nothing," he replied, offended that I had not shown more delight in the dolphins.

"Did you get it caught in a machine?" I insisted.

"What ever are you going on about machines for? I cut it off myself."

"Yourself? Why?"

"You can't understand, boss!" he said, shrugging his shoulders. "I told you I had been in every trade. Once I was a potter. I was mad about that craft. D'you realize what it means to take a lump of mud and make what you will out of it? Ffrr! You turn the wheel and the mud whirls round, as if it were possessed while you stand over it and say: I'm going to make a jug, I'm going to make a plate, I'm going to make a lamp and the devil knows what more! That's what you might call being a man: freedom!"

He had forgotten the sea, he was no longer biting the lemon, his eyes had become clear again.

"Well?" I asked. "What about your finger?"

"Oh, it got in my way in the wheel. It always got in the middle of things and upset my plans. So one day I seized a hatchet. . ."

"Didn't it hurt you?"

"What d'you mean? I'm not a tree trunk. I'm a man. Of course it hurt me. But it got in my way at the wheel, so I cut it off."

The sun went down and the sea became calmer. The clouds dispersed. The evening star shone, I looked at the sea, I looked at the sky and began to reflect. . . To love like that to take the hatchet and chop and feel the pain. . . . But I hid my emotion.

"A bad system that, Zorba!" I said, smiling. "It reminds me of the ascetic who, according to the Golden Legend, once saw a woman who disturbed him physically, so he took an axe. . ."

"The devil he didn't!" Zorba interposed, guessing what I was going to say. "Cut that off! To hell with the fool! The poor benighted innocent, that's never an obstacle!"

"But," I insisted, "it can be a very great obstacle!"

"To what?"

"To your entry into the kingdom of heaven."

Zorba glanced sideways at me, with a mocking air, and said: "But, you fool, that is the key to paradise!"

He raised his head, looked at me closely, as if he wanted to see what was going on in my mind: future lives, the kingdom of heaven, women, priests. But he did not seem to be able to gather much. He shook his great grey head guardedly.

"The maimed don't get into paradise," he said, and then fell silent.

QUESTIONS

4. Does the "I" point of view always represent the same character in this selection? Explain.

_____

_____

5. The author's purpose in this selection is to reveal something of Zorba's character. What sort of person does Zorba appear to be?

_____

_____

6. The author presents several examples of significance (important meaning) in this narration, including a concept (idea) of freedom and concern with the conflict between the body and the spirit. Review the selection and explain these "significances" in your own words.

_____

_____

7. The author reveals *changes of emotion* in this selection, particularly within the character, Zorba. Trace some of these changes by referring to the text.

_____

_____

_____

ANSWERS: 4. Sometimes the "I" refers to Zorba and sometimes to the unnamed character through whose "eyes" the author is looking; 5. and 6. are for class discussion after you prepare your answers; 7. prepare your answer for class discussion

Second Person Point of View

The writer uses "you," the second person point of view, to draw himself and the reader closer to his writing. With this technique, the author writes as if he knew the reader personally. Look at the following example from Antoine de Saint-Exupéry's *The Little Prince.* In this story, a flier, whose plane has crashed in the Sahara Desert, meets a child, the little prince, who has had many strange experiences. The flier, the point of view through which the author himself "speaks," presents the details of his adventure informally.

THE LITTLE PRINCE
Antoine de Saint-Exupéry

I had thus learned a second fact of great importance: this was that the planet the little prince came from was scarcely any larger than a house!

But that did not really surprise me much. I knew very well that in addition to the great planets . . . to which we have given names, there are also hundreds of others, some of which are so small that one has a hard time seeing them through the telescope. When an astronomer discovers one of these he does not give it a name, but only a number. He might call it, for example, "Asteroid 325."

I have serious reason to believe that the planet from which the little prince came is the asteroid known as B-612.

This asteroid has only once been seen through the telescope. That was by a Turkish astronomer, in 1909.

On making his discovery, the astronomer had presented it to the International Astronomical Congress, in a great demonstration. But he was in Turkish costume, and so nobody would believe what he said.

Grown-ups are like that. . . .

If I have told you these details about the asteroid, and made a note of its number for you, it is on account of the grown-ups and their ways. Grown-ups love figures. When you tell them that you have made a new friend, they never ask you questions about essential matters. They never say to you, "What does his voice sound like? What games does he love best? Does he collect butterflies?" Instead, they demand: "How old is he? How many brothers has he? How much does he weigh? How much money does his father make?" Only from these figures do they think they have learned anything about him.

QUESTIONS

8. The author uses two techniques of drawing himself closer to the reader. The first is in paragraph two and it involves the use of the pronoun_____. The second is in the last paragraph and involves_____ .

9. To whom does "we" refer in paragraph two?_____

10. To whom does "you" refer in the last paragraph, first line?_____

ANSWERS: 8. we; 9. the writer and you (all of us); 10. the reader

Third Person Point of View

The third person point of view is used to show characters behaving in their environment. The author shows the characters acting independently of him and of the reader. Third person is shown by use of "he," "she," "it," "they," or any noun. Examine the following excerpt from *Another Country*.

ANOTHER COUNTRY
James Baldwin

Seven months ago, a lifetime ago, he had been playing a gig in one of the new Harlem spots owned and operated by a Negro. It was their last night. It had been a good night, everybody was feeling good. Most of them, after the set, were going to make it to the home of a famous Negro singer who had just scored in his first movie. Because the joint was new, it was packed. Lately, he had heard, it hadn't been doing so well. All kinds of people had been there that night, white and black, high and low, people who came for the music and people who spent their lives in joints for other reasons. There were a couple of minks and a few near-minks and a lot of God-knows-what shining at wrists and ears and necks and in the hair. The colored people were having a good time because they sensed that, for whatever reason, this crowd was solidly with them; and the white people were having a good time because nobody was putting them down for being white. The joint, as Fats Waller would have said, was jumping.

QUESTIONS

11. The following pronouns appear in this selection: he, it, everybody, them, his, their. Many

nouns are included too. What is the point of view of all these words?_____

12. What kind of narrative hook is the first sentence?_____

13. What is the significance of the selection? It deals with white-black relations. Explain.

_____

_____

14. What is the emotional revelation shown?

_____

_____

ANSWERS: 11. all are third person; 12. five-way sentence; 13. If the proper environment exists, all types of people can get along well together; 14. Everyone was having a good time—but not necessarily for the same reasons. The Blacks felt accepted; the whites were pleased that their color wasn't held against them.

Omniscient Point of View

By using the omniscient point of view, the writer assumes the power of God. He knows what every character is thinking and doing because he can see into the minds and hearts of all. A writer may act omnisciently (all-knowing) no matter what variety in point of view he shows to develop his story. The following example illustrates.

"WHERE DID YOU GO?" "OUT." "WHAT DID YOU DO?" "NOTHING."

Robert Paul Smith

You go to your mother and say, "I owe Charlie Pagliaro one hundred and forty-four marbles." Your mother says, "I told you not to play for keeps." You go to your father and you say, "I owe Charlie Pagliaro one hundred and forty-four marbles." Your father says, "One hundred and forty-four? Well, tell him you didn't mean to go that high."

You go to your best friend. He believes that Charlie Pagliaro will cut your head off. He lends you three immies and a steelie, which, if I remember, was worth five immies, or if big enough, ten, if the guy you were swapping with wanted a steelie at all. Two copies of *The Boy Allies* and a box of blank cartridges, a seebackroscope you got from the Johnson Smith catalog, and a promise to Charlie Pagliaro that you will do his homework for the rest of your life, twenty-five cents in cash, and that's it. Charlie takes the stuff, and all you owe him now is fifteen immies. He knows you have a realie. Realies are worth more than diamonds. It is not a good thing to have Charlie mad at you. There goes the realie. You are alive, but poverty-stricken for all time.

QUESTIONS

15. Does the writer know the thoughts and acts of you, I, Mother, Father, the best friend, and of

Charlie Pagliaro?_____

16. When a writer knows the thoughts and acts of all characters in his work, he is using the

_____ point of view.

ANSWERS: 15. yes; 16. omniscient

Objective Point of View

Objective point of view is shown through dialogue, the reproduction of human speech, in which each character is shown expressing himself in true-to-life fashion. Thus, we may say that each character has an identity independent of the author and the reader. Dialogue is always narrative because the author uses it to show what the character is saying. Read the following example from Ernest Hemingway's "A Clean, Well-Lighted Place." In the excerpt, two waiters are talking about a drunk, deaf old man who is in the cafe where they work. One waiter is serving the old man as the excerpt begins.

A CLEAN, WELL-LIGHTED PLACE
Ernest Hemingway

The waiter took the brandy bottle and another saucer from the counter inside the cafe and marched out to the old man's table. He put down the saucer and poured the glass full of brandy.

"You should have killed yourself last week," he said to the deaf man. The old man motioned with his finger. "A little more," he said. The waiter poured on into the glass so that the brandy slopped over and ran down the stem into the top saucer of the pile. "Thank you," the old man said. The waiter took the bottle back inside the cafe. He sat down at the table with his colleague again.

"He's drunk now," he said.

"What did he want to kill himself for?"

"How should I know."

"How did he do it?"

"He hung himself with a rope."

"Who cut him down?"

"His niece."

"Why did they do it?"

"Fear for his soul."

"How much money has he got?"

"He's got plenty."

"He must be eighty years old."

"Anyway I should say he was eighty."

"I wish he would go home. I never get to bed before three o'clock. What kind of hour is that to go to bed?"

"He stays up because he likes it."

"He's lonely. I'm not lonely. I have a wife waiting in bed for me."

"He had a wife once too."

"A wife would be no good to him now."

"You can't tell. He might be better with a wife."

QUESTIONS

17. Is each character independent of you and of the author?_____ (yes or no)

18. Dialogue is_____point of view.

ANSWERS: 17. yes; 18. objective

Stream-of-Consciousness Point of View

Not too commonly used is the technique of stream of consciousness, the writer's attempt to show what is passing through the mind of a character. The technique is difficult to accomplish, requiring great understanding of the often complicated way in which humans think. Furthermore, the result often *seems to be* a "jumble" of unrelated ideas. The following example may give you a "taste."

George, look out for the river! My God, did I turn off the stove? You always cut corners when you turn left, George. Will he remember? What a beautiful view from the hill. George, are you sure you have the tickets? Mae bought a new dress. Trouble with high school reunions; will he recognize me? That's right, George, turn left at the river fork.

QUESTIONS

19. What seems to be happening?_____

_____

20. Who is the main character?_____

_____

21. Can you construct a relationship among the various ideas shown?_____

_____

_____

ANSWERS: 19. two or more people are driving to an affair; 20. an unnamed person, "I," related to George; 21. prepare answer for class discussion

The Importance of Being Consistent in Point of View

When a writer selects a point of view to show or tell his ideas, he does so *deliberately* because he feels that some particular view will serve his purposes best. Once he has made his decision, furthermore, he tries to be *consistent* in point of view because he knows that if he shifts a view for no clear reason, he may confuse his reader. Thus, "I" remains "I"; "you" remains "you"; "he" remains "he"; "Tom" remains "Tom" or may change to "he"; "Mary"-and-"Joe" remain "Mary"-and-"Joe" or may change to "they"; and "someone" remains "someone" or may change to "he" or "she."

The point is that when a noun or pronoun is used, it should refer *clearly* to the person intended by the writer. Finally, to be certain that he is clear, the writer is consistent in person (first, second, third), in number (singular: he, she, it; or plural: we, they) and in gender (masculine, feminine, or neuter).

REVIEW QUESTIONS

Read the following lettered items concerning point of view. Select *one* of the lettered items to identify each numbered statement of definition which follows.

Lettered Items
  a. stream of consciousness
  b. first person
  c. objective
  d. second person
  e. first person minor
  f. third person
  g. omniscient

22. The writer assumes familiarity with the reader, and addresses him directly. _____

23. The writer reproduces the thoughts going through the mind of a character._____

24. The writer himself is the major character. _____

25. The writer shows a character behaving in his environment._____

26. The writer is himself a character but this character is *minor* in the story. Someone or some-thing else is the major character._____

27. The writer reproduces human speech through dialogue._____

28. The author writes like God, showing complete knowledge of the motivations and behavior of all characters in a story as well as of their environment._____

ANSWERS: 22. d; 23. a; 24. b; 25. f; 26. e; 27. c; 28. g

Identify the point of view of the following words. Your answers will be either *first, second, or third* person.

29. Mary_____	34. someone_____	38. table_____
30. you _____	35. I _____	39. he _____
31. we_____	36. her _____	40. automobile_____
32. him_____	37. themselves_____	41. it _____
33. they_____		

ANSWERS: 29. third; 30. second; 31. first; 32. third; 33. third; 34. third; 35. first; 36. third; 37. third; 38. third; 39. third; 40. third; 41. third

Identify the point of view of the following sentences. Mark them first, second, third, objective, omniscient, stream of consciousness, or first person minor.

42. I didn't want to tell the secret. _____

43. We helped him aboard. _____

44. Jack said, "I missed the boat." _____

45. He missed the shot at the rabbit. _____

46. I watched him closely as he spoke to us saying, "You know me." _____

47. Helen and Bob each thought the other was fooling. _____

ANSWERS: 42. first; 43. first; 44. objective; 45. third; 46. first minor; 47. omniscient

Read the following paragraphs from *The Sensitives* by Louis Charbonneau. Judging each paragraph individually, identify its point of view.

48. While he occasionally commented bitterly to Tina about being kept in a box by the agency, Adam Cooper was too blissfully happy with her to dwell on his complaints or to become deeply resentful. He studied languages with specialists at the agency, displaying a remarkable and previously unknown facility. Occasionally he conducted interrogations. Then the time came when he was called in on a critical case involving a suspected defector. Cooper read the man's guilt easily and was able to direct other agents toward the evidence that gave ironclad proof of treason, and toward the traitor's accomplices. The agency seemed pleased. More important assignments were talked of, and a few began to trickle through, each success leading to another.

_____

49. But somewhere along the way came the subtle change in Tina's (his wife's) behavior, unnoticed until the chance detection of her uneasiness came to him one night in spite of his fatigue and self-absorption. Reluctantly he began to pay more attention to her moods and movements—a more critical attention. He began to see a woman he had never really known, the one who lived beneath that golden sheath of flesh. Finally the ugly suspicion was born. For a telepath, proof was not hard to find.

_____

50.   Adam Cooper heard a horn bleat outside on Hennessy Road in Wan Chai. Inside the bar a juke box was playing American-style rock featuring a Japanese singer with a shrill teenager's voice. Cooper drained his glass. His hand was shaking.

---

51.   That was when he started drinking—after the accident. Nothing seemed to matter as much. The CIA continued to make use of him on increasingly important assignments, though still without complete trust, still uncertain how to exploit his talent for knowing what other people were thinking.

---

52. Is a writer deliberate in selecting a point of view when he writes?_____ (yes or no)

53. If a writer shifts a point of view for no clear reason, is the reader likely to be confused?_____(yes or no)

54. When a word such as a pronoun (he, she, it) is used, must it refer clearly to the person which the writer intends? _____(yes or no)

55. If a writer uses a pronoun to refer to a noun and the noun is singular, must the pronoun be singular too?_____(yes or no)

56. If the writer uses a pronoun to refer to something neuter, such as table, chair, apple, must the pronoun be neuter too?_____(yes or no)

57. What pronoun would be used to refer to a word like *apple*? _____(fill in)

58. What pronoun would be used to refer to something like *John*?_____(fill in)

59. What pronoun would be used to refer to something like *Florence*?_____ (fill in)

60. What pronoun would refer to *Mary and I*? _____ (fill in)

61. What pronoun would refer to the singular indefinite word *someone*?_____ (fill in)

ANSWERS: 48. third person; 49. omniscient; 50. third person; 51. omniscient; 52. yes; 53. yes; 54. yes; 55. yes; 56. yes; 57. it; 58. he; 59. she; 60. we; 61. he or she

---

Writing Sample Number Four: Go back to the list you made of memorable experiences on page 52. Pick one as a basis for writing. Write one from your memory and check it against the Narrative Checklist. Write a second draft and check it against the list too. Then go to the Assignment-Evaluation sheet on the next page before you write your final draft.

WRITING SAMPLE 4—EVALUATION

Write to re-create a moment of experience in narrative style, but use a point of view *other than* first person.
Length: approximately 200 words

Required in Contents	Full	Earned	For Study
1. Use narrative hook	20		
2. Use imagism	20		
3. Show emotional revelation	20		
4. Make significance clear to reader as well as to character in narrative	20		
5. Show a single point of view but not first person	20		
PROOFREAD YOUR WORK CAREFULLY!	0		
TOTAL	100		

Instructor's Comments:

ENGLISH MECHANICS: Instructor Assigns Values for Criteria

Content Areas	Full	Earned	For Study
ORGANIZATION: Introduction	————		Chapter 13
Chronological Organization	————		Chapter 15
Topical Organization	————		Chapter 16
Rational Organization	————		Chapter 17
Smooth Development	————		Chapter 14
Termination	————		Chapter 18
PARAGRAPHING: Introduction	————		Page 163
Development (unity)	————		Page 165
Development (coherence)	————		Page 168
SENTENCES: completeness; variety; economy; use of modifiers; pronouns; agreement; use of verbs, phrases, clauses	————		
USE OF LANGUAGE: Level of usage / Idiomatic usage / Vividness	————		Chapter 8
PUNCTUATION AND CAPITALIZATION and related graphics: Quotation marks	————		Chapter 7
SPELLING:			
TOTAL	100		

Mechanics not in this text are assigned in supplementary text.

Dialogue: The Drama of Speech

Dialogue, the objective point of view (see Chapter 6), is the author's tool for re-creating the drama of human speech. It is always narrative in style, for no matter what verbs are contained *within the spoken words* of the characters in a story, it is the characters who speak (act); they are not being described.

Do you recall the excerpt from Ernest Hemingway's story, "A Clean, Well-Lighted Place"? In it, two waiters are seen talking about a deaf old man. Was Hemingway telling us about the waiters or was he showing their exchange of words?

However, dialogue does have limitations. Although the author may use it to show a character speaking, he cannot use dialogue *alone* to show facial expressions, gestures, moods, tension, or other relevant details. Unless he is writing a play and expects to use live actors and a stage setting to show us these qualities, the author must mix dialogue with other passages to complete the illusion of an exchange of words among living people.

There are several mechanical devices which a writer uses to avoid confusion between dialogue and related passages. First, he places the words being spoken within quotation (") marks. Second, he shows the speaker, the verb and other necessary words which reveal *how* the dialogue is spoken outside the quotation marks. Sometimes the related passages are within the same sentence as the dialogue, but separated by quotation marks ("). Often the related passages are in separate sentences altogether. Third, whenever one speaker "breaks off" and another begins, the author changes to a new paragraph. To observe these devices, let us look at a brief sample from *Zorba The Greek*. The paragraphs are numbered for your convenience.

I. "Dolphins!" he (Zorba) exclaimed joyously.

II. I noticed for the first time that almost half of the index finger on his left hand was missing. I started and felt sick.

III. "What happened to your finger, Zorba?" I cried.

IV. "Nothing," he replied, offended that I had not shown more delight in the dolphins.

V. "Did you get it caught in a machine?" I insisted.

VI. "What ever are you going on about machines for? I cut it off myself."

QUESTIONS ABOUT THE EXCERPT FROM *ZORBA THE GREEK*

1. Look at the following verbs from paragraphs I, III, and V: "exclaimed, cried, insisted." Do they show *how* the speaker spoke even though they are not part of the dialogue?

   _____(yes or no)

2. Look at the verb, "replied" in paragraph IV. Does this verb alone show how the speaker

   spoke?_____(yes or no)

3. In paragraph IV, what technique *other than the verb* does the author use to show how the speaker spoke?

   _____

   _____

   _____

4. What kind of verbs are those shown in questions one and two above?

5. Do the spoken words alone in paragraphs I, III, IV, and V show how the speaker spoke?

   Explain._____

   _____

   _____

   _____

ANSWERS: 1. yes; 2. no; 3. He uses description beginning with the word "offended," an adjective; 4. narrative or active; 5. No, for the author used verbs and modifiers outside the quotation marks to show the speakers' moods.

Mood: A Character's Emotional Attitude

Mood is a character's emotional state, his attitude toward his surroundings. In writing emphasizing the spoken word, it is revealed at first through a combination of dialogue and related passages. However, once an author has established a character's mood successfully, he may "carry" it with dialogue alone.

Look back to the final line of the excerpt from *Zorba The Greek*. The author built very carefully to this line. Notice that there is no verb or modifier to show how the words are spoken. The author had developed the "word play" to a point where it was unnecessary to show how the words are spoken; the reader can imagine the mood of the final line because it follows naturally from the earlier lines.

Figure 6. How would you describe this mood in words? "The Lovers" by Fred C. Money, Jr.; property of authors.

First, you saw Zorba "joyous" at the sight of dolphins. Then you saw the character represented by "I" (the author in a first person minor point of view) ignoring Zorba's joy, which annoyed Zorba. The "I" character persisted in ignoring Zorba's joy and the final line of dialogue shows the resulting change in Zorba's mood.

QUESTIONS ABOUT MOOD

You will find the information to answer the following questions in the six-paragraph excerpt from *Zorba The Greek.*

6. In paragraph I, which word reveals Zorba's mood?_____

7. In which paragraph is there evidence of the mood of the character represented by "I"?

_____

8. In which paragraph is there evidence of a change in Zorba from his initial mood?

_____

9. What word shows the change from Zorba's initial mood?

10. Describe the mood shown in paragraph VI.

_____

_____

_____

ANSWERS: 6. joyously; 7. paragraph II; 8. paragraph IV; 9. "offended"; 10. Zorba was annoyed or disgusted at being ignored when he showed pleasure at sight of the dolphins.

Creation of Tension Between Characters

Tension is a state of emotional strain between personalities. It results from differences in their attitudes (moods) or their failure to understand one another. Tension, furthermore, is important in good dialogue.

In the earlier consideration of mood, you saw how Zorba's emotional attitude changed when he felt that his feeling of joy was being ignored. On the other hand, the "I" character was unable to share Zorba's joy because he was sickened by Zorba's half-missing finger.

Thus, you saw tension develop as the moods of the characters conflicted, and they were unable to communicate. Furthermore, the author built tension so well that in his final line of dialogue (paragraph VI), he didn't have to show Zorba's emotion; you could interpret it from the dialogue alone.

QUESTIONS ABOUT TENSION

Read the following lines of dialogue and answer questions about them.

"Mary, I love you!" he exclaimed.

"John, you need a breath freshener," she murmured.

11. Are the two characters sharing similar moods? _____ (yes or no)

12. What are their two different moods?_____

13. Would additional lines of dialogue which followed *logically* from these show the development

    of tension?_____(yes or no)

14. Add two more lines of dialogue which show the logical or natural development of tension.

_____

_____

_____

_____

_____

ANSWERS: 11. no; 12. love and concern (annoyance or sympathy); 13. yes; 14. for class review and discussion

PUNCTUATION OF DIALOGUE

Examine the following lines of dialogue and related passages carefully. Then answer the questions which follow.

I. "Johnny cried bitterly when he lost his ball," Mother said sadly.

II. "Couldn't anything be done to replace it?" Mrs. Ables asked. "Poor boy!"

III. "There is no store nearby. I'm afraid there's nothing we can do until next week," Father declared.

IV. Mother sighed, "I wish we could do something sooner."

15. Are all the spoken words in paragraphs I through IV surrounded by quotation marks?

_____(yes or no)

16. At various places, the comma, question mark, exclamation point, and period are used with quotation marks to connect dialogue with words which show *how* the dialogue is spoken. Are

    these punctuation marks placed before or after the quotation marks? _____

17. In paragraph number I, is a comma used to close the dialogue itself?_____ (yes or no)

18. What punctuation marks are used to close dialogue in paragraph number II?_____

19. How many sentences (complete or incomplete) are there in paragraph number II?_____

20. What punctuation mark is used to conclude the first sentence in paragraph number II?

    _____

21. In paragraph number III, what concludes the dialogue?

22. What punctuation is used to separate sentences *within* dialogue in paragraph number III?

    _____

23. In paragraph IV, what punctuation mark introduces the dialogue?

24. In paragraph number IV, what punctuation mark concludes the dialogue?

25. In paragraph number IV, what punctuation mark concludes the sentence?

ANSWERS: 15. yes; 16. before; 17. yes; 18. question mark, exclamation point (? !); 19. two; 20. period; 21. comma; 22. period; 23. comma; 24. period; 25. period

A FEW CONCLUSIONS ABOUT PUNCTUATION OF DIALOGUE

1. Dialogue is surrounded by quotation marks.

2. Punctuation is used with quotation marks to separate dialogue from the words which show how it is spoken. This related punctuation *precedes* the quotation marks. Look at the examples which follow.
   a. "Help!" said John. *(! before ")*
   b. John asked, "Will you help?" *(, and ? before ")*
   c. "I hope," said he, "to help." *(, and . before ")*

3. When dialogue is part of a sentence, the sentence has its own punctuation; this serves to separate different sentences containing dialogue from each other.
   a. "James can help me," said Bill. "At least, I think he can," he added. *(. after Bill)*

4. In the unusual situation when there is dialogue in which the speaker quotes someone else's words, the practice is to use single quotation marks (') within the double quotation marks (").
   a. James said, "I heard my neighbor say, 'Stop making so much noise here,' so I turned my car radio down to a lower level."

5. Whenever there is a change of speaker in dialogue, it is necessary to start a new paragraph.

FINAL REVIEW

Read the following segments of dialogue. Notice how punctuation differs between Dialogue A, which contains only the spoken word, and Dialogue B, which contains the spoken word and related passages. The paragraphs are numbers for your convenience.

Dialogue A

I. "Today, class, we shall talk about dialogue."

II. "That's what you think!"

III. "Dialogue is characterized by tension."

IV. "But how do you write it?"

V. "Mike, please raise your hand and be recognized before you speak in class."

VI. "I mean, how do you put it on paper?"

VII. "Mike, you must raise your hand and be recognized!"

VIII. "He means the 'he said' and the 'she said' and those things, Mr. Abalone."

IX. "I know what Mike means, Joe. You don't have to interpret for him. And raise your hand before you speak."

X. "Oh, Joe doesn't have any manners anyway, Mr. Abalone."

XI. "Thank you, Roberta, but Joe doesn't have to be reminded."

XII. "But how do you write it?"

XIII. "He doesn't know!"

Dialogue B

I.   "Today, class, we shall talk about dialogue," said Mr. Abalone, clipping the words off in a precise tone, effecting a pseudo-British accent.

II.   "That's what you think!" shot back a whisper from the rear.

III.   "Dialogue," continued Mr. Abalone, "is characterized by tension." He paused to permit the words to sink in, his eyes probing the back rows of the class for the heckler.

IV.   "But how do you write it?" blurted out Mike from his front row seat.

V.   "Mike, please raise your hand when you have a question."

VI.   "I mean, how do you put it on paper?"

VII.   "Mike, you must raise your hand and be recognized before you speak in this class," persisted Mr. Abalone, the color rising in his face.

VIII.   "He means the 'he said' and the 'she said' and those things, Mr. Abalone."

IX.   "I know what Mike means, Joe. You don't have to interpret for him. And raise your hand before you speak!"

X.   "Oh, Joe doesn't have any manners anyway, Mr. Abalone."

XI.   "Thank you, Roberta, but Joe doesn't have to be reminded," he shot back coldly, his eyes merry with the opportunity to strike back.

XII.   "But how do you write it?" persisted Mike.

XIII.   "He doesn't know," answered a whisper from the back.

QUESTIONS ABOUT DIALOGUES A AND B

26. Look at the first paragraph of A and B. Does the dialogue in each case end with the same

punctuation?_____ (yes or no)

27. Why is the final punctuation for paragraph II, Dialogue A, different from the final punctuation

for paragraph II, Dialogue B? _____

_____

_____

_____

28. Which, Dialogue A or B, is more informative about how the words are spoken?_____

29. Which gives greater information about mood, A or B?_____

ANSWERS: 26. no; 27. In IIA, the dialogue (spoken word) is the entire sentence; in IIB, the dialogue is only part of a larger sentence; 28. B; 29. B

PRACTICE IN PUNCTUATING DIALOGUE

Punctuate the following sentences to separate dialogue from related passages.

30. Help she cried

31. I like only modern novels said John

32. I'll read the poem volunteered William

33. Karen asked which way shall I go

34. Show her John exclaimed

*After you check your answers on the following page,
turn to the next page, and read the selection.*

ANSWERS: 30. "Help!" she cried.
                31. "I like only modern novels," said John.
                32. "I'll read the poem," volunteered William.
                33. Karen asked, "Which way shall I go?"
                34. "Show her!" John exclaimed.

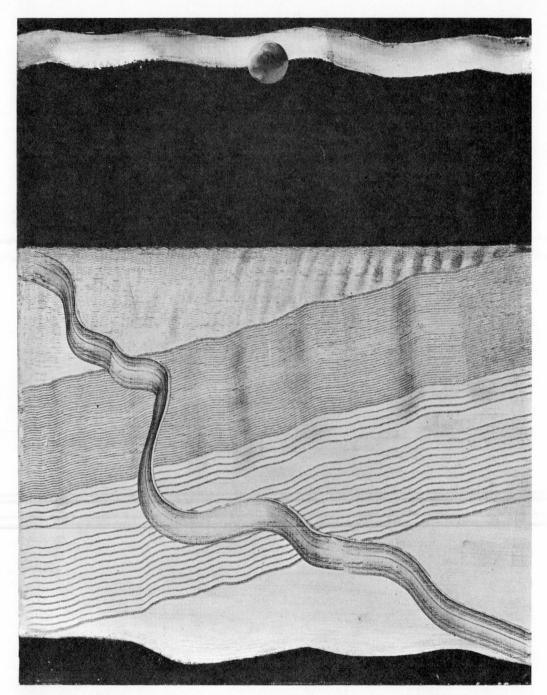

Figure 7. "La Mer" by Max Ernst. Mr. and Mrs. William Preston Harrison Collection. Permission from Los Angeles County Museum of Art.

AUGUST 2002: NIGHT MEETING

Ray Bradbury

Before going up into the blue hills, Tomás Gomez stopped for gasoline at the lonely station.

"Kind of alone out here, aren't you, Pop?" said Tomás.

The old man wiped off the windshield of the small truck. "Not bad."

"How do you like Mars, Pop?"

"Fine. Always something new. I made up my mind when I came here last year I wouldn't expect nothing, nor ask nothing, nor be surprised at nothing. We've got to forget Earth and how things were. We've got to look at what we're in here, and how *different* it is. I get a hell of a lot of fun out of just the weather here. It's *Martian* weather. Hot as hell daytimes, cold as hell nights. I get a big kick out of the different flowers and different rain. I came to Mars to retire and I wanted to retire in a place where everything is different. An old man needs to have things different. Young people don't want to talk to him, other old people bore hell out of him. So I thought the best thing for me is a place so different that all you got to do is open your eyes and you're entertained. I got this gas station. If business picks up too much, I'll move on back to some other old highway that's not so busy, where I can earn just enough to live on and still have time to feel the *different* things here."

"You got the right idea, Pop," said Tomás, his brown hands idly on the wheel. He was feeling good. He had been working in one of the new colonies for ten days straight and now he had two days off and was on his way to a party.

"I'm not surprised at anything any more," said the old man. "I'm just looking. I'm just experiencing. If you can't take Mars for what she is, you might as well go back to Earth. Everything's crazy up here, the soil, the canals, the natives (I never saw any yet, but I hear they're around), the clocks. Even my clock acts funny. Even *time* is crazy up here. Sometimes I feel I'm here all by myself, no one else on the whole damn planet. I'd take bets on it. Sometimes I feel about eight years old, my body squeezed up and everything else tall. Jesus, it's just the place for an old man. Keeps me alert and keeps me happy. You know what Mars is? It's like a thing I got for Christmas seventy years ago—don't know if you ever had one—they called them kaleidoscopes, bits of crystal and cloth and beads and pretty junk. You held it up to the sunlight and looked in through at it, and it took your breath away. All the patterns! Well, that's Mars. Enjoy it. Don't ask it to be nothing else but what it is. Jesus, you know that highway right there, built by the Martians, is over sixteen centuries old and still in good condition? That's one dollar and fifty cents, thanks and good night."

Tomás drove off down the ancient highway, laughing quietly.

It was a long road going into darkness and hills and he held to the wheel, now and again reaching into his lunch bucket and taking out a piece of candy. He had been driving steadily for an hour, with no other car on the road, no light, just the road going under, the hum, the roar, and Mars out there, so quiet. Mars was always quiet, but quieter tonight than any other. The deserts and empty seas swung by him, and the mountains against the stars.

There was a smell of Time in the air tonight. He smiled and turned the fancy in his mind. There was a thought. What did Time smell like? Like dust and clocks and people. And if you wondered what Time sounded like it sounded like water running in a dark cave and voices crying and dirt dropping down upon hollow box lids, and rain. And, going further, what did Time *look* like? Time looked like snow dropping silently into a black room or it looked like a silent film in an ancient theater, one hundred billion faces falling like those New Year balloons, down and down into nothing. That was how Time smelled and looked and sounded. And tonight—Tomás shoved a hand into the wind outside the truck—tonight you could almost *touch* Time.

He drove the truck between hills of Time. His neck prickled and he sat up, watching ahead.

He pulled into a little dead Martian town, stopped the engine, and let the silence come in around him. He sat, not breathing, looking out at the white buildings in the moonlight. Uninhabited for centuries. Perfect, faultless, in ruins, yes, but perfect, nevertheless.

He started the engine and drove on another mile or more before stopping again, climbing out, carrying his lunch bucket, and walking to a little promontory where he could look back at that dusty city. He opened his thermos and poured himself a cup of coffee. A night bird flew by. He felt very good, very much at peace.

Perhaps five minutes later there was a sound. Off in the hills, where the ancient highway curved, there was a motion, a dim light, and then a murmur.

Tomás turned slowly with the coffee cup in his hand.

And out of the hills came a strange thing.

It was a machine like a jade-green insect, a praying mantis, delicately rushing through the cold air, indistinct, countless green diamonds winking over its body, and red jewels that glittered with multifaceted eyes. Its six legs fell upon the ancient highway with the sounds of a sparse rain which dwindled away, and from the back of the machine a Martian with melted gold for eyes looked down at Tomás as if he were looking into a well.

Tomás raised his hand and thought Hello! automatically but did not move his lips, for this *was* a Martian. But Tomás had swum in blue rivers on Earth, with strangers passing on the road, and his weapon had always been his smile. He did not carry a gun. And he did not feel the need of one now, even with the little fear that gathered about his heart at this moment.

The Martian's hands were empty too. For a moment they looked across the cool air at each other.

It was Tomás who moved first.

"Hello!" he called.

"Hello!" called the Martian in his own language.

They did not understand each other.

"Did you say hello?" they both asked.

"What did you say?" they said, each in a different tongue.

They scowled.

"Who are you?" said Tomás in English.

"What are you doing here?" In Martian; the stranger's lips moved.

"Where are you going?" they said and looked bewildered.

"I'm Tomás Gomez."

"I'm Muhe Ca."

Neither understood, but they tapped their chests with the words and then it became clear.

And then the Martian laughed. "Wait!" Tomás felt his head touched, but no hand had touched him. "There!" said the Martian in English. "That is better!"

"You learned my language so quick!"

"Nothing at all!"

They looked, embarrassed with a new silence, at the steaming coffee he had in one hand.

"Something different?" said the Martian, eying him and the coffee, referring to them both, perhaps.

"May I offer you a drink?" said Tomás.

"Please."

The Martian slid down from his machine.

A second cup was produced and filled, steaming. Tomás held it out.

Their hands met and—like mist—fell through each other.

"Jesus Christ!" cried Tomás, and dropped the cup.

"Name of the gods!" said the Martian in his own tongue.

"Did you see what happened?" they both whispered.

They were very cold and terrified.

The Martian bent to touch the cup but could not touch it.

"Jesus!" said Tomás.

"Indeed." The Martian tried again and again to get hold of the cup, but could not. He stood up and thought for a moment, then took a knife from his belt. "Hey!" cried Tomás. "You misunderstand, catch!" said the Martian, and tossed it. Tomás cupped his hands. The knife fell through his flesh. It hit the ground. Tomás bent to pick it up but could not touch it, and he recoiled, shivering.

Now he looked at the Martian against the sky.

"The stars!" he said.

"The stars!" said the Martian, looking, in turn, at Tomás.

The stars were white and sharp beyond the flesh of the Martian, and they were sewn into his flesh like scintillas swallowed into the thin, phosphorescent membrane of a gelatinous sea fish. You could see stars flickering like violet eyes in the Martian's stomach and chest, and through his wrists, like jewelry.

"I can see through you!" said Tomás.

"And I through you!" said the Martian, stepping back.

Tomás felt of his own body and, feeling the warmth, was reassured. *I* am real, he thought.

The Martian touched his own nose and lips. "*I* have flesh," he said, half aloud. "*I* am alive."

Tomás stared at the stranger. "And if *I* am real, then *you* must be dead."

"No, you!"

"A ghost!"

"A phantom!"

They pointed at each other, with starlight burning in their limbs like daggers and icicles and fireflies, and then fell to judging their limbs again, each finding himself intact, not, excited, stunned, awed, and the other, ah yes, the other over there, unreal, a ghostly prism flashing the accumulated light of distant worlds.

I'm drunk, thought Tomás. I won't tell anyone of this tomorrow, no, no.

They stood there on the ancient highway, neither of them moving.

"Where are you from?" asked the Martian at last.

"Earth."

"What is that?"

"There." Tomás nodded to the sky.

"When?"

"We landed over a year ago, remember?"

"No."

"And all of you were dead, all but a few. You're rare, don't you *know* that?"

"That's not true."

"Yes, dead. I saw the bodies. Black, in the rooms, in the houses, dead. Thousands of them."

"That's ridiculous. We're *alive!*"

"Mister, you're invaded, only you don't know it. You must have escaped."

"I haven't escaped; there was nothing to escape. What do you mean? I'm on my way to a festival now at the canal, near the Eniall Mountains. I was there last night. Don't you see the city there?" The Martian pointed.

Tomás looked and saw the ruins. "Why, that city's been dead thousands of years."

The Martian laughed. "Dead. I slept there yesterday!"

"And I was in it a week ago and the week before that, and I just drove through it now, and it's a heap. See the broken pillars?"

"Broken? Why, I see them perfectly. The moonlight helps. And the pillars are upright."

"There's dust in the streets," said Tomás.

"The streets are clean!"

"The canals are empty right there."

"The canals are full of lavender wine!"

"It's dead."

"It's alive!" protested the Martian, laughing more now. "Oh, you're quite wrong. See all the carnival lights? There are beautiful boats as slim as women, beautiful women as slim as boats, women the color of sand, women with fire flowers in their hands. I can see them, small, running in the streets there. That's where I'm going now, to the festival; we'll float on the waters all night long; we'll sing, we'll drink, we'll make love. Can't you *see* it?"

"Mister, that city is as dead as a dried lizard. Ask any of our party. Me, I'm on my way to Creen City tonight; that's the new colony we just raised over near Illinois Highway. You're mixed up. We brought in a million board feet of Oregon lumber and a couple dozen tons of good steel nails and hammered together two of the nicest little villages you ever saw. Tonight we're warming one of them. A couple rockets are coming in from Earth, bringing our wives and girl friends. There'll be barn dances and whiskey—"

The Martian was not disquieted. "You say it is over *that* way?"

"There are the rockets." Tomás walked him to the edge of the hill and pointed down. "See?"

"No."

"Damn it, there they *are!* Those long silver things."

"No."

Now Tomás laughed. "You're blind!"

"I see very well. You are the one who does not see."

"But you see the new *town*, don't you?"

"I see nothing but an ocean, and water at low tide."

"Mister, that water's been evaporated for forty centuries."

"Ah, now, now, that *is* enough."

"It's true, I tell you."

The Martian grew very serious. "Tell me again. You do not see the city the way I describe it? The pillars very white, the boats very slender, the festival lights—oh, I see them *clearly!* And listen! I can hear them singing. It's no space away at all."

Tomás listened and shook his head. "No."

"And I, on the other hand," said the Martian, "cannot see what you describe. Well."

Again they were cold. An ice was in their flesh.

"Can it be. . .?"

"What?"

"You say 'from the sky'?"

"Earth."

"Earth, a name, nothing," said the Martian. "*But* . . . as I came up the pass an hour ago. . ." He touched the back of his neck. "I felt. . ."

"Cold?"

"Yes."

"And now?"

"Cold again. Oddly. There was a thing to the light, to the hills, the road," said the Martian. "I felt the strangeness, the road, the light, and for a moment I felt as if I were the last man alive on this world. . ."

"So did I!" said Tomás, and it was like talking to an old and dear friend, confiding, growing warm with the topic.

The Martian closed his eyes and opened them again. "This can only mean one thing. It has to do with Time. Yes. You are a figment of the Past!"

"No, you are from the Past," said the Earth Man, having had time to think of it now.

"You are so *certain*. How can you prove who is from the Past, who from the Future? What year is it?

"Two thousand and one!"

"What does that mean to *me?*"

Tomás considered and shrugged. "Nothing."

"It is as if I told you that it is the year 4462853 S.E.C. It is nothing and more than nothing! Where is the clock to show us how the stars stand?"

"But the ruins prove it! They prove that *I* am the Future, *I* am alive, *you* are dead!"

"Everything in me denies this. My heart beats, my stomach hungers, my mouth thirsts. No, no, not dead, not alive, either of us. More alive than anything else. Caught between is more like it. Two strangers passing in the night, that is it. Two strangers passing. Ruins, you say?"

"Yes. You're afraid?"

"Who wants to see the Future, who *ever* does? A man can face the Past, but to think—the pillars *crumbled*, you say? And the sea empty, and the canals dry, and the maidens dead, and the flowers withered?" The Martian was silent, but then he looked on ahead. "But there they *are*. I *see* them. Isn't that enough for me? They wait for me now, no matter *what* you say."

And for Tomás the rockets, far away, waiting for *him*, and the town and the women from Earth. "We can never agree," he said.

"Let us agree to disagree," said the Martian. "What does it matter who is Past or Future, if we are both alive, for what follows will follow, tomorrow or in ten thousand years. How do you know that those temples are not the temples of your own civilization one hundred centuries from now, tumbled and broken? You do not know. Then don't ask. But the night is very short. There go the festival fires in the sky, and the birds."

Tomás put out his hand. The Martian did likewise in imitation.

Their hands did not touch; they melted through each other.

"Will we meet again?"

"Who knows? Perhaps some other night."

"I'd like to go with you to that festival."

"And I wish I might come to your new town, to see this ship you speak of, to see these men, to hear all that has happened."

"Good-by," said Tomás.

"Good night."

The Martian rode his green vehicle quietly away into the hills. The Earth Man turned his truck and drove it silently in the opposite direction.

"Good lord, what a dream that was," sighed Tomás, his hands on the wheel, thinking of the rockets, the women, the raw whisky, the Virginia reels, the party.

How strange a vision was that, thought the Martian, rushing on, thinking of the festival, the canals, the boats, the women with golden eyes, and the songs.

The night was dark. The moons had gone down. Starlight twinkled on the empty highway where now there was not a sound, no car, no person, nothing. And it remained that way all the rest of the cool dark night.

Appreciation of Style

1. The language of the passages not included in dialogue itself shows a strong tone (the author's attitude or emotion toward his subject). Identify Bradbury's tone through reference to specific passages outside dialogue.

2. What mood (characters' attitude or emotion) does Bradbury develop through the dialogue between Tomás and the Martian?

3. Give examples of specific details which contribute to the development of tone (the author's attitude) and mood (the characters' attitudes).

4. How did Bradbury build tension between Tomás and the Martian?

Test Your Comprehension

1. How do the Martian and Tomás manage to communicate *or do* they communicate?
2. Can you formulate a general statement from this selection about communication between people of different cultural backgrounds?
3. Can you prepare a definition of reality based upon this selection? Refer to the text to support your ideas.
4. What is Bradbury's overall theme in this selection?

Vocabulary for Study

phosphorescent   scintillas   gelatinous   disquieted

A MAN AND THE UNIVERSE

Stephen Crane

A man said to the universe:
"Sir, I exist!"
"However," replied the universe,
"The fact has not created in me
A sense of obligation."

Appreciation of Style

1. Dialogue can be very efficient. In this little poem, Crane has packed a great deal of meaning because he used dialogue. Would you care to estimate how much writing you would have to do to say as much by different techniques?

Test Your Comprehension

1. What is the attitude (mood) of the man?
2. What is the attitude of the universe?
3. How do you feel about the philosophy expressed here?

Writing Sample Number Five: Return to the list you made of your memorable experiences. Follow the directions for a dialogue sample on the Assignment-Evaluation sheet on the next page.

WRITING SAMPLE 5—EVALUATION

Write primarily dialogue in re-creating a moment of experience in narrative style.
Length: approximately 200 words

Required in Contents	Full	Earned	For Study
1. Use narrative hook (may be dialogue)	17		
2. Use imagism (emphasize speech)	17		
3. Show emotional revelation	17		
4. Make significance clear to reader	17		
5. Stress use of dialogue and choose verbs carefully to show *how* words are spoken; show development of *tension* between characters	17		
6. Use special mechanics: a. paragraph change of speaker b. quotation marks around words in dialogue c. punctuation within quotation marks as needed d. punctuate sentence stops of sentences containing speech	15		
TOTAL	100		

Instructor's Comments: REMEMBER TO PROOFREAD CAREFULLY!

ENGLISH MECHANICS: Instructor Assigns Values for Criteria

Content Areas	Full	Earned	For Study
ORGANIZATION: Introduction Chronological Organization Topical Organization Rational Organization Smooth Development Termination	—————— —————— —————— —————— —————— ——————		Chapter 13 Chapter 15 Chapter 16 Chapter 17 Chapter 14 Chapter 18
PARAGRAPHING: Introduction Development (unity) Development (coherence)	—————— —————— ——————		Page 163 Page 165 Page 168
SENTENCES: completeness; variety; economy; use of modifiers; pronouns; agreement; use of verbs, phrases, clauses	—————		
USE OF LANGUAGE: Level of usage Idiomatic usage Vividness	—————		Chapter 8
PUNCTUATION AND CAPITALIZATION and related graphics: Quotation marks	—————		Chapter 7
SPELLING:			
TOTAL	100		

Mechanics not in this text are assigned in supplementary text.

Figure 8. Variety of Texture: comparison and contrast.

Sense Impressions:
To See or to Perish

In his famous book, *The Phenomenon of Man*, Teilhard de Jardin says that human survival is dependent upon understanding of the environment. Man's cultivation of his senses is necessary to his well-being.

If every man must cultivate his senses to assure his well-being, certainly the writer must do so, for how else can the writer communicate except on the basis of deep understanding?

The author learns to "feel" his environment keenly before he writes about it. He tries to be sensitive in order to perceive (see, hear, feel) *accurately* before he writes. Furthermore, when he writes, he uses his language as effectively as he can. Knowing that the written word has many limitations, the writer exercises ingenuity in order to accomplish his purpose. He often invents new applications of existing words, makes use of colorful comparison and contrast, and strives for clear, sharp detail.

Novel Uses of Words

Because there are virtually no standard verbs in English which show taste, sound, sight, or feeling, the writer must be creative when he wishes to communicate what his senses have enabled him to learn. He knows that he must be concrete and specific in recording sensory detail. How does he do so?

Let us consider some statements about common experiences:

1. I smelled the rain.
2. John tasted ice cream.
3. The man heard a meadow lark.
4. Susan looked at the red picture.

Are these statements re-creations of the experiences with which they deal? Are the sentences vivid?

Suppose the ice cream which John tasted, and which the writer reported in the sentence above, was pineapple and had a tart taste, would your perception of the experience improve if the writer said, "The pineapple ice cream 'tarted' my

95

tongue."? Whether you liked the creation of the verb "tarted" or not, would you agree that it shows a sharp sensation on the tongue?

Why would it be correct to suggest that this particular use of "tarted" is novel? The answer is that the writer used a word which is ordinarily an adjective (*tart* taste) or a noun (ice cream *tart*) as a verb. He created this verb as his way of *showing* you the experience he had when he tasted pineapple ice cream.

A problem the writer often faces is communicating experience which may be unfamiliar to the reader. If he is wise, he deals with the problem by using language which the reader knows. For example, at one time, when most people lived on farms, a plow passing through the earth was a common experience, but the motion of a ship passing over the sea was not. One writer saw this comparison: "A ship is a sea plow." This kind of sentence, as you know, is descriptive-expository. How could the idea be made more vivid through narrative style? The writer solved the problem in this way: "The ship plowed the sea."

What did the writer do? He used the *source* of the sense perception—the ship, as the actor in his sentence. Finally, he used the verb, plow, in a new way, to compare the action of a ship on water with that of a plow on land. By use of narrative style, the writer encouraged the reader to imagine his own sense perception, "to see" the ship behaving. Let us look at two examples which accomplish the same purpose of encouraging the reader to see, hear, and feel through novel uses of existing verbs:

1. The jetliner chewed its way across the sky.

   Source or actor? _____jetliner_____

   Action? _____chewed_____

2. The automobile horn poked the pedestrian along.

   Source? _____horn_____

   Action? _____poked_____

Making Comparisons: The Metaphor

When a writer seeks a fresh approach to words, he uses comparison of similar or dissimilar things to make his idea clear. Occasionally, this approach results in what are called figures of speech, and the metaphor is one particular type. Let us look at the examples we used in the earlier section on novel uses of words.

1. The ice cream tarted my tongue.

You were told that "tart" is ordinarily an adjective (a word which describes nouns and pronouns) or a noun. Furthermore, if you understand the meaning of tart as an adjective, "sharp," you may appreciate the sensation which the writer's tongue experienced. What the writer really did in this sentence was to *compare* the taste of the ice cream with the reader's general idea of "tartness" or "sharpness." Finally, the author's comparison was *indirect* or *suggested*. Were you clearly aware that this was so? Let us look at some more of our earlier examples.

2. The ship was a sea plow.
3. The ship plowed the sea.

In these examples, another comparison is made between a ship and a plow. Is the comparison direct or is it merely suggested?

4. The jetliner chewed its way across the sky.
5. The automobile horn poked the pedestrian along.

Can a jetliner "chew" or is it being compared to someone or something which can? Can an automobile horn "poke" or is it being compared to someone or something which can?

All of examples one through five show the use of one type of figure of speech, the *metaphor*, which is defined as *implied* or *suggested* comparison. It is particularly useful in communicating sensory impressions in narrative style because the writer may use it to make comparisons through the verb (plowed, tarted, chewed).

Making Comparisons: The Simile

Another technique for communicating sense impressions is the *simile* which, unlike the metaphor, makes a *direct* comparison through the use of "like" or "as." Here are two examples:

1. John is *like* a roaring lion.
2. John eats *as* a wolf eats.

Would it be useful to contrast the simile and metaphor further by rewriting the examples of metaphors we used earlier in the form of similes?

3. The tart flavor of the ice cream affected my tongue *like* a thousand little needles.
4. The jetliner moved across the sky *like* a hungry animal chewing everything in its path.
5. The automobile horn startled me *as* a poke in the ribs would have done.

REVIEW QUESTIONS

1. Is the comparison made in a simile direct or suggested?_____

2. Look at the examples of simile again. How were comparisons made? _____

3. Which figure of speech shows comparisons made through the verb? _____

4. Which, the metaphor or the simile, is more effective for use in narrative style? _____

ANSWERS: 1. direct; 2. through like or as; 3. metaphor; 4. metaphor

Comparing the Metaphor and the Simile

Perhaps it would be profitable to compare the metaphor and simile side-by-side. Remember, the metaphor implies or suggests comparison by stating that something *is* something else or acts in an unusual way. The simile, on the other hand, states that something is *like* or acts *as* something else, a direct comparison. Look at the following.

METAPHOR   John is a roaring lion.
                      or
                 John roared his anger at his pride of relatives.

SIMILE   John roars *like* a lion.
                      or
                 John's voice is *as* threatening *as* a lion's.

METAPHOR   The bread is an old boot.
                      or
                 The bread booted my tongue.

SIMILE   The bread tasted *like* an old boot.
                      or
                 The bread is *as* tough *as* an old boot.

REVIEW QUESTIONS

Identify the figures of speech in the following sentences. Mark "M" for metaphor and "S" for simile.

5. Mary's lamb had fleece as white as snow.   _____

6. The lawn was a green carpet.   _____

7. The breeze kissed her brow gently.   _____

8. Jane is as tall as a giraffe.   _____

9. Hunger is a curse to be avoided.   _____

10. The boat flattened the waves like a steamroller.   _____

11. The man is as dependable as the Rock of Gibraltar.   _____

12. The leaves danced in the wind.   _____

13. The nurse's hand is down to the touch.   _____

14. His sneer rattles a warning when he enters the room.   _____

ANSWERS: 5. S; 6. M; 7. M; 8. S; 9. M; 10. S; 11. S; 12. M; 13. M; 14. M

Now that you have identified metaphors and similes in questions five through fourteen, return to these same sentences and rewrite them. If a sentence now has a metaphor, rewrite the metaphor as a simile. If a simile is now used, rewrite it as a metaphor.

15. (#5) _____

_____

16. (#6) _____

_____

17. (#7) _____

_____

18. (#8) _____

_____

19. (#9) _____

_____

20. (#10) _____

_____

21. (#11) _____

_____

22. (#12) _____

_____

23. (#13) _____

_____

24. (#14) _____

_____

ANSWERS: 15. Mary's lamb had snowy fleece; 16. The lawn was like a green carpet; 17. The breeze touched her brow gently like a kiss; 18. Jane is a giraffe in height; 19. Avoid hunger like a curse; 20. The boat steamrolled the waves; 21. The man is a Rock of Gibraltar; 22. The leaves moved like dancers in the wind; 23. The nurse's hand feels like down; 24. His sneer is like a rattler's warning when he enters the room

Now that you have identified metaphors and similes in questions five through fourteen and rewritten them in questions fifteen through twenty-four, return to questions five through fourteen and examine them for style. Mark each "D" for descriptive or "N" for narrative.

25.   sentence 5._____   30.   sentence 10._____

26.   sentence 6._____   31.   sentence 11._____

27.   sentence 7._____   32.   sentence 12._____

28.   sentence 8._____   33.   sentence 13._____

29.   sentence 9._____   34.   sentence 14._____

ANSWERS: 25. N; 26. D; 27. N; 28. D; 29. D; 30. N; 31. D; 32. N; 33. D; 34. N

35. In which of the ten questions, numbered five through fourteen, are comparisons made through

the verb?_____

36. Sentences containing comparisons made through the verb are_____sentences.

37. Figures of speech which show comparisons made through the verb are _____ .

38. Figures of speech which make use of "like" or "as" are _____ .

39. Which figure of speech is more effective in narrative style, the metaphor or simile?_____

_____

ANSWERS: 35. 7; 12, 14, 36. narrative; 37. metaphors; 38. similes; 39. metaphor

Figure 9. A sharp detail may represent the whole well.

Use of Detail to Communicate Sense Impressions

An important element in good writing is the effective use of detail. This means that the writer tries to be as specific and concrete as possible. He avoids general statements unless he plans to clarify or support them through appropriate detail. Perhaps a comparison between a detailed poetic statement and a generalized prose passage about the same subject may serve to illustrate.

Example of Generalized Prose Passage

Birches are thin, light-colored trees which bend frequently. The action of weather or the efforts of small boys who swing on birch trunks can sometimes make birches fold down so their leaves are close to the ground.

Example of Detailed Poetic Statement

BIRCHES

Robert Frost

1. When I see birches bend to left and right
2. Across the lines of straighter darker trees,
3. I like to think some boy's been swinging them.
4. But swinging doesn't bend them down to stay
5. As ice storms do. Often you must have seen them
6. Loaded with ice a sunny winter morning
7. After a rain. They click upon themselves
8. As the breeze rises, and turn many-colored
9. As the stir cracks and crazes their enamel.
10. Soon the sun's warmth makes them shed crystal shells
11. Shattering and avalanching on the snow crust—
12. Such heaps of broken glass to sweep away
13. You'd think the inner dome of heaven had fallen.
14. They are dragged to the withered bracken by the load,
15. And they seem not to break; though once they are bowed
16. So low for long, they never right themselves:
17. You may see their trunks arching in the woods
18. Years afterwards, trailing their leaves on the ground
19. Like girls on hands and knees that throw their hair
20. Before them over their heads to dry in the sun.

Now that you have read this excerpt from "Birches," can you compare it with the more generalized statement which preceded it? Return to the poem as needed and refer to the numbers of the lines when you answer the questions which follow. Find the lines of the poem which show *details* of the statements contained in questions 40 to 44.

40. "Birches are thin, light-colored trees." The lines from the poem are:_____.

41. Birches "bend frequently." Lines: _____.

42. The weather folds birches down. Lines: _____.

43. Small boys swing on and fold birches. Lines: _____.

44. Birches which have been folded down have their leaves close to the ground. Lines: _____ .

ANSWERS: 40. lines 1 & 2; 41. lines 1, 3, 4; 42. lines 5, 6; 43. line 3; 44. lines 18, 19, 20

Now, answer these other questions about the poem.

45. Can you identify a simile in any of the lines?_____

46. Can you identify a metaphor which involves the use of the word "enamel"?_____

47. Return to the poem again. Make a brief list of the expressions which you think are particularly appealing sense impressions because they help you visualize aspects of the subject of the poem.

ANSWERS: 45. lines 18, 19, 20; 46. ice is compared to enamel; 47. class discussion

OTHER TECHNIQUES OF VIVID WRITING

In addition to novel uses of words, effective comparisons, and emphasis upon specific detail, writers use other techniques too; a variety of techniques contributes to an interesting overall style.

Onomatopoeia

Onomatopoeia is an appeal to the sense of hearing. It involves the use of words which, when spoken, resemble the sounds they represent. Listen to the sounds of the underlined words in the sentences which follow.

1. The mother said, "Hush" to her child.
2. The rain pattered on the roof.
3. The cannon boomed dangerously.
4. The birds chirped merrily.
5. Angrily, the lion roared to warn us.

QUESTIONS FOR REVIEW

Create five sentences of your own which show the use of onomatopoeia.

48. _____

49. _____

50. _____

51. _____

52. _____

ANSWERS: 48. through 52. for class review

Use of Contrast

Contrast is comparison through the use of opposites. Earlier, you learned about the use of comparison through emphasis on similar characteristics; but, sometimes, the use of sharply contrasting characteristics makes an explanation clear. Let us look at two examples.

EXAMPLE

The human race shows enormous variations in size. To appreciate these variations, one need only contrast a pygmy tribe averaging four feet in height with the tribe of giants living in the fabled Solomon's mines country of Africa. These "giants" average well over six feet in height.

EXAMPLE

Solutions to the problem of crime were hard to choose. Some people suggested a humane approach which stressed rehabilitation of even the most hardened criminals. Others preferred the old Hammurabi Code which shows the concept of "an eye for an eye, a tooth for a tooth," the implication of which are such measures as amputating the hand of a thief.

QUESTIONS FOR REVIEW

53. What is the contrast in the example dealing with variations in human size?

    _____

    _____

54. What is the contrast in the paragraph dealing with crime?

    _____

    _____

    _____

55. Now, write two or three related sentences which show the effective use of contrast.

_____

_____

_____

_____

ANSWERS: 53. four-foot pygmies with "giants" averaging over six feet in height; 54. rehabilitation versus harsh punishment of criminals; 55. for class review and discussion

A Brief Review and a Few Precautions

It is important to man's survival that he be sensitive to his environment, and no one knows this more than the writer, who must be both sensitive and able to communicate his perceptions effectively.

Some of the techniques which the writers uses to communicate sense perceptions are (1) novel uses of words (the ship plowed); (2) figures of speech like the metaphor (John is a lion) and the simile (John is like a lion); (3) emphasis upon vivid, concrete detail; (4) onomatopoeia (hiss, shush); and (5) contrast (humane versus harsh law enforcement).

If you use techniques such as those reviewed in this lesson, you may improve your writing, but you should not use them excessively. To explain, one simile may be effective, but two similes may be too much. Novel use of words may be helpful, but too many novel uses may make the reader wonder about your knowledge of standard English vocabulary. Contrast may heighten the reader's ability to visualize your ideas, but *never* should the reader have to ask himself if "that particular comparison (contrast) was necessary."

In short, do not use an exaggerated style, one which *calls attention to itself* instead of to the story or the ideas which you are expressing. Enjoy your writing, but always remember: good writing shows harmony between style and idea. Now, read the three selections which follow for appreciation of style and for comprehension of ideas.

FEBRUARY 2002: THE LOCUSTS
Ray Bradbury

The rockets set the bony meadows afire, turned rock to lava, turned wood to charcoal, transmitted water to steam, made sand and silica into green glass which lay shattered mirrors reflecting the invasion, all about. The rockets came like drums, beating in the night. The rockets came like locusts, swarming and settling in blooms of rosy smoke. And from the rockets ran men with hammers in their hands to beat the strange world into a shape that was familiar to the eye, to bludgeon away all the strangeness, their mouths fringed with nails so that they resembled steel-toothed carnivores, spitting them into their swift hands as they hammered up frame cottages and scuttled over roofs with shingles to blot out the eery stars, and fit green shades to pull against the night. And when the carpenters had hurried on, the women came in with flowerpots and chintz and pans and set up a kitchen clamor to cover the silence that Mars made waiting outside the door and the shaded window.

In six months a dozen small towns had been laid down upon the naked planet, filled with sizzling neon tubes and yellow electric bulbs. In all, some ninety thousand people come to Mars, and more, on Earth, were packing their grips. . . .

Appreciation of Style

1. Does Bradbury use detail to show sense impressions effectively? Select examples to illustrate.
2. Identify some similes.
3. Find evidence of the use of contrast.
4. Is the excerpt narrative or expository?
5. Look at the word "fringed" in line eleven. Is this an unusual use for the word, perhaps novel?

Test Your Comprehension

1. The simile, "The rockets came like locusts. . ." is a clue to the author's attitude, the tone he sets, toward what is happening. How does he feel?
2. What are the people doing to their new environment?
3. What theme (big idea) does Bradbury want us to draw from this excerpt?

Vocabulary for Study

transmitted   scuttled   bludgeon   clamor

MACARTHUR PARK

Jimmy Webb

I

Spring was never waiting for us, girl, it ran one step
    ahead as we followed in a dance
between the parted pages, and were pressed in Love's
    hot fevered iron
like a striped pair of pants.

(Chorus)

MacArthur Park is melting in the dark
all the sweet, green icing flowing down.
Someone left the cake out in the rain.
I don't think I can make it
'cause it took so long to bake it
And I'll never have the recipe again, oh no.

II
I recall the yellow cotton dress
foaming like a wave on the ground around your knees
the birds like tender babies in your hands
and the old men playing checkers by the trees.

(Repeat Chorus)

III
There will be another song for me, for I will sing it.
There will be another dream for me; someone will
        bring it.
I will drink the wine while it is warm
and never let you catch me looking at the sun.
But after all the loves of my life,
you'll still be the one.
I will take my life into my hands, and I will use it.
I will win the worship in their eyes, and I will lose it.
I will have the things that I desire, and my passions
        flow like rivers to the sky,
But after all the loves of my life, oh, after all
        the loves of my life,
I'll be thinking of you and wondering why.

(Repeat Chorus)

Appreciation of Style

1. What things are compared in the following quotes:
   a. "... Park is melting in the dark..."
   b. "we ... were pressed in Love's ... iron like a ... pair of pants."
   c. "the sweet, green icing flowing down."

2. Is the use of "foaming" in connection with "yellow cotton dress" in stanza two effective in stimulating your senses? What picture do you get?

3. The chorus is an extended metaphor. What "large" comparison is made?

4. Is the poem narrative or expository?

Test Your Comprehension

1. What is the author's emotion (tone) in this poem?

2. Briefly, summarize the story in your own words.

3. Does the author expect you to share his feelings? Why?

MOTHER TO SON
Langston Hughes

Well, son, I'll tell you:
Life for me ain't been no crystal stair,
It's had tacks in it,
And splinters,
And boards torn up,
And places with no carpets on the floor—
Bare.

Figure 10. "Black Child" by Schain. Permission of the artist.

But all the time
I'se been a-climbin' on
And reachin' landin's
And turnin' corners,
And sometimes goin' in the dark
Where there ain't been no light.
So, boy, don't you turn back.
Don't you set down on the steps
"Cause you find it kinder hard.
Don't you fall now—
For I'se still goin', honey,
I'se still climbin'
And life for me ain't been no crystal stair.

Appreciation of Style

1. Much of the language is concrete and appeals sharply to the senses in creating pictures. Select examples.
2. There is effective contrast within lines 1-4. Identify.
3. Why does the poet use nonstandard English?
4. From what point of view was the poem written?

Test Your Comprehension

1. Describe the character of the speaker.
2. What advice does the speaker give? Is it good advice?
3. What is the author's purpose in this poem?

Final Practice Exercise

In separate sentences, write twenty sense impressions of your environment. Use a narrative style chiefly and emphasize sharp, concrete detail. Include samples of comparison and contrast; metaphor and simile; creative and interesting uses of words; and onomatopoeia. Do not use any one technique more than you do others.

1. _____

_____

2. _____

_____

3. _____

_____

4. _____

_____

5. _____

_____

6. _____

_____

7. _____

_____

8. _____

_____

9. _____

_____

10. _____

_____

11. _____

_____

12. _____

_____

13. _____

_____

14. _____

_____

15. _____

_____

16._____

_____

17._____

_____

18._____

_____

19._____

_____

20._____

_____

*After you finish this practice exercise,
turn to page 113 and read the story.*

Figure 11. "For all that, it is the truth!" From "Studies of Expressions for 'Battle of Anghiari'" by Da Vinci, Budapest Museum of Fine Arts.

(handwritten margin note: DESCRIBE MAN AS IF HE WERE AN ANIMAL)

THE PIECE OF STRING*

Guy de Maupassant

It was market-day, and over all the roads around Goderville the peasants and their wives were coming towards the town. The men walked easily, lurching the whole body forward at every step. Their long legs were twisted and deformed by the slow, painful labors of the country:—by bending over to plough, which is what also makes their left shoulders too high and their figures crooked; and by reaping corn, which obliges them for steadiness' sake to spread their knees too wide. Their starched blue blouses, shining as though varnished, ornamented at collar and cuffs with little patterns of white stitch-work, and blown up big around their bony bodies, seemed exactly like balloons about to soar, but putting forth a head, two arms, and two feet.

(handwritten margin notes: BIG EVENT / EVERYONE PUTING ON A SHOW)

Some of these fellows dragged a cow or a calf at the end of a rope. And just behind the animal, beating it over the back with a leaf-covered branch to hasten its pace, went their wives, carrying large baskets from which came forth the heads of chickens or the heads of ducks. These women walked with steps far shorter and quicker than the men; their figures, withered and upright, were adorned with scanty little shawls pinned over their flat bosoms; and they enveloped their heads each in a white cloth, close fastened round the hair and surmounted by a cap.

Now a char-à-banc passed by, drawn by a jerky-paced nag. It shook up strangely the two men on the seat. And the woman at the bottom of the cart held fast to its sides to lessen the hard joltings.

In the market-place at Goderville was a great crowd, a mingled multitude of men and beasts. The horns of cattle, the high and long-napped hats of wealthy peasants, the head-dresses of the women, came to the surface of that sea. And voices clamorous, sharp, shrill, made a continuous and savage din. Above it a huge burst of laughter from the sturdy lungs of a merry yokel would sometimes sound, and sometimes a long bellow from a cow tied fast to the wall of a house.

(handwritten margin notes: COMPARES MEN & ANIMALS)

It all smelled of the stable, of milk, of hay, and of perspiration, giving off that half-human, half-animal odor which is peculiar to the men of the fields.

Maître Hauchecorne, of Bréauté, had just arrived at Goderville, and was taking his way towards the square, when he perceived on the ground a little piece of string. Maître Hauchecorne, economical, like all true Normans, reflected that everything was worth picking up which could be of any use; and he stooped down—but painfully, because he suffered from rheumatism. He took the bit of thin cord from the ground, and was carefully preparing to roll it up when he saw Maître Malandain, the harness-maker, on his door-step, looking at him. They had once had a quarrel about a halter, and they had remained angry, bearing malice on both sides. Maître Hauchecorne was overcome with a sort of shame at being seen by his enemy looking in the dirt so for a bit of string. He quickly hid his find beneath his blouse; then in the pocket of his breeches; then pretended to be still looking for something on the ground which he did not discover; and at last went off towards the market-place, with his head bent forward, and a body almost doubled in two by rheumatic pains.

He lost himself immediately in the crowd, which was clamorous, slow, and agitated by interminable bargains. The peasants examined the cows, went off, came back, always in great perplexity and fear of being cheated, never quite daring to decide, spying at the eye of the seller, trying ceaselessly to discover the tricks of the man and the defect in the beast.

(handwritten margin notes: HE HAD BEEN JUDGED LIKE AN ANIMAL)

The women, having placed their great baskets at their feet, had pulled out the poultry, which lay upon the ground, tied by the legs, with eyes scared, with combs scarlet.

They listened to propositions, maintaining their prices, with a dry manner, with an impassible face; or, suddenly, perhaps, deciding to take the lower price which was offered, they cried out to the customer, who was departing slowly:

"All right, I'll let you have them, Maìt' Anthime."

---

*A translation by Jonathan Sturges, from *The Odd Number: Thirteen Tales by Guy de Maupassant* (New York: Harper and Brothers, 1889), pp. 73-87.

Then, little by little, the square became empty, and when the *Angelus* struck mid-day those who lived at a distance poured into the inns.

At Jourdain's the great room was filled with eaters, just as the vast court was filled with vehicles of every sort—wagons, gigs, char-à-bancs, tilburys, tilt-carts which have no name, yellow with mud, misshapen, pieced together, raising their shafts to heaven like two arms, or it may be with their nose in the dirt and their rear in the air.

Just opposite to where the diners were at table the huge fireplace, full of clear flame, threw a lively heat on the backs of those who sat along the right. Three spits were turning, loaded with chickens, with pigeons, and with joints of mutton; and a delectable odor of roast meat, and of gravy gushing over crisp brown skin, took wing from the hearth, kindled merriment, caused mouths to water.

All the aristocracy of the plough were eat-ing there, at Maît' Jourdain's, the innkeeper's, a dealer in horses also, and a sharp fellow who had made a pretty penny in his day.

The dishes were passed round, were emptied, with jugs of yellow cider. Every one told of his affairs, of his purchases and his sales. They asked news about the crops. The weather was good for green stuffs, but a little wet for wheat.

All of a sudden the drum rolled in the court before the house. Every one, except some of the most indifferent, was on his feet at once, and ran to the door, to the windows, with his mouth still full and his napkin in his hand.

When the public crier had finished his tattoo he called forth in a jerky voice, making his pauses out of time:

"Be it known to the inhabitants of Goderville, and in general to all—persons present at the market, that there has been lost this morning, on the Beuzeville road, between—nine and ten o'clock, a pocket-book of black leather, containing five hundred francs and business papers. You are re-quested to return it—to the mayor's office, at once, or to Maître Fortuné Houlbreque, of Manneville. There will be twenty francs reward."

Then the man departed. They heard once more at a distance the dull beatings on the drum and the faint voice of the crier.

Then they began to talk of this event, reckoning up the chances which Maître Houlbrèque had of finding or of not finding his pocket-book again.

And the meal went on.

They were finishing their coffee when the corporal of gendarmes appeared on the threshold. He asked:

"Is Maître Hauchecorne, of Bréauté, here?"

Maître Hauchecorne, seated at the other end of the table, answered:

"Here I am."

And the corporal resumed:

"Maître Hauchecorne, will you have the kindness to come with me to the mayor's office? M. le Maire would like to speak to you."

The peasant, surprised and uneasy, gulped down his little glass of cognac, got up, and, even worse bent over than in the morning, since the first steps after a rest were always particularly difficult, started off, repeating:

"Here I am, here I am."

And he followed the corporal.

The mayor was waiting for him, seated in an arm-chair. He was the notary of the place, a tall, grave man of pompous speech.

"Maître Hauchecorne," said he, "this morning, on the Beuzeville road, you were seen to pick up the pocket-book lost by Maître Houlbrèque, of Manneville."

The countryman, speechless, regarded the mayor, frightened already by this suspicion which rested on him he knew not why.

"I, I picked up that pocket-book?"

"Yes, you."

"I swear I didn't even know nothing about it at all."

"You were seen."   JUDGED BY APEARANCES

"They saw me, me? Who is that who saw me?"

"M. Malandain, the harness-maker."

Then the old man remembered, understood, and, reddening with anger:

"Ah! he saw me, did he, the rascal? He saw me picking up this string here, M'sieu' le Maire."

And, fumbling at the bottom of his pocket, he pulled out of it the little end of string.

But the mayor incredulously shook his head:

"You will not make me believe, Maître Hauchecorne, that M. Malandain, who is a man worthy of credit, has mistaken this string for a pocket-book."

The peasant, furious, raised his hand and spit as if to attest his good faith, repeating:

"For all that, it is the truth of the good God, the blessed truth, M'sieu' le Maire. There! on my soul and my salvation I repeat it."

The mayor continued:

"After having picked up the thing in question, you even looked for some time in the mud to see if a piece of money had not dropped out of it."

The good man was suffocated with indignation and with fear:

"If they can say!-if they can say . . . such lies as that to slander an honest man! If they can say!—"

He might protest, he was not believed.

He was confronted with M. Malandain, who repeated and sustained his testimony. They abused one another for an hour. At his own request Maître Hauchecorne was searched. Nothing was found upon him.

At last, the mayor, much perplexed, sent him away, warning him that he would inform the public prosecutor, and ask for orders.

The news had spread. When he left the mayor's office, the old man was surrounded, interrogated with a curiosity which was serious or mocking as the case might be, but into which no indignation entered. And he began to tell the story of the string. They did not believe him. They laughed.

He passed on, button-holed by every one, himself button-holing his acquaintances, beginning over and over again his tale and his protestations, showing his pockets turned inside out to prove that he had nothing.

They said to him:

"You old rogue, *va!*"

And he grew angry, exasperated, feverish, in despair at not being believed, and always telling his story.

The night came. It was time to go home. He set out with three of his neighbors, to whom he pointed out the place where he had picked up the end of string; and all the way he talked of his adventure.

That evening he made the round in the village of Bréauté, so as to tell every one. He met only unbelievers.

He was ill of it all night long.

The next day, about one in the afternoon, Marius Paumelle, a farm hand of Maître Breton, the market-gardener at Ymauville, returned the pocket-book and its contents to Maître Houlbrèque, of Manneville.

This man said, indeed, that he had found it on the road; but not knowing how to read, he had carried it home and given it to his master.

The news spread to the environs. Maître Hauchecorne was informed. He put himself at once upon the go, and began to relate his story as completed by the *dénouement.* He triumphed.

"What grieved me," said he, 'was not the thing itself, do you understand; but it was the lies. There's nothing does you so much harm as being in disgrace for lying."

All day he talked of his adventure, he told it on the roads to the people who passed; at the cabaret to the people who drank; and the next Sunday, when they came out of church. He even stopped strangers to tell them about it. He was easy, now, and yet something worried him without his knowing exactly what it was. People had a joking manner while they listened. They did not seem convinced. He seemed to feel their tittle-tattle behind his back.

On Tuesday of the next week he went to market at Goderville, prompted entirely by the need of telling his story.

Malandain, standing on his door-step, began to laugh as he saw him pass. Why?

He accosted a farmer of Criquetot, who did not let him finish, and, giving him a punch in the pit of his stomach, cried in his face: "Oh you great rogue, *va!*" Then turned his heel upon him.

Maître Hauchecorne remained speechless, and grew more and more uneasy. Why had they called him "great rogue"?

When seated at table in Jourdain's tavern he began again to explain the whole affair.

A horse-dealer of Montivilliers shouted at him:

"Get out, get out you old scamp; I know all about your string!"

Hauchecorne stammered:

"But since they found it again, the pocket-book!"

But the other continued:

"Hold your tongue, daddy; there's one who finds it and there's another who returns it. And no one the wiser."

The peasant was choked. He understood at last. They accused him of having had the pocket-book brought back by an accomplice, by a confederate.

He tried to protest. The whole table began to laugh.

He could not finish his dinner, and went away amid a chorus of jeers.

He went home, ashamed and indignant, choked with rage, with confusion, the more cast-down since from his Norman cunning, he was, perhaps, capable of having done what they accused him of, and even of boasting of it as a good trick. His innocence dimly seemed to him impossible to prove, his craftiness being so well known. And he felt himself struck to the heart by the injustice of the suspicion.

Then he began anew to tell of his adventure, lengthening his recital every day, each time adding new proofs, more energetic protestations, and more solemn oaths which he thought of, which he prepared in his hours of solitude, his mind being entirely occupied by the story of the string. The more complicated his defence, the more artful his arguments, the less he was believed.

"Those are liars' proofs," they said behind his back.

He felt this; it preyed upon his heart. He exhausted himself in useless efforts.

He was visibly wasting away.

The jokers now made him tell the story of "The Piece of String" to amuse them, just as you make a soldier who has been on a campaign tell his story of the battle. His mind, struck at the root, grew weak.

About the end of December he took to his bed.

He died early in January, and, in the delirium of the death-agony, he protested his innocence, repeating:

"A little bit of string—a little bit of string—see, here it is, M'sieu' le Maire."

Appreciation of Style

1. Guy de Maupassant made very effective use of specific detail to communicate sense impressions. Refer to examples in the story to prove that this is so.
   a. The setting or environment
   b. Descriptions of characters in the story
   c. Details of the actions of characters
   d. The language of dialogue

2. Identify the tone (author's attitude) of the story.

3. What comparison is made in the following sentence:

"Their starched blue blouses, shining as though varnished, ornamented at collar and cuffs with little patterns of white stitch-work, and blown up around their bony bodies, seemed exactly like balloons about to soar, but putting forth a head, two arms, and two feet."

4. Is the language of the story particularly emotional? How would you describe the language?

5. In which character do you see the greatest change in mood? Why?

Test Your Comprehension

1. Why aren't we surprised that Hauchecorne would stoop to pick up a piece of string?

2. Why is it important to the story that Hauchecorne kept looking at the ground after he had already picked up the string?

3. The story has a twist of irony: after the wallet has been returned by someone else, people still believe that Hauchecorne is guilty. Can you explain this?

4. What is the theme of this story?

Vocabulary for Study

adorned	clamorous	confronted
scanty	perplexity	environs
din	indignation	denouement

Narrative—Mood Sequence

A narrative-mood sequence shows a series of events in which a character's experiences in his environment cause his mood (emotional attitude) and, thus, his behavior to change. The narrative-mood sequence has a certain form:

1. The character *shows* the beginning of a recognizable mood (love, anger, frustration) through the way he behaves.
2. He is stimulated by his own thoughts, actions, or by people or things in his environment.
3. He reacts to his experience and he reveals changes in his mood.
4. He performs an act which is his final response to his change in mood.

Example of a Narrative-Mood Sequence

Let us look at an example of a brief narrative-mood sequence which you, as a student, may find familiar.

Derek arose early the day following spring final exams, his eyes reddened from a sleepless night. He washed the scale from his eyes, dressed, and went to the kitchen. There, coffee perked, filling the bright room with morning incense. Derek nodded absently to his mother who was turning some sizzling bacon. He sat at the kitchen table, his eyes refusing to focus on the morning paper spread by his plate.

As he glanced repeatedly at his watch, the coffee in his cup cooled and the bacon and eggs lay untouched on his plate. He barely responded to his mother's cheerful comments as he focused on his wrist, watching the hands of his watch march slowly, minute by minute, toward the time for his departure for school.

Smiling apologetically when it was time to leave, Derek opened the kitchen door and stepped out into a brilliant day, the air country sweet and alive with morning sounds. Slowly, he backed his car from the garage.

He drove down the hill to the highway, up the highway for three miles, and into the student parking area at school. Feeling more and more anxious, with even a tinge of nausea, Derek walked immediately to the Administration building where final grades were posted.

At the bulletin board, he found many students seeking the information he sought. After some jostling, he came close enough to see:

Geology III

Moore, Derek . . . . B

"B!" he thought, a widening of his lips, a crinkling of his eyes, a scintillating of the nerves in his back accompanying this knowledge. "Whoopee, I made it!" he shouted as he ran down the corridor to call home.

QUESTIONS ABOUT THE NARRATIVE-MOOD SEQUENCE

1. What is Derek's initial mood shown in the narrative hook and the balance of the first paragraph?

   _____

   _____

   _____

2. How does Derek react to most things in his environment? Why?

   _____

   _____

   _____

   _____

3. What causes Derek's change in mood?

   _____

   _____

4. Describe Derek's new mood.

   _____

   _____

5. Does he do something to show his change of mood?

   _____

   _____

6. What value is served by the author's use of such details as "odor of fresh coffee," and "brilliant day, the air sweet. . ."?

   _____

7. Is Derek's failure to react to ordinarily pleasant sense impressions consistent with his initial

   mood?_____(yes or no)

8. Is Derek's reaction to the one stimulus which changes his mood believable?_____(yes or no)

ANSWERS: 1. fearful, preoccupied; 2. His mood prevents him from reacting to most things around him; he shows apathy; 3. He got a good grade in geology; 4. joyful, excited; 5. He shouts, smiles and runs to call home; 6. They provide contrast with Derek's mood; 7. yes; 8. yes

TWO ADDITIONAL EXAMPLES

Let us look at two more brief narrative-mood sequences. In each, notice, first, how the chief character is shown in one mood. Second, observe how sense impressions "crowd in on" each character, creating a gradual build-up of relatively mild emotional reaction, mostly within the characters. Third, notice how the burden of his impressions finally causes a definite change in each character's mood. Fourth, look for the obvious action of the character which shows his change in mood.

John turned his head sideways, cupped his hand over his ear and concentrated on the television picture.

"Our tour will take us to Rome on the fourteenth day," Martha announced.

John leaned toward the set, his eye and uncovered ear concentrating on the simulated moon landing, as the commentator announced the rate of descent and the altitude of the Lunar Excursion Module. The oven clock clamored the passing of a set hour, and John scooted to the edge of his chair to hear the intervals as they came from the set.

"Listen to this! Listen to this!" Martha exclaimed, reading from the tour guide. John poked a finger into his ear and squinted deliberately at the set. A dog bounded into the room, jumped into John's lap, and tried to lick his face. Pushing the dog from his lap, John focused on the set once again.

"One hundred feet altitude; 17.5 feet per minute descent; sixty feet per minute horizontal," the announcer briefed the audience.

John bent over the dog, cradling his arms on the floor to get nearer the set.

"Oh what a nice poochy," said Martha.

"Isn't he growling?" asked George. "Look, he wants to kiss John."

Inching out on the floor, John cupped his hands to focus both ears on the television, his eyes fighting to lock onto the picture.

"Why don't they have actual pictures?" Martha asked. "This is silly," she exclaimed, her voice drowning the announcer's.

"Fifty feet," said the announcer as George interrupted once again.

"Don't they have any cameras on board?"

John snaked onto his stomach to move nearer the set.

"Seventeen feet from touchdown," the announcer exclaimed feverishly.

"Now here is the high point of our trip," Martha gushed, reading from the brochure. John rose, ran to the bedroom, turned on the second television set and locked the door.

QUESTIONS FOR REVIEW

9. Identify John's original mood. _____

_____

10. Identify the semse impressions which irritate him in order of their appearance. _____

_____

_____

11. What are John's gradual, mild responses to his sense impressions? Be specific.

_____

_____

_____

_____

12. What finally shows the change in John's mood?

_____

_____

_____

13. What do you think the tone (writer's attitude) of the selection is?

_____

_____

_____

ANSWERS: 9. He was trying to concentrate; 10. Martha's talk, oven clock, dog, George's talk; 11. cupping hand over ear, leaning toward television, scooting to edge of chair, quieting dog, inching onto the floor, moving on stomach to set; 12. He leaves room and locks himself in with another set; 13. The writer sympathizes with John's discomfort at the interruptions.

Ernie anxiously studied the typewriter keys, his face locked in a determined scowl. He caught himself humming in tune with the air conditioner and looked over to the blank space in his notes. Outside, a dog barked at a cat who returned the challenge, and Ernie shook his head.

A car squeaked to a stop in the street opposite his front door, but Ernie, determinedly, looked back at the typewriter keys, trying to refocus his mind. Then, as if in rebuke, a stereo set from the parked car faintly ground out an erotic love call. Ernie closed his eyes as if to shut out the music.

He shuddered as shortly thereafter, the kitchen sink began to pound out its own melody of drops. His eyes scanned the notes leading to the blank page.

He winced as a passing car blew a tribute to the lovers in the parked car. Finally, he slammed the cover on his notes, rose and went to bed.

QUESTIONS FOR REVIEW

Analyze this narrative-mood sequence, dealing with the same information called for in questions nine through thirteen. Write your analysis in the form of a paragraph.

_____

_____

_____

_____

_____

_____

_____

_____

A Few Additional Comments

A narrative-mood sequence reveals change in a character's emotion (mood) as a direct result of his experiences (sense impressions). The actions which follow this change of mood must seem consistent with that mood or the reader will not believe in them.

The writer uses a narrative-mood sequence to reveal change, good or bad, in a character and to show his own attitude (tone) toward what is happening. The writer accomplishes these purposes through careful selection of the particular sense impressions which are shown affecting the characters in a story.

Such a sequence may deal with a single event from the life of a character, as do the examples you have just read, or it may extend over a longer period of time. However, the critical factor is structure: a character is shown with a beginning mood which develops or changes logically as a result of his sense impressions. Finally, as the character's mood reaches a strong or intense state, he is *compelled* to act.

Now, two reading selections follow. As you read them, try to be sensitive to their *structure* and meaning.

THE GIRLS IN THEIR SUMMER DRESSES

Irwin Shaw

Fifth Avenue was shining in the sun when they left the Brevoort. The sun was warm, even though it was February, and everything looked like Sunday morning—the buses and the well-dressed people walking slowly in couples and the quiet buildings with the windows closed.

Michael held Frances' arm tightly as they walked toward Washington Square in the sunlight. They walked lightly, almost smiling, because they had slept late and had a good breakfast and it was Sunday. Michael unbuttoned his coat and let if flap around him in the mild wind.

easy- free —

"Look out," Frances said as they crossed Eighth Street. "You'll break your neck." Michael laughed and Frances laughed with him.

"She's not so pretty," Frances said. "Anyway, not pretty enough to take a chance of breaking your neck."

Michael laughed again. "How did you know I was looking at her?"

Frances cocked her head to one side and smiled at her husband under the brim of her hat. "Mike, darling," she said.

"O.K.," he said. "Excuse me."

Frances patted his arm lightly and pulled him along a little faster toward Washington Square. "Let's not see anybody all day," she said. "Let's just hang around with each other. You and me. We're always up to our neck in people, drinking their Scotch or drinking our Scotch; we only see each other in bed. I want to go out with my husband all day long. I want him to talk only to me and listen only to me."

"What's to stop us?" Michael asked.

"The Stevensons. They want us to drop by around one o'clock and they'll drive us into the country."

"The cunning Stevensons," Mike said. "Transparent. They can whistle. They can go driving in the country by themselves."

"Is it a date?"

"It's a date."

Frances leaned over and kissed him on the tip of the ear.

"Darling," Michael said, "this is Fifth Avenue."

"Let me arrange a program," Frances said. "A planned Sunday in New York for a young couple with money to throw away."

"Go easy."

"First let's go to the Metropolitan Museum of Art," Frances suggested, because Michael had said during the week he wanted to go. "I haven't been there in three years and there are at least ten pictures I want to see again. Then we can take the bus down to Radio City and watch them skate. And later we'll go down to Cavanagh's and get a steak as big as a blacksmith's apron, with a bottle of wine, and after that there's a French picture at the Filmarte that everybody says—say, are you listening to me?"

"Sure," he said. He took his eyes off the hatless girl with the dark hair, cut dancer-style like a helmet, who was walking past him.

"That's the program for the day," Frances said flatly. "Or maybe you'd just rather walk up and down Fifth Avenue."

"No," Michael said. "Not at all."

"You always look at other women," Frances said. "Everywhere. Every damned place we go."

"No, darling," Michael said, "I look at everything. God gave me eyes and I look at women and men in subway excavations and moving pictures and the little flowers of the field. I casually inspect the universe."

"You ought to see the look in your eye," Frances said, "as you casually inspect the universe on Fifth Avenue."

"I'm a happily married man." Michael pressed her elbow tenderly. "Example for the whole twentieth century—Mr. and Mrs. Mike Loomis. Hey, let's have a drink," he said, stopping.

"We just had breakfast."

"Now listen, darling," Mike said, choosing his words with care, "it's a nice day and we both feel good and there's no reason why we have to break it up. Let's have a nice Sunday."

"All right. I don't know why I started this. Let's drop it. Let's have a good time."

They joined hands consciously and walked without talking among the baby carriages and the old Italian men in their Sunday clothes and the young women with Scotties in Washington Square Park.

"At least once a year everyone should go to the Metropolitan Museum of Art," Frances said after a while, her tone a good imitation of the tone she had used at breakfast and at the beginning of their walk. "And it's nice on Sunday. There're a lot of people looking at the pictures and you get the feeling maybe Art isn't on the decline in New York City, after all—"

"I want to tell you something," Michael said very seriously. "I have not touched another women. Not once. In all the five years."

"All right," Frances said.

"You believe that, don't you?"

"All right."

They walked between the crowded benches, under the scrubby city-park trees.

"I try not to notice it," Frances said, "but I feel rotten inside, in my stomach, when we pass a woman and you look at her and I see that look in your eye and that's the way you looked at me the first time. In Alice Maxwell's house. Standing there in the living room, next to the radio, with a green hat on and all those people."

"I remember the hat," Michael said.

"The same look," Frances said. "And it makes me feel bad. It makes me feel terrible."

"Sh-h-h, please, darling, sh-h-h."

"I think I would like a drink now," Frances said.

They walked over to a bar on Eighth Street, not saying anything, Michael automatically helping her over curbstones and guiding her past automobiles. They sat near a window in the bar and the sun streamed in and there was a small, cheerful fire in the fireplace. A little Japanese waiter came over and put down some pretzels and smiled happily at them.

"What do you order after breakfast?" Michael asked.

"Brandy, I suppose," Frances said.

"Courvoisier," Michael told the waiter. "Two Courvoisiers."

The waiter came with the glasses and they sat drinking the brandy in the sunlight. Michael finished half his and drank a little water.

"I look at women," he said. "Correct. I don't say it's wrong or right. I look at them. If I pass them on the street and I don't look at them, I'm fooling you, I'm fooling myself."

"You look at them as though you want them," Frances said, playing with her brandy glass. "Every one of them."

"In a way," Michael said, speaking softly and not to his wife, "in a way that's true. I don't do anything about it, but it's true."

"I know it. That's why I feel bad."

"Another brandy," Michael called. "Waiter, two more brandies."

He sighed and closed his eyes and rubbed them gently with his fingertips. "I love the way women look. One of the things I like best about New York is the battalions of women. When I first came to New York from Ohio that was the first thing I noticed, the million wonderful women, all over the city. I walked around with my heart in my throat."

"A kid," Frances said. "That's a kid's feeling."

"Guess again," Michael said. "Guess again. I'm older now. I'm a man getting near middle age, putting on a little fat, and I still love to walk along Fifth Avenue at three o'clock on the east side of the street between Fiftieth and Fifty-seventh Streets. They're all out then, shopping, in their furs and their crazy hats, everything all concentrated from all over the world into seven blocks— the best furs, the best clothes, the handsomest women, out to spend money and feeling good about it."

The Japanese waiter put the two drinks down, smiling with great happiness.

"Everything is all right?" he asked.

"Everything is wonderful," Michael said.

"If it's just a couple of fur coats," Frances said, "and forty-five dollar hats—"

"It's not the fur coats. Or the hats. That's just the scenery for that particular kind of woman. Understand," he said, "you don't have to listen to this."

"I want to listen."

"I like the girls in the offices. Neat, with their eyeglasses, smart, chipper, knowing what everything is about. I like the girls on Forty-fourth Street at lunchtime, the actresses, all dressed up on nothing a week. I like the salesgirls in the stores, paying attention to you first because you're a man, leaving lady customers waiting. I got all this stuff accumulated in me because I've been thinking about it for ten years and now you've asked for it and here it is."

"Go ahead," Frances said.

"When I think of New York City, I think of all the girls on parade in the city. I don't know whether it's something special with me or whether every man in the city walks around with the same feeling inside him, but I feel as though I'm at a picnic in this city. I like to sit near the woman in the theatres, the famous beauties who've taken six hours to get ready and look it. And the young girls at the football games, with the red cheeks, and when the warm weather comes, the girls in their summer dresses."

He finished his drink. "That's the story."

Frances finished her drink and swallowed two or three times extra. "You say you love me?"

"I love you."

"I'm pretty, too," Frances said. "As pretty as any of them."

"You're beautiful," Michael said.

"I'm good for you," Frances said, pleading. "I've made a good wife, a good housekeeper, a good friend. I'd do any damn thing for you."

"I know," Michael said. He put his hand out and grasped hers.

"You'd like to be free to—" Frances said.

"Sh-h-h."

"Tell the truth." She took her hand away from under his.

Michael flicked the edge of his glass with his finger. "O.K.," he said gently. "Sometimes I feel I would like to be free."

"Well," Frances said, "any time you say."

"Don't be foolish." Michael swung his chair around to her side of the table and patted her thigh.

She began to cry silently into her handkerchief, bent over just enough so that nobody else in the bar would notice. "Someday," she said, crying, "you're going to make a move."

Michael didn't say anything. He sat watching the bartender slowly peel a lemon.

"Aren't you?" Frances asked harshly. "Come on, tell me. Talk. Aren't you?"

"Maybe," Michael said. He moved his chair back again. "How the hell do I know?"

"You know," Frances persisted. "Don't you know?"

"Yes," Michael said after a while, "I know."

Frances stopped crying then. Two or three snuffles into the handkerchief and she put it away and her face didn't tell anything to anybody. "At least do me one favor," she said.

"Sure."

"Stop talking about how pretty this woman is or that one. Nice eyes, nice breasts, a pretty figure, good voice." She mimicked his voice. "Keep it to yourself. I'm not interested."

Michael waved to the waiter. "I'll keep it to myself," he said.

Frances flicked the corners of her eyes. "Another brandy," she told the waiter.

"Two," Michael said.

"Yes, Ma'am, yes sir," said the waiter, backing away.

Frances regarded Michael coolly across the table. "Do you want me to call the Stevensons?" she asked. "It'll be nice in the country."

"Sure," Michael said. "Call them."

She got up from the table and walked across the room toward the telephone. Michael watched her walk, thinking what a pretty girl, what nice legs.

★ ★ ★

Appreciation of Style

1. Identify the points of view the author uses in this story.
2. What is the emotional tone of the setting (physical environment) shown in the first paragraph?
3. Identify the initial moods of the characters. Do the moods match the emotional tone of the setting?
4. What are the sense impressions shown which stimulate changes in mood?
5. Is the final mood of the two characters the same as the initial mood?
6. What is the act which completes the narrative-mood sequence? Is it believable?
7. Can you find examples of sharp, colorful use of words and detail?

Test Your Comprehension

1. Shaw draws his characterization well. Find a single modifier (adjective) to describe Frances' character. Support your choice by referring to details from the story.
2. Does Shaw show Michael as a basically honest person? Prove your answer by referring to the story.
3. Did Shaw re-create an experience which is, perhaps, common in male-female relationships in our society? Prepare a brief comment.

Vocabulary for Study

evacuation   chipper   scrubby

DOG

Lawrence Ferlinghetti

The dog trots freely in the street
        and sees reality.
And the things he sees are bigger
        than himself,
And the things he sees are his reality;
        drunks in doorways,
        moons on trees.
The dog trots freely through the streets,
And the things he sees are smaller
        than himself:
        Fish on newsprint;
        Ants in holes;
        Chickens in China Town windows,
        their heads a block away.
The ·log trots freely in the street
        and the things he smells
        smell something like himself.
The dog trots freely in the street
        past puddles and babies;
        cats in cigars;
        poolrooms and policemen.

He doesn't hate cops; he merely has
    no use for them.
    He goes past them,
    past the dead cows hung up whole
    in front of the San Francisco meat market.
He would rather eat a tender cow than a tough
    policeman, though either might do.
He goes past the Romeo Ravioli Factory.
    Past Coit's tower,
    Past Congressman Doyle.*
He's afraid of Coit's tower, but he's not
    afraid of Congressman Doyle.
Although, what he hears is very discouraging,
    very depressing, very absurd,
To a sad young dog like himself, to a
    serious young dog like himself,
But he has his own free world to live in,
    his own fleas to eat.
    He will not be muzzled.
Congressman Doyle is just another fire hydrant to him.
The dog trots freely in the street
And has his own dog's life to live,
Touching and tasting and testing everything,
    investigating everything
    without benefit of perjury.
A real realist, with a real tale to tell,
And a real tail to tell it with.
A real, live, barking, democratic dog,
Engaged in real, free enterprise,
With something to say about ontology,
With something to say about reality,
    And how to see it,
    And how to hear it,
With his head cocked sideways at street corners
As if he is just about to have his picture
    taken for Victor Records,
Listening for his master's voice,
And looking like a living question mark
    into the great Gramophone of
    puzzling existence,
With its wondrous hollow horn
Which always seems just about to spout
Forth some victorious answer to
    everything.

Appreciation of Style

1. In this narrative poem, the poet uses a dog to symbolize himself. The dog sets out on a tour of his environment with, perhaps, no stronger emotion (mood) than curiosity. What is the *final* mood of the dog?

---

*Doyle was the head of the House of Representatives un-American Activities Committee at the time.

2. Identify some of the dog's experiences (sense impressions), including some he liked and some he didn't like, as well as some he scarcely noticed.

3. Is the language of the poem appropriate to the subject?

4. Is this poem a narrative-mood sequence? Support your opinion.

Test Your Comprehension

1. What was the author's reason for selecting a dog to symbolize himself?

2. Interpret the meaning of the following lines:
   a. "But he has his own free world to live in, his own fleas to eat.
      He will not be muzzled."

   b. "Touching and tasting and testing everything,"
   c. "A real, live, barking, democratic dog,
      Engaged in real, free enterprise,"

3. The poem has a strong theme. Identify it and support your opinion by referring to the text.

Vocabulary for Study

perjury   ontology   wondrous

> **Writing Sample Number Six:** Follow the directions for writing a narrative-mood sequence, including those on the Assignment-Evaluation sheet.

Directions for Planning a Narrative-Mood Sequence

1. Select a character in a clear emotional state (angry, loving, sad), who is in a particular environment.

2. Choose some sense impressions appropriate to his environment to stimulate your character. You may find that a review of the sense impressions you wrote in Chapter 8 will help you to make some choices.

3. Select your sense impressions to satisfy, irritate, or contrast with your character's initial mood in order to build the changed mood you hope to show.

4. Write a narrative hook which shows your character acting out his beginning mood.

5. Introduce your sense impressions, showing your character reacting to them individually or collectively. Try *to show* the character's emotional build-up through his reactions to stimuli.

6. After you show the character's change in mood as a result of his sense impressions, conclude the sequence with the character acting in a way that is consistent with his change of mood.

7. Write a first draft to develop the sequence of sense impression-emotional development. Then rewrite to refine it. Finally, get a reaction to your work from someone before you prepare a final draft to correct all errors of content and English mechanics.

Now, turn to the Assignment-Evaluation sheet.

WRITING SAMPLE 6—EVALUATION

Write a narrative-mood sequence showing a third person character experiencing an emotion which builds gradually until he is compelled to act.
Length: approximately 200 words

Required in Contents	Full	Earned	For Study
1. Use narrative hook to show character's initial emotion	20		
2. Provide sense impressions in some believable sequence to stimulate the character	20		
3. Show character reacting gradually to sense impressions to reveal their influence on him	20		
4. Use character's reactions to sense impressions to show change in his emotional state	20		
5. Show character committing an obvious act which is consistent with his change of mood	20		
PROOFREAD YOUR WORK CAREFULLY!	0		
TOTAL	100		

Instructor's Comments:

ENGLISH MECHANICS: Instructor Assigns Values for Criteria

Content Areas	Full	Earned	For Study
ORGANIZATION: Introduction Chronological Organization Topical Organization Rational Organization Smooth Development Termination	——— ——— ——— ——— ——— ———		Chapter 13 Chapter 15 Chapter 16 Chapter 17 Chapter 14 Chapter 18
PARAGRAPHING: Introduction Development (unity) Development (coherence)	——— ——— ———		Page 163 Page 165 Page 168
SENTENCES: completeness; variety; economy; use of modifiers; pronouns; agreement; use of verbs, phrases, clauses	———		
USE OF LANGUAGE: Level of usage Idiomatic usage Vividness	——— ——— ———		Chapter 8
PUNCTUATION AND CAPITALIZATION and related graphics: Quotation marks	———		Chapter 7
SPELLING:			
TOTAL	100		

Mechanics not in this text are assigned to supplementary text.

Figure 12. Crossing over. The Story of Meek by Roger Johnson.

Narration to Exposition: Comparing Them

For some time, you have been writing narrative compositions; it is now time to apply some of the techniques you have learned to expository writing, the type that is most common in school or daily life. Before you proceed, however, you may find a few reminders worthwhile. Good writing, whether narrative or expository, has certain characteristics:

1. It is clear in meaning.
2. It stimulates interest.
3. It deals with ideas or experiences which are worth the reader's attention.
4. It fulfills the writer's purpose.

In order to attain these characteristics, the writer does a variety of things, including:

1. He writes from personal experience or about ideas he understands.
2. He collects and organizes necessary information *before* he writes.
3. He expresses himself clearly through effective introduction, development, and termination.
4. He uses lively language with concrete words and specific detail to stimulate the reader.
5. He makes *deliberate* choices of content, language, and style to accomplish his purpose.

To amplify further, let us compare samples of narration and exposition. Do you recall the earlier distinction made between showing and telling? You read that the author uses narration to show experience, re-creating it so that the reader may abstract meaning from the experience *by himself.* On the other hand, the author uses exposition to tell the reader the author's interpretation of experience, but does not necessarily re-create the experience itself. Let us examine two passages dealing essentially with the same subject.

Narrative Example

John had not hit the ball that broke Mr. Jones' window. On the day in question, the young man left his house and slowly crossed the street to visit his friend, Charley.

"Get out of the way, kid," the boys playing street ball shouted. "You're holding up the game."

John hurried to get out of the way. He had started up the block toward Charley's house when he heard a window explode nearby. He looked around and saw the ballplayers disappear under hedges and between houses. He shrugged his shoulders as if to say, "Well, it's none of my business," and continued walking.

A few minutes later, John felt a firm hand on his arm. "I've got you, you rotten kid! You kids got no respect for people's property. All you do is make noise, clog up the streets and break things. This time I've got you good and you're going to be sorry by the time I get through with you."

John, too shocked to respond at first, finally got out, "Do what? I didn't do anything! What do you want from me? Let me go!"

"Let you go? Sure I'll let you go—in the police station. Come with me, you brat."

Comments on the Narrative Example

In this little "slice" of narrative, the author has presented a brief sequence of events to demonstrate a common type of conflict. He used dialogue to show the characters' moods and reactions, with other narrative passages to connect the dialogue. The author used this narration to re-create an experience so that the reader could draw his own conclusions. Now, let us examine below how the same author might have presented the kernel of truth inherent in narration had he chosen to use an expository style.

Expository Example

Young people often play in public streets, sometimes annoying their elders and being destructive. These annoyances and petty forms of destruction occasionally cause people to behave in irrational ways to youngsters, even to committing distinct acts of injustice. I know of a youngster who was arrested because a neighborhood man accused him of breaking a window which, in fact, he had not broken.

Comparison Between Narrative and Expository Examples

In the narrative passage, a bit of experience was shown in order to give you the opportunity to "live" it. Do you see how the narrative experience differs from the expository passage dealing with the same subject? Do you recognize that in the narrative passage, the author stated only one objective fact which might be considered expository: "John had not hit the ball that broke Mr. Jones' window." During the rest of the narrative, furthermore, the author simply re-created the details of the experience. Finally, you, the reader, must conclude the meaning of this experience.

How, on the other hand, is the expository passage different from the narrative? In exposition, experience is not shown, and you must *imagine* the real-life basis for the author's statements. Next, in exposition, the author does not free you to judge for yourself as to the kernels of truth (theme) present in experience; instead, *he tells you what he thinks.* Third, the exposition is more direct and economical than the narration because it is a distillation of experience. Fourth, the author uses exposition to give *generalizations based upon experience* and supports them by offering specific facts and/or detail. For example, the expository general statements, ". . . annoying their elders and being destructive." and ". . . cause people to behave in irrational ways . . ." are supported by the specific fact, "I know of a youngster who was arrested because a neighborhood man accused him of breaking a window which, in fact, he had not broken."

Finally, if narration and exposition are used by authors for different purposes, are they always isolated from each other? The answer is no, for authors often mix these styles. Thus, what is essentially narration may contain exposition too, and *vice versa*. Look at the following excerpt from a novel, essentially a narrative form. Be careful, as you read, of this distinction: the difference between *showing* and *telling*, the contrast between "watching" a character behave and having the author tell us about this character. In addition, see if you are clever enough to recognize for what purposes the author uses narration and for what purposes exposition. For your convenience, all verbs have been underlined and paragraphs numbered.

THE SENSITIVES
Louis Charbonneau

I. In fact Adam Cooper was never completely accepted within the intelligence organization. He was theirs, but he was not exactly one of them.

II. Once, in assessing the failure of intelligence sources to predict direct Chinese intervention in the Korean War, hordes of Communist volunteers having poured into the battle against unprepared United Nations forces in December of 1950, CIA director Allen Dulles put the agency's crying need facetiously as one for "mind readers." But when they found one, Adam Cooper learned, they did not quite know what to do with him.

III. Powerful figures in the agency argued that Adam Cooper was at least as much a threat to the United States as he was to any of its enemies. A man who could read minds, it was said, turned loose inside the Central Intelligence Agency of this country, would very shortly know too damned much! Few people in the agency knew a great deal of what was going on throughout the complex organization; a degree of departmental autonomy and secrecy was essential for security. No one, not even the Director, knew everything. Surely an unknown Quality like Adam Cooper could not be entrusted with that knowledge. To put him in the position of acquiring it at will violated the most elementary principles of security.

IV. One result of this debate was an elaborate system of precautions to keep Cooper from gaining access to too much information. Seldom was he allowed to visit the awesome immensity of the CIA's headquarters at Langley, not far from Washington. When he did go there he was never allowed beyond minimum security areas and he was closely attended. Normally he worked out of the old group of buildings the agency continued to maintain on E Street in the Foggy Bottom section of the capital. Even here his range of contacts was carefully limited.

QUESTIONS FOR REVIEW

1. Is paragraph I narrative or expository? _____

2. Is paragraph II narrative or expository?_____

3. Is paragraph III narrative or expository?_____

4. Is paragraph IV narrative or expository?_____

5. Is the overall purpose of these paragraphs to show or to tell about Cooper's position within the

   intelligence organization?_____(to show, to tell, both)

6. Are there many sentences *within* the narrative paragraphs which contain linking rather than

   active verbs?_____(yes or no)

7. Which linking verb is frequently used within the narrative paragraphs?_____

8. Are the two styles, narration and exposition, mixed throughout the four paragraphs?_____
   (yes or no)

9. Are the two sentence types, descriptive and active, intermixed within the same paragraphs?___

   _____(yes or no)

ANSWERS: 1. expository; 2. narrative; 3. narrative; 4. expository*; 5. both; 6. yes; 7. was (a form
of "to be"); 8. yes; 9. yes

A Review: Building Bricks of Writing

You have looked at many samples of professional writing. You have also written samples which show many of the elements or "bricks" which writers use in
novels, essays, short stories, and poems. For example, in your study of narration,
you learned how to recognize and use narrative hooks and imagism; to record sense
impressions through effective use of language and detail; to re-create experience
through emphasis upon the active verb; to show the drama of speech through dialogue; to reveal changes in human character and emotion through the narrative-
mood sequence; and to emphasize the significance (theme) of human experience.

In your expository writing, when you wrote about your reaction to the introductions of your classmates, you learned about the importance of gathering, organizing, and presenting information effectively. You also learned how to make a suitable
blending of generality and specific detail when you reported your reaction, as well as
how to describe a process when you revealed how you obtained the information.
Finally, in your second expository assignment, you defined your goals for accom-
plishment in this course after you learned of the importance of formulating goals
through study of the story, "Young Man Axelbrod."

---

*This is passive voice, for despite *appearance* of action (was . . . allowed *or* was . . . attended) the
subject isn't acting but is having *something done to him.*

Throughout, you have been encouraged to look at all writing, your own and that of professional writers, from the writers' point of view. Furthermore, a consistent focus of this course has been your developing appreciation of style, the author's *deliberate* use of language to accomplish his purpose.

What did your writing experiences demonstrate thus far which is true of both narration and exposition? The answer is, you dealt with *limited purposes*. For example, you wrote about *moments* of experience from your life when you wrote narratively, and about *single subjects* when you wrote expositorily. Can we relate your experiences with those of writers in general?

The primarily narrative writer tells *one story,* however long, by showing (recreating) experience a moment at a time, connecting these moments directly if appropriate or filling time gaps between them through exposition.

The primarily expository writer, on the other hand, deals with a *limited subject*, developing his ideas appropriately, a step at a time, until he fulfills his purpose. He may sometimes use narration if he wishes to show a sequence, as in a process, or if he wishes to make his ideas especially lively and concrete.

Indeed, whether a writer wishes to tell a story or write an article about a subject; whether his purpose is to argue, to describe or to define, he may use exposition or narration or any combination of both. It is essential, in any case, that he form a clear purpose either *to show* a limited continuum of experience through narration or *to tell about* a limited unified subject through exposition. Finally, although narration and exposition are not the same, they do have similarities which are worth knowing. Study the chart on the following page which shows parallels among the elements of these two styles of writing.

QUESTIONS FOR REVIEW

Answer the following questions *true* or *false.*

10. Expository writing may include narration too. _____

11. Narrative writing emphasizes use of linking verbs. _____

12. Narration distills experience; exposition shows it. _____

13. Narration shows sequences of events which are often tied together through exposition. _____

14. Imagism is a narrative technique which is similar to specific detail in exposition. _____

15. Significance is the theme or meaning of human experience which is shown in narration. _____

16. A writer's work is a reflection of his purpose. _____

17. A writer of exposition should select a carefully limited subject for his writing. _____

ELEMENTS OF NARRATION	ELEMENTS OF EXPOSITION
1. *Purpose:* Tell a story	1. *Purpose:* Write about a subject
2. *Beginning:* Narrative hook to awaken interest	2. *Beginning:* Introduction to define and limit subject.
3. *Plot Development:* a. moments of experience shown in sequence b. expository passages to fill gaps in time between moments of experience and describe elements of the setting (environment) c. dialogue d. point of view	3. *Appropriate Development:* a. rational or logical organization to demonstrate reasoning b. topical breakdown to explain subject by convenient subdivision c. chronological development in narrative style to show processes; in expository style "to tell"
4. *Characterization:* a. emotional revelation b. narrative-mood sequences to show changes in characters and their moods c. dialogue	4. *No comparable element* unless the subject is a person
5. *Significance:* (Theme) to show meaning of experience	5. *Theme:* (Central Idea) to emphasize most important aspect of the subject
6. *Effectiveness of Language:* a. imagism b. figurative language to show sense impressions c. blend of narration and exposition; emphasis on actives verbs *to show*	6. *Effectiveness of Language:* a. use of concrete detail b. specific words to explain concepts clearly c. blend of exposition and narration
7. *Conclusion:* To bring together all elements of story in purposeful way	7. *Termination:* Appropriately, to summarize, form conclusion, or make recommendation

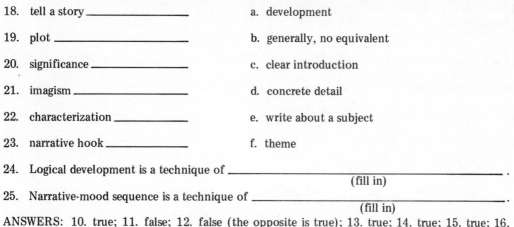

Match the lettered expository elements to the numbered narrative elements.

18. tell a story _____   a. development

19. plot _____   b. generally, no equivalent

20. significance _____   c. clear introduction

21. imagism _____   d. concrete detail

22. characterization _____   e. write about a subject

23. narrative hook _____   f. theme

24. Logical development is a technique of _____ .
                                              (fill in)

25. Narrative-mood sequence is a technique of _____ .
                                              (fill in)

ANSWERS: 10. true; 11. false; 12. false (the opposite is true); 13. true; 14. true; 15. true; 16. true; 17. true; 18. e; 19. a; 20. f; 21. d; 22. b; 23. c; 24. exposition; 25. narration

Additional Emphasis: Limiting a Subject

Whether you use narration or exposition, you *must always limit your subject to what you can actually accomplish.* For example, if you were writing a 500 word (about two typed pages) essay about Abraham Lincoln, could you deal with his entire life, from birth to death, thoroughly? On the other hand, could you do an effective job with the subject, "Lincoln's Gettysburg Address"? Obviously, "Lincoln's Gettysburg Address" is a more fitting subject for a short essay than his entire life, although even the "Gettysburg" subject could be too broad for only 500 words.

Let us consider another possibility. If you were writing a short story, no more than 1250 words (about five pages), could you show *most* of the important experiences of your chief character's entire life? Would the experience, "John's First Date," be better suited to a short story than his entire life?

In short, whether you write an essay or a story, in narrative or expository style, you must select your subject carefully so you can actually deal with it.

REVIEW QUESTIONS

Examine each of the subjects on the following page. If you think you could handle it *well* in a short essay or story, write SHORT on the line next to it. If you think the subject would require considerable length, thousands of words or a complete book, to handle well, write LONG on the line.

26. The Sun _____

27. The Effect of Sunspots on Radio Waves _____

28. John's Four Years in College _____

29. John's Difficulty with A Math Final _____

30. The Effects of Smog on Life _____

31. The Effects of Smog on A Tree in My Yard _____

ANSWERS: 26. long; 27. short; 28. long; 29. short; 30. long; 31. short

Now, examine each broad subject below. Compose a narrow topic *within the same subject area* that you think you could handle well in a short essay or story.

EXAMPLE

Baseball

Babe Ruth's Sixtieth Home Run

32. Martin Luther King

_____

_____

33. The Milky Way

_____

_____

34. Campus Problems

_____

_____

_____

Check answers below, then go to the next page to read.

ANSWERS: 32. *Example:* "King Used Civil Disobedience as an Effective Tool," 33. *Example:* "The Milky Way Is Only One Galaxy among A Vast Number," 34. *Example:* "Students Should Share in Planning Their Course Contents"

THE SENSITIVES
Louis Charbonneau

In fact Adam Cooper was never completely accepted within the intelligence organization. He was theirs, but he was not exactly one of them.

Once, in assessing the failure of intelligence sources to predict direct Chinese intervention in the Korean War, hordes of Communist volunteers having poured into the battle against unprepared United Nations forces in December of 1950, CIA director Allen Dulles put the agency's crying need facetiously as one for "mind readers." But when they found one, Adam Cooper learned, they did not quite know what to do with him.

Powerful figures in the agency argued that Adam Cooper was at least as much a threat to the United States as he was to any of its enemies. A man who could read minds, it was said, turned loose inside the Central Intelligence Agency of this country, would very shortly know too damned much! Few people in the agency knew a great deal of what was going on throughout the complex organization; a degree of departmental autonomy and secrecy was essential for security. No one, not even the Director, knew *everything*. Surely an unknown Quality like Adam Cooper could not be entrusted with that knowledge. To put him in the position of acquiring it at will violated the most elementary principles of security.

One result of this debate was an elaborate system of precautions to keep Cooper from gaining access to too much information. Seldom was he allowed to visit the awesome immensity of the CIA's headquarters at Langley, not far from Washington. When he did go there he was never allowed beyond minimum security areas and he was closely attended. Normally he worked out of the old group of buildings the agency continued to maintain on E Street in the Foggy Bottom section of the capital. Even here his range of contacts was carefully limited.

While he occasionally commented bitterly to Tina about being kept in a box by the agency, Adam Cooper was too blissfully happy with her to dwell on his complaints or to become deeply resentful. He studied languages with specialists at the agency, displaying a remarkable and previously unknown facility. Occasionally he conducted interrogations. Then the time came when he was called in on a critical case involving a suspected defector. Cooper read the man's guilt easily and was able to direct other agents toward the evidence that gave ironclad proof of treason, and toward the traitor's accomplices. The agency seemed pleased. More important assignments were talked of, and a few began to trickle through, each success leading to another.

But somewhere along the way came the subtle change in Tina's (his wife's) behavior, unnoticed until the chance detection of her uneasiness came to him one night in spite of his fatigue and self-absorption. Reluctantly he began to pay more attention to her moods and movements—a more critical attention. He began to see a woman he had never really known, the one who lived beneath that golden sheath of flesh. Finally the ugly suspicion was born. For a telepath, proof was not hard to find.

Her accident—sudden, terrible and unpredictable—ended worry, confusion, anger, but not the heartache, not the knowledge of betrayal and loss, not the shattering conviction of personal failure. . . .

Adam Cooper heard a horn bleat outside on Hennessy Road in Wan Chai. Inside the bar a juke box was playing American-style rock featuring a Japanese singer with a shrill teenager's voice. Cooper drained his glass. His hand was shaking.

That was when he started drinking—after the accident. Nothing seemed to matter as much. The CIA continued to make use of him on increasingly important assignments, though still without complete trust, still uncertain how to exploit his talent for knowing what other people were thinking.

Well, they needed him now. Now, because they were worried, maybe a little desperate. Now, because the Red Chinese were up to something.

Suddenly Cooper wondered if all of Britain's Special Branch people in the Far East were unavailable to him because of the emergency situation or because the British, too, were more than a little afraid of him. They wouldn't want all their secrets plucked from the minds of their top agents.

Everybody keep back, Adam Cooper thought sourly. Here comes the freak!

An awareness of intrusion came to him even before sensory warning. The image was vivid and feminine and very close. A strong flower fragrance made it physical.

"You wish to dance?" the girl asked.

A smile pulled at the corners of Cooper's mouth. "I don't, but it's the best invitation I've had all day."

The Chinese girl had beautiful teeth, small, even and very white. She was small-breasted, slight of figure, a neat package very tightly wrapped in a fitted *cheongsam* with an exaggerated side slit. Cooper suspected that the slit improved on the traditional style by about six revealing inches. It all went to prove that you did not need a mountainous bosom and a low-cut neckline to be sexy, Cooper thought. It was the kind of reflection he began to get after about a half dozen afternoon drinks.

"You like?"

"I like very much. But I'd hate to see it doing the frug."

"We dance old style, maybe?" The girl suggested, still smiling but now uncertain about him, not sure how to interpret his bemused responses. "Very Close?"

Cooper shook his head sadly. "You've pegged me, all right, but I'll still have to sit this one out. My shoes would slosh."

"Slosh? I do not know this slosh."

"It's not a big thing to know."

The girl hesitated. In her uncertainty she was even more appealing. She was small, as most of them were, although he had been in one bar the night before, over on the Kowloon side of the harbor, where the girls, all Oriental, had been unusually tall. The bar had been named, in a blatant and a bit too obvious appeal to American visitors, *Tall in the Saddle.* This girl was just average in size, barely five feet tall, among the Thais, Koreans, Chinese and others who filled the innumerable bars. A sexier Barbie doll, Cooper thought. Her heavily made-up eyes, dominating a delicately-featured face, seemed larger than most he had seen in the Hong Kong bars. He wondered if she had had the lids cut, as some did.

"You buy me a drink?" the girl ventured.

"What's your name?"

"Kou Yen." She brightened. "They call me Koo-Koo."

"I'll bet they do."

"You may call me Koo-Koo. You buy me a drink."

"You're too young to drink, honey. Besides, I was just leaving."

"You think I am too young." Kou Yen glanced toward a cluster of girls at tables on the far side of the room, waiting in various attitudes of boredom or passive acceptance for someone to come in. Like a doll collection, Cooper thought. "I have a friend, she is. . ."

"You've got it all wrong," Cooper interrupted. "You're the right age. Just right."

"Then what—what is wrong with me?"

"Not you." He smiled, but the smile didn't quite come off. He slid from his stool. "The trouble is with me."

It had occurred to him that he should be trying to read Koo-Koo's mind. He did not find the thought very pleasant. She sure as hell wasn't a Red Chinese agent, and never mind the fact that the men she met probably did a lot of talking. Using a girl as a plant of this kind was common enough, but not Koo-Koo. She might not be innocent of very many things, but she was of this.

His was getting to be an uglier world than hers.

Appreciation of Style

1. This excerpt from the novel, *The Sensitives*, mixes exposition with narration. Identify examples of this mixture of styles in three different paragraphs.
2. What figure of speech is the following: "A smile pulled at the corners of Cooper's mouth."
3. What points of view are shown in this selection? Give examples to illustrate.
4. Much of this excerpt provides *background* for action which is shown as happening "now." Where does the background stop and the current action begin?
5. Which is more narrative, the background or the current action? Why?
6. Identify several examples of effective use of imagism or specific detail.

Test Your Comprehension

1. Cooper's career has been an unhappy one. Why?
2. In the dialogue between Cooper and Koo-Koo, Cooper rejects both himself and her, but for different reasons. Why does he reject her?
3. Interpret the meaning of the following: "His was getting to be an uglier world than hers."
4. What is the author's purpose *in this excerpt* from *The Sensitives*?

Vocabulary for Study

assessing	elaborate	bemused
complex	accomplice	blatant
autonomy	intrusion	

Elements of Exposition

Purposes and Techniques
of Exposition

Earlier in the text you studied a comparison between narration and exposition. In this and succeeding chapters, you will have the opportunity to learn more about purposes, techniques, structure, and types of expository writing.

Purposes of Exposition

At its most basic level, expository writing fulfills the author's purpose *to tell* the reader about a given limited subject. However, now that we are moving on from our earlier emphasis upon narration, as distinguished from exposition, we shall consider expository purposes in greater detail. In the future, therefore, when you are reading or writing, bear this most important idea in mind: if an author's purpose is *to tell what he thinks about his subject,* as opposed to showing experience in imitation of life, then he is writing exposition. Finally, it is quite common for authors to use a variety of styles and techniques, including narration, for the purpose of telling readers what they think.

To return to the purposes of exposition, we must begin to identify some of the specific reasons an author might have for *telling.* He might write expository material *to define* an object or idea, or he might wish, instead, *to describe* the appearance of a person, place, or thing. These are but two particular purposes an author might have. Let us look at some others. Pretend, first, that you wished to make clear the nature of a pencil for someone whose culture was different from yours. What would you do? Below are several purposes which you could legitimately formulate and which would influence the writing techniques and styles you used.

GENERAL EXPOSITORY PURPOSE: To tell about the nature of a pencil

Specific Purpose I: Define pencil

Procedure or Technique	A. Explain *what a pencil is* by use of clear simple words, selected because they are familiar to the reader.
	B. Use comparison and/or contrast to clarify.

Specific Purpose II: Describe pencil

Procedure
or
Technique

    A. Define pencil.

    B. Give data about size, shape, color, and other relevant aspects of the physical appearance.

    C. Use comparison and/or contrast.

Specific Purpose III: Analyze pencil

Procedure
or
Technique

    A. Define pencil.

    B. Describe physical appearance.

    C. Identify components of construction, including variations of materials, to whatever extent is necessary to purpose.

    D. Use comparison and/or contrast.

Specific Purpose IV: Show how pencil is used (a process)

Procedure
or
Technique

    A. Define pencil.

    B. Describe pencil.

    C. Use narrative style to give the step-by-step sequence by which someone uses a pencil.

        a. how to grasp it

        b. how to move it across paper

Specific Purpose V: Argue for the use of pencils

Procedure
or
Technique

    A. Define pencil and relate to importance of written communication.

    B. Present evidence: give variety of uses, support economy, and give other relevant ideas to persuade.

    C. Use example.

    D. Use comparison and/or contrast.

As you can see, selection of *what* to do and *how much* to do in a particular piece of expository writing is very much a function of the author's purpose. The possibilities are quite diverse and may include such approaches as definition, description, analysis, comparison and contrast, narration, argumentation, and use of example. Following, now, are paragraph examples of various purposes for exposition.

DEFINITION: WHAT SOMETHING IS

Purpose: To define the nature of isolation in society.

Controlling or Central Idea: Isolation is caused by poor communication among people.

Characteristics of Definition: Definition tells *what something is.* It should reveal the use of words which are likely to be familiar to the reader. A definition which shows use of complex words may be more confusing than helpful and may, in effect, not define at all.

EXAMPLE

Isolation is a state of existence in which individuals or groups do not communicate with each other. It may be a form of escape or a vacuum of interpersonal relationships. It may be the cold remaining when human warmth and concern are lacking, or when outstretched hands fail to touch. It may show the mutual ignorance of parent and child, of scientist and humanist, of educator and student.

DESCRIPTION: HOW SOMETHING LOOKS

Purpose: To describe the diverse characteristics of a crowd as the author reacts to it.

Controlling or Central Idea: I (the author) felt uncomfortable about the character of a crowd I saw witnessing executions.

Characteristics of Description: Description gives the *physical appearance* or *outward characteristics* of something. It goes beyond definition by providing such data as size, shape, even emotional qualities, depending upon the author's purpose.

EXAMPLE

I saw the crowd at the executions as a composite of types. The "gawker," the fellow who must satisfy his urge for blood, stared in fascination. The righteous type, too, attended; and every groan of pain, every plea for mercy which he saw, was punctuated on righteous-man's face by an "Amen." Many officials occupied positions of prominence; some were expressionless, some showed zeal, some had a fine efficiency of manner. Although I looked hard, nowhere did I see compassion. Was there, indeed, not a single person who found suffering repugnant? I hoped, as I moved away slowly, that some compassionate ones were in the crowd too.

ANALYSIS: DEFINITION AND DESCRIPTION WITH MORE DETAIL

Purpose: To define, describe, and identify the materials of which a dart and blow gun are composed.

Controlling or Central Idea: A blow gun is a dangerous weapon consisting of a long, hollow tube and a dart.

Characteristics of Analysis: Analysis *includes* definition and description and goes beyond them by providing greater detail including data about makeup or composition. The *extent* of an analysis depends upon the author's purpose. An analysis may be very detailed and complete or it may focus only upon the minimum elements needed to communicate a central idea. In the following example, the author could have dealt with variations of wood instead of merely "hardwood" or types of metal instead of merely "metal." Furthermore, in truly complex analysis, the author could concern himself with even chemical composition. However, read the following limited analysis and see if you have a reasonable understanding of the nature of a blow gun.

EXAMPLE

A blow gun is a dangerous weapon consisting of a long, hollow tube and a dart. The tube may range in length from twelve to twenty-four inches and may be constructed of wood, such as bamboo, or a variety of metals. The dart is approximately four to six inches in length and may be made of a narrow sliver of pointed hardwood or of a metal tip inserted into a wooden shank. In either case, the dart has feathers of natural or artificial material inserted into the end opposite the point. The feathers help to stabilize the dart while it is in flight.

The blow gun tube is like an ordinary drinking straw; the dart is similar to the dart used in ordinary parlor games. If you can remember when, as a child, you placed a small wad of moistened paper into a straw and blew it at the back of your friend's neck, you will understand how a blow gun is used.

DESCRIPTION: A PROCESS IN NARRATIVE STYLE

Purpose: To identify the materials and show the operations needed to attach stamps to envelopes.

Controlling or Central Idea: There is an easy way to attach stamps to envelopes without licking the stamps.

Characteristics of Description of a Process: Description of a process shows the chronological procedure, step-by-step, necessary to perform a job. Because it is sequential, it resembles the sequence of events shown in a narrative; but the author's primary purpose in process description is *to tell.* An important part of this procedure is identification of the materials necessary to perform the process. Finally, another term used for process description is "operational definition."

EXAMPLE

I have found a way to moisten stamps for attachment to envelopes which is efficient and eliminates the need to lick them. All one needs to do the job is a sponge, a small dish, and some water. First, I place some water in the dish. Then, I place the sponge in the dish of water, allowing it to absorb enough water to become moist. Finally, I take each stamp, press it lightly on the moist sponge to make its glue tacky and, then, I apply it firmly to an envelope.

ARGUMENTATION: USE OF REASON OR LOGIC TO PERSUADE

Purpose: To reveal the consequences of limiting free expression.

Controlling or Central Idea: Limiting a man's free expression destroys his ability to function in a free society.

Characteristics of Argumentation: The author uses argument to persuade the reader to adopt his point of view. He shows logical relationships among the facts and reasons he presents to appeal to the reader's sense of judgment.

EXAMPLE

If you wish to destroy a man's ability to function as a member of a free society, limit his ability to express himself. Let him know that there are only certain things which he may say and that *you* must agree with them. Then you will succeed in throttling controversy and in assuring the maintenance of things as you wish them to be. Do not be surprised, however, if this limitation causes the minds of many men to resemble cookies from a factory, with similar texture, color, size, weight, odor, and taste. Would such a "diet," culinary or intellectual, appeal to you?

Techniques Used in Exposition

Whatever reason a writer has for using exposition, he may use a variety of techniques to accomplish his purpose. Many of these techniques have already been reviewed in Chapter 8, *Sense Impressions,* but consideration of concrete versus abstract words, comparison and contrast, and the effective use of example is given here.

Concrete Versus Abstract Words

A concrete word is more specific and tangible than an abstract word. It conveys an image (sense impression) to the reader more readily than does an abstract; thus, it communicates more effectively. A general useful rule to follow is: Avoid the use of abstract words when concrete words may be used instead!

On the other hand, when you cannot avoid an abstract word, try to clarify it through use of comparison and/or contrast with words likely to be familiar to your reader, or give concrete examples which you believe your reader will know. For example, do you remember the paragraph defining isolation? Did you notice the use of the familiar word "escape" and the comparison between isolation and "the failure of outstretched hands to touch"? Did these techniques contribute to the definition?

Let us look at a few additional examples. Which stimulate your senses more and are easier to understand, the sentences containing the concrete words or the sentences containing the abstract words?

ABSTRACT: Practice *economy* in your life.
CONCRETE: You can buy a $7.00 shirt for $5.00 if you wait for next week's sale.

ABSTRACT: When he was little, John was always *good.*
CONCRETE: When he was little, John always told the truth and obeyed his parents.

ABSTRACT: The oasis was a *blessing* when we reached it.
CONCRETE: The oasis provided us with cool water and comfortable shade from the sun.

ABSTRACT: Elmer is a *patriotic* man.
CONCRETE: Elmer always salutes the flag, argues for the government and Constitution against all who attack it, and has served in the army willingly.

Use of Example

The use of example is the presentation of concrete instances or samples to make a word or concept easier to understand. Do you recall the description of the crowd earlier in this lesson? Didn't the author present a number of examples in his effort to explain the character of the crowd witnessing the executions? Do you remember the "gawker," the righteous type, and the variety of officials?

Comparison and Contrast

The author uses comparison and contrast to clarify ideas. He compares and/or contrasts what he wishes to explain by relating it to something he believes is likely to be familiar to the reader.

EXAMPLE OF COMPARISON

A blow gun is a dangerous weapon consisting of a long hollow tube and a dart. The tube is something like an ordinary straw used for sipping a drink; the dart is similar to the dart used in ordinary parlor games. If you can remember when, as a child, you placed a small wad of moistened paper in a straw and blew it at the back of your friend's neck, you will understand how a blow gun is used.

EXAMPLE OF CONTRAST

Bamboo is a member of the same family as ordinary lawn grass, but they are very different. Bamboo may attain a height of 100 feet or more, while lawn grass rarely reaches one foot. Bamboo is a shade of white when mature; grass is green. Bamboo grows in almost impenetrable thickets which are difficult to control, but lawn grass is easily adapted for human comfort and convenience. Bamboo is extremely hardy in a friendly environment while many lawn grasses require careful cultivation if they are to survive.

A Brief Summary

Exposition may be used by a writer to fulfill a variety of purposes. These purposes include definition, description, analysis, process description, argumentation. Whether a writer uses one or more type depends upon his purpose.

A distinction should be made between a writer's purpose and the techniques he uses to achieve his purpose. You studied a number of such techniques in Chapter 8, *Sense Impressions*, including effective use of words, simile and metaphor, importance of sharp detail, and comparison and contrast. In this lesson, you read about concrete versus abstract words, the use of example, and more about comparison and contrast.

Perhaps the most important idea in this lesson is the importance of having a clear purpose. You had the opportunity to observe how such a "simple" subject as a pencil could vary widely in its treatment, depending upon the writer's purpose.

QUESTIONS FOR REVIEW

Match the numbered purposes for exposition at the left with the lettered statements on the right.

1. narration _____   a. used to tell *how something looks*

2. argumentation _____   b. used to identify *what something is*

3. description _____   c. used to show the operations in a process

4. analysis _____   d. used to convince a reader to accept the author's viewpoint

5. definition _____   e. used to examine something in detail, including its parts

6. An author's purpose for writing and the techniques he uses to fulfill his purpose are identical.

   _____(true or false)

7. Analysis may include definition too._____(true or false)

8. Argumentation may include analysis too._____(true or false)

9. Definition should involve the use of words which are familiar to the reader._____
   (true or false)

10. The use of examples may help to clarify analysis, description and narration._____
    (true or false)

11. Contrast is a technique of explanation through emphasis upon similar characteristics._____
    (true or false)

12. "Liberty" is an abstract word._____(true or false)

13. Concrete words are more specific than abstract words._____(true or false)

14. Comparison and contrast may be used together or separately in exposition._____
    (true or false)

ANSWERS: 1. c; 2. d; 3. a; 4. e; 5. b; 6. false; 7. true; 8. true; 9. true; 10. true; 11. false; 12. true;
          13. true; 14. true

Give *concrete examples* to clarify the following abstract terms underlined in the sentences. Study the examples given before you write your own.

15. He is a good student.

    Example: He attends classes faithfully.

    _____

    _____

16. He follows <u>sound ecological practice</u>.

   Example: He doesn't litter highways with garbage.

   _____

   _____

   _____

17. He is an <u>effective</u> teacher.

   Example: His lectures are easy for me to understand.

   _____

   _____

   _____

ANSWERS: questions 15 through 17 are for class discussion.

   Provide a *contrasting word or statement* for each of the following words. Note examples given.

18. generous

   Example: He is *miserly*; he wouldn't give a penny to a starving man.

   _____

   _____

19. durable

   Example: The car is *flimsy*; I had it only a month when the steering gear broke.

   _____

   _____

20. safety

   Example: The building is *dangerous*; a ceiling tile fell and hit me on the head.

   _____

   _____

ANSWERS: questions 18 through 20 are for class discussion

   Provide a word or statement which *compares with* (is similar to) each of the following. Study the examples given.

21. generous

    Example: He is *charitable*, giving ten per cent of his income to the poor.

    _____

    _____

22. durable

    Example: Some cars are *long-lasting*; mine is twenty years old.

    _____

    _____

23. safety

    Example: That building is *like a baby's crib* for its residents. It was the only one to withstand the hurricane.

    _____

    _____

ANSWERS: questions 21 through 23 are for class discussion

Write a sentence which contains a *concrete example* of each of the following abstract terms. For example, you might write, "He salutes the flag" or "He supports the government against all attackers" as substitutes for the word "patriotic."

24. moral _____

    _____

25. beautiful _____

    _____

26. cruel _____

    _____

ANSWERS: questions 24 through 26 are for class discussion

On the following page are listed several possible subjects for expository essays. *First,* decide if each subject is narrow enough for an essay of about 500 words (two typed pages); if not narrow enough, select a more limited subject yourself. *Second,* select a controlling or central idea for the essay. *Third,* select the procedures or techniques you would use to develop the subject. For example, you might decide to define it, to describe it, to analyze it, to show how to use it, or to argue for or against it. Finally, you might decide to use concrete examples, comparison and/or contrast or any other devices that would be appropriate. Study the example first.

EXAMPLE

> *Subject*—Abraham Lincoln
>
> Narrow The Subject—*Lincoln's "Gettysburg Address"*
>
> Select Your Purpose—*To deal with the "Gettysburg Address" as an example of constructive appeal*
>
> Select Controlling or Central Idea—*Lincoln made his speech to stimulate unity among the American people.*
>
> Procedures and Techniques—*An argument that Lincoln emphasized honoring the dead rather than damning the enemy Confederate troops who killed the Union soldiers.*
>> 1. *contrast*—Lincoln could have denounced the enemy
>> 2. *example*—select brief examples from speech to emphasize unity and honor
>> 3. *definition*—use Lincoln's definition of the character of the American government as of, by and for the people

27. a newspaper

    a.   narrow subject _____

_____

    b.   select purpose _____

_____

    c.   controlling or central idea _____

_____

    d.   procedures—techniques _____

_____

_____

_____

_____

28. the sun

    a.   narrow subject _____

_____

b. select purpose _____

_____

c. controlling or central idea _____

_____

d. procedures—techniques _____

_____

_____

_____

_____

29. capital punishment

a. narrow subject _____

_____

b. select purpose _____

_____

c. controlling or central idea _____

_____

d. procedures—techniques _____

_____

_____

_____

_____

_____

ANSWERS: questions 27 through 29 are for class discussion

Read the correlated reading which follows.

TRUTH IS A RED HERRING
Arthur Hoppe

I speak to you today, friends, as President of the American Council Against Truth in Advertising, a vigorous anti-Communist organization. It is our credo that Truth in Advertising is not only unAmerican, but a Communist plot.

Turn, if you will, to the current issue of *Newsweek*, which carries an authoritative article on the insidious advertising methods in Communist Russia today. Let me, with a shudder, read you a typical socko Communist ad for Communist Caspian herring:

"The quality of this herring is in no way inferior to other brands of herring."

That, friends, is Truth in Advertising. And, before it is too late, let every good American ask himself the soul-searching question: "So who needs it?"

Imagine what our lives would be like under Communist advertising. There you are, leaping out of bed after a night of sleeping on a mattress that is like sleeping on a mattress. You light up your first cigarette of the day and you stumble into the kitchen to brew a cup of instant coffee. Which tastes as good as instant coffee.

You get your 15th shave from your razor blade even though the label warns that you may well slash yourself to ribbons. Which, lacking confidence, you do. You apply a deodorant guaranteed to "make you smell a little better for a little while. If you like the smell." And you don your synthetic shirt which requires no ironing unless you don't care much for random pleats.

Rumpled and uneasy, you stagger out to your car which, it's been drummed into you, "is about the same as most new cars, except it has only two seats in front and two in back, plus an old-fashioned stick shift." Muttering a prayer for your new battery, which "should usually start most engines in moderate weather unless something goes wrong," you turn the ignition key. And off you sputter to work, timid and apprehensive, a brand of gasoline in your tank.

You have a fairly good lunch in a restaurant ("Fairly Good Food, Our Specialty") and, as shadows fall, you come home defeatedly to make yourself a couple of drinks ("This whiskey will make you as drunk as any other whiskey and, if mixed with ginger ale, doesn't taste too bad"). Finally, you brush your teeth with a toothpaste which 43 per cent of the people in clinical tests liked as well as any other tooth paste and off you go to bed to dwell sleeplessly on the dreary, lackluster ordinariness of your misspent life.

That, friends, is life under communism.

Oh, how much better it is to sleep on a cloud, inhale rich enjoyment and drink real tasting coffee! Feeling sharp, smelling lovely, impeccably groomed, you leap into your personality-changing racing car and roar off with a tiger in your tank! Surfeited by a day of gourmet viands and real sipping pleasure, you finally whip into bed after giving the mirror one last sparkling smile.

That, friends, is the American way of life. Let us each labor to preserve the glamor, excitement and pleasure that the creativity of Madison Avenue daily brings us. Join our Council. Help stamp out the gravest menace of them all—Truth in Advertising.

Appreciation of Style

1. Identify the use of the following in the essay:
   a. Definition
   b. Narration
   c. Comparison and Contrast
   d. Example
2. What point of view does the author emphasize in this essay? Is it effective? Why?
3. Analyze the language of the essay. Is it more abstract than concrete? Why?
4. The author is *satirical*, that is, he pokes fun at a problem. He may be using *irony*, that is, saying the opposite of what he really means. Is this an effective technique or would a more direct statement have been better? Why?

5. This essay is essentially an argument. Why is this a true statement of the author's purpose?

Test Your Comprehension

1. What is the problem identified in this essay? Explain.
2. State the theme of the essay.
3. Compare Communist- and American-style advertising. Use the author's ideas but your own words.

Vocabulary for Study

credo	insidious	random	viand	impeccable
apprehensive	gourmet	lackluster	surfeited	rumpled

FATHER AND SON
Art Seidenbaum

My father was an advertising man, which may be why I'm a newspaper man.

My father was a natural dancer. I have taken few sober steps to music.

My father loved to act, tell narrative jokes and wear costumes. I have, I'm afraid, always loved myself too much to perform.

My father died three days ago and I'm in New York helping with some of those necessary dreary things to legalize death instead of serenading life.

Life: He was a complicated man who took his pleasures simple. Theater, movies, cards, TV (especially the football-baseball sweat set), books and all word games.

He didn't play with little children (with me) until they learned to talk. And then he word-played with them (with me) constantly. Anagrams when I was young, Scrabble when I was older.

Scrabble may have been invented for him. He could play it all night with my mother, intermittently nodding off in a chair, dangling an arc of ash off his cigar.

What he did he was excellent at doing: drawing, writing, extroverting. My friends grew up liking my father.

What he was not excellent at doing—or was afraid he would not be excellent at doing—he tried not to do at all: household chores, keeping books, operating machines.

I'm almost certain my father never learned to drive a car because he didn't want to go through the training procedure—he hated to be a grown novice at anything.

He was a dominant husband, verbally. He was an extraordinarily dependent husband, logistically. My mother always brought him a plate at informal dinners. I don't think he trusted himself to balance buffets any better than books.

His dependence made him a fiercely loyal husband. And he moralized about other men's fidelity or their lack thereof.

Self-made success in advertising made him extremely patriotic, in a dues-paying sense. While he usually voted as a Democrat, many of his emotional ties were really to the right.

We used to argue foreign policy, unions, demonstrations and about who the villains really are in this society. He argued well; he listened politely; he rarely changed his mind. Conservative loyalty came out in funny ways. If he found a restaurant he liked, he hardly went anywhere else for the next month. He didn't like to travel; if I hadn't taken his grandchildren to California, I think he could have lived his 69 years within a 100-mile radius of home.

He didn't want to be a novice about new places.

To Bill Seidenbaum's credit, I had the freedom to fail that he never gave himself. He supported my freedom for a lot of years and he did it so gracefully that I didn't feel guilt or resentment.

I loved my father partly because this proud, competitive man let me compete with his wishes and then encouraged me to think that I could win.

I suppose only a spoiled only child could write so much about himself upon his father's death. But there is so much of him—good him, not-so-good him—in me. And because one of his best games was encouragement, I can live with it.

Appreciation of Style

1. This essay is an analysis. Prove that this statement is true.
2. Identify the use of comparison, contrast and example.
3. What point of view is emphasized?
4. Give the tone of the essay.

Test Your Comprehension

1. Prove these statements:
   a. Seidenbaum's father was good with words.
   b. He was a stubborn man.
   c. He was both dominant and dependent.
2. Make a brief list of the outstanding characteristics of Bill Seidenbaum.

Vocabulary for Study

sober	anagram	extrovert
dreary	intermittently	conservative

Writing Sample Seven: Take one of the subjects on pages 156 and 157 for which you formulated a purpose and selected techniques and procedures for writing; write an expository paper on this subject. However, *first*, select from the criteria on the Assignment-Evaluation sheet on the next page. By now, you are used to writing papers on the basis of specific criteria, but this time *you* will select the criteria on which your work is graded. Before you start, read a FEW WORDS OF CAUTION BELOW.

A Few Words of Caution

When performing any expository assignment, a writer should be *deliberate* about certain things. These include:

1. Formulating his own clear purpose for writing.
2. Dealing with a narrow enough subject to handle it well.
3. Selecting a controlling or central idea to which the entire paper is related.
4. Collecting and arranging needed data before writing.
5. Deciding what writing techniques will best suit his purpose.
6. Writing with emphasis upon clear, specific words.
7. Preparing as many drafts of copy as necessary.

WRITING SAMPLE 7—EVALUATION

Write: (Select own *limited* subject) _____

_____

Length: optional _____

Required in Contents	Full	Earned	For Study
1. Limit subject	20		
2. Identify purpose (define, describe, analyze, argue) _____ _____	20		
3. Select clear controlling or central idea _____ _____	20		
4. Assign point values only to the techniques you use: a. *concrete* vs abstract b. specific detail c. comparison d. contrast e. narrative style f. expository style g. other: _____	_____ _____ _____ _____ _____ _____ _____		
TOTAL	100		

Instructor's Comments:

ENGLISH MECHANICS: Instructor Assigns Values for Criteria

Content Areas	Full	Earned	For Study
ORGANIZATION: Introduction Chronological Organization Topical Organization Rational Organization Smooth Development Termination	_____ _____ _____ _____ _____ _____		Chapter 13 Chapter 15 Chapter 16 Chapter 17 Chapter 14 Chapter 18
PARAGRAPHING: Introduction Development (unity) Development (coherence)	_____ _____ _____		Page 163 Page 165 Page 168
SENTENCES: completeness; variety; economy; use of modifiers; pronouns; agreement; use of verbs, phrases, clauses	_____		
USE OF LANGUAGE: Level of usage Idiomatic usage Vividness	_____		Chapter 8
PUNCTUATION AND CAPITALIZATION and related graphics: Quotation marks	_____		Chapter 7
SPELLING:			
TOTAL	100		

Mechanics not in this text are assigned in supplementary text.

The Paragraph: Showing Development of Thought

The paragraph is an essay or composition in miniature. It is the smallest unit which you may use to show the *development* of your thoughts from a general idea to specific ideas or from the abstract to the concrete. In another sense, you may consider the paragraph as several sentences which deal with *one limited controlling idea* and which has two basic parts, the topic sentence and the body or development. Finally, when a paragraph is well-structured, it has the characteristics of unity and coherence and deals with a very limited subject.

The Topic Sentence: The Controlling Idea

The topic sentence is the general statement in a paragraph. It is most commonly used to introduce the specific sentences which support it with details. Its other functions are to state the controlling or limited idea (purpose) and to confine the subject to what can actually be accomplished within the length of a paragraph. Now, look at some samples of topic sentences which are repeated from paragraphs in Chapter 11.

Sample Topic Sentences

1. Isolation is a state of existence in which individuals or groups do not communicate with each other.

   Controlling Idea: Defines isolation in terms of poor communication.

2. I saw the crowd at the executions as a composite of types.

   Controlling Idea: Introduces a description of the different types of people the author saw witnessing some executions.

3. I have found a way to moisten stamps for attachment to envelopes which is efficient and eliminates the need to lick them.

   Controlling Idea: Introduces a process for attaching stamps to envelopes.

4. If you wish to destroy a man's ability to function as a member of a free society, limit his ability to express himself.

   Controlling Idea: Argues that a man can't function in a free society if his freedom of expression is limited.

5. A blow gun is a dangerous weapon consisting of a long hollow tube and a dart.

Controlling Idea: Defines and describes a blow gun.

6. Bamboo is a member of the same family as ordinary lawn grass, but they are very different.

Controlling Idea: Defines bamboo as grass and introduces a contrast with lawn grasses.

Each of the topic sentences above makes a general statement. Each introduces the controlling idea of the paragraph. Following each would be specific sentences which provide the details necessary to complete the author's interpretation of the controlling idea. Now, try the questions which follow to see if you can distinguish among a number of statements those which could be topic sentences and those which would be otherwise.

REVIEW QUESTIONS

Read the following and mark with a "T" those statements which you think are general and could be topic sentences; mark specific ideas with an "S."

1. I had a good time at the ball game. _____

2. There are other errors besides lack of unity. _____

3. The spectator stared in anticipation. _____

4. Furthermore, the chair is broken. _____

5. You must learn to distinguish between a smile and a smirk. _____

6. I found a sock in the drawer too. _____

7. His stationery drawer is a mess. _____

8. Tom Jones caught the pass. _____

9. The meat is in the refrigerator. _____

10. The game started with a lot of action. _____

ANSWERS: 1. T; 2. T; 3. T; 4. S; 5. T; 6. S; 7. T; 8. S; 9. S; 10. T

After you review the answers to the questions you have just completed, read the following general statements to determine if they are possible *topics of paragraph length*. If they are possible, mark them "yes"; if they are too broad, mark them "no." The question is could you *develop* these ideas in one paragraph?

11. Man's world is threatened by pollution.   _____

12. A hamburger is made of two pieces of bread and a patty of meat. _____

13. Communism and capitalism are different economic systems.   _____

14. The umpire's decision at the plate was inaccurate.   _____

15. I've seen cheating in all my schools.   _____

16. The construction of the modern automobile is complex.   _____

17. The diamond is the hardest substance.   _____

18. Electricity is the servant of mankind.   _____

19. It took three years to build Hoover Dam.   _____

20. George Bernard Shaw was a vegetarian.   _____

ANSWERS: 11. no; 12. yes; 13. no; 14. yes; 15. yes; 16. no; 17. yes; 18. no; 19. no; 20. yes

Paragraph Development: Unity

The development or body of a paragraph contains a number of sentences each of which makes a *different specific* statement related to the *limited* controlling idea in the topic sentence. When a paragraph shows this coordination between the topic and specific sentences, it has unity. On the other hand, unity is lacking when any sentence is included that does not directly and clearly relate to all of the other sentences in a paragraph. Let us look at a sample paragraph and answer some questions about it. Each sentence is identified by a letter for your convenience.

(A) I've seen cheating in each school in which I was enrolled, in areas as widely separated as the southern, eastern, and western parts of the country. (B) Everywhere, I saw term papers for sale on every conceivable subject. (C) I also observed students using "crib" sheets on examinations, copying from each other's papers, and whispering when they were supposed to be silent.

21. Which is the topic sentence?_____

22. Which sentence states the controlling idea?_____

23. What is the controlling idea of the paragraph?_____

_____

_____

24. Which sentences develop the controlling idea of the paragraph?_____

25. Do all of the sentences you identified in question 24 deal with the controlling idea in some particular way? (yes or no) _____

26. Briefly, summarize the specific information of each sentence in the body of the paragraph.

    B. _____

    _____

    C. _____

    _____

27. Do any of the sentences in the body repeat the same information as any of the other sentences? (yes or no) _____

ANSWERS: 21. A; 22. A; 23. Cheating occurred in every school I attended; 24. B, C; 25. yes; 26. B. I saw term papers for sale everywhere; C. I saw crib sheets, copying, and whispering; 27. no

    Consider the following paragraph to see if it has unity too. For your convenience, each sentence has a letter.

    (A) I had a good time at the ball game. (B) Joe and Bill, my best friends, went with me. (C) I have known them all my life, and we go everywhere together. (D) Joe is a good storyteller; the best times I have are those when Joe relates a joke he heard or tells about some experience he had. (E) Joe and Bill are very sincere people. (F) I think that sincerity is the most important quality in a friend. (G) If the world had more sincere people, there would not be so much bigotry and war.

28. What is the central idea of this paragraph?

    (A, B, C, D, E, F, G, None, Uncertain) _____

29. Are all the sentences related to a central idea? (yes or no) _____

30. Does the paragraph have unity? (yes or no) _____

31. Some of the sentences in the paragraph are somewhat related; others are not. Using the letters which precede each sentence, group all sentences to show which could be related to each other. Any sentence <u>may</u> appear in more than one group.

32. Is it possible to invent a controlling idea which relates to all of the sentences in the paragraph and, thus, unifies them? (yes or no) _____

33. List the separate subjects which you can identify in this group of sentences.

_____

_____

_____

_____

_____

_____

ANSWERS: 28. uncertain; 29. no; 30. no; 31. A, B-C, D, B-E-F, F-G, others?; 32. no; 33. good time at ball game, relationship of sincerity to friendship, relationship of sincerity to world conditions, Joe's ability to tell stories or jokes, others?

Now, examine a paragraph from the following:

THE PRIVATE WORLD OF THE MAN WITH A BOOK
Harold Taylor

Whenever we take a writer out of his natural element, that is, treat him as other than a human being who is writing what he knows, we run the risk of destroying his value to the reader by making him represent a category of thought to which he has been assigned after the fact, usually after his death. In graduate schools, this unnatural treatment of writers leads to the continual preoccupation with tracing influences, classifying authors into categories, and otherwise drawing attention away from the writer himself. The writer must be allowed to stand on his own feet. Indeed, his greatness is established by the fact that he continues to stand on his own feet from generation to generation, and that he is perpetually rediscovered for himself and for what he has to say.

34. State the controlling idea in your own words.

_____

_____

_____

_____

35. In which sentence is the controlling idea?_____

36. Does each of the sentences in the body of the paragraph contribute something specific to help

develop the controlling idea? (yes or no) _____

37. Does the paragraph have unity? (yes or no) _____

ANSWERS: 34. We mistreat a writer when we make him represent a category of thought; 35. the first (topic) sentence; 36. yes; 37. yes

Paragraph Development: Coherence

Thus far, you have learned that a paragraph has two basic parts, a topic sentence and a body. The topic sentence makes a general statement which includes the controlling idea; the body is composed of a number of sentences, each specific and related to the topic sentence. When these parts of the paragraph work together, the result is a unified treatment of the subject. However, there is another important element which is a technique rather than a definite part of a paragraph: coherence.

Coherence is the technique of relating sentences smoothly through the use of transitional words and phrases. By transitional is meant the process of "crossing over" from the meaning of one sentence to the meaning in the next sentence. If transition is lacking or poor, the shift in meaning between sentences is too abrupt and the effect, rough. The sentences, then, do not stick together well to provide unity in the paragraph—even if each sentence is a specific detail of the controlling idea.

Let us draw a comparison between coherence and something familiar. Think of a highway several miles long which is crossed at right angles by several small roads. Pretend that some of the small roads are not yet paved, resulting in rough, uneven intersections at the places where they cross the highway. How would you feel if you were driving a car on the smooth highway at, say, fifty miles per hour and you suddenly entered one of these unpaved intersections? Do you think you would notice the difference in road surface? Now, look at the illustration below; see if it helps to clarify further.

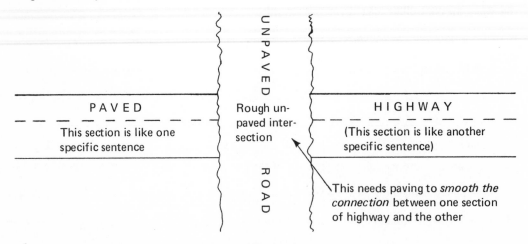

Figure 13.

Is the symbolism clear? The job of the writer is to "pave the intersection" among all his sentences in order to "smooth the connections." Now, let's look at a sample paragraph to see how the sentences are related. Pay particular attention to the underlined words and phrases which are examples of the transitions among the sentences.

(A) John is a good man. (B) He has never been less than kind and considerate to me. (C) Furthermore, I have seen John perform acts of remarkable kindness on behalf of strangers. (D) Last week, for example, he returned $5.00 to a clerk who had given him too much change. (E) Another example of John's goodness is his great tolerance of the dishonesty of others. (F) Once, at a restaurant, he refused to become angry when a waiter obviously tried to overcharge him. (G) Instead, John made an excuse that the waiter was so busy that he had made a mistake. (H) This remarkable man also accepts ordinary human weaknesses with calm. (I) That is to say, such phenomena as insincerity, thoughtlessness, and ingratitude do not affect his loving nature.

38. What element of the paragraph is sentence (A)?_____

_____

39. To which word in sentence (A) does the underlined word "he" in sentence (B) refer?_____

_____

40. Does "he" help to relate (B) to (A)?_____

41. How many times does "John" appear in the paragraph?_____

42. Does the repetition of "John" help to relate sentences (A) through (I)?_____

43. Is "John" in sentence (G) the same person as "John" in sentence (A)?_____

44. Does the use of the same "John" throughout the paragraph keep the point of view clear?_____

_____

45. Does "furthermore" in sentence (C) help to relate sentences (C) and (B)? (yes or no) _____

_____

46. "Furthermore" serves as a _____word between (C) and (B).

47. Which two sentences does "Another" serve as a transitional word?_____

48. Which two sentences does "That is to say" serve as a transitional clause? _____

49. How does "also" serve sentences (H) and (G)?_____

50. Does the grouping of sentences (A) through (I) have coherence as well as unity because

transitional words and phrases are used to relate them gracefully?_____

ANSWERS: 38. topic sentence and controlling idea; 39. John; 40. yes; 41. four; 42. yes; 43. yes; 44. yes; 45. yes; 46. transitional or connective; 47. (E) and (D); 48. (I) and (H); 49. as a transition; 50. yes

Now, for the sake of contrast, let us examine the same paragraph about John, this time with many of the transitions removed. *No attempt has been made to destroy all sentence coherence, only to weaken some of it.* See if what has been removed weakens the paragraph structure.

(A) John is a good man. (B) He has never been less than kind and considerate to me. (C) I have seen him perform acts of remarkable kindness on behalf of strangers. (D) Last week he returned $5.00 to a clerk who had given him too much change. (E) His goodness includes great tolerance of the dishonesty of others. (F) At a restaurant, he refused to become angry when a waiter obviously tried to overcharge him. (G) John made an excuse that the waiter was so busy that he had made a mistake. (H) This remarkable man accepts ordinary human weaknesses with calm. (I) Such phenomena as insincerity, thoughtlessness, and ingratitude do not affect his loving nature.

51. Many transitional words and phrases have been removed from this paragraph. Let us compare the two paragraphs about John by referring to the matching sentences in each. For example, in sentence (C), "furthermore" was removed from the second paragraph; this missing word suggests *an addition* to the meaning of the previous sentence, (B). Identify the other missing words and phrases.

   a.   Sentence (D)_____

   b.   Sentence (E)_____

   c.   Sentence (F)_____

   d.   Sentence (G)_____

   e.   Sentence (H)_____

   f.   Sentence (I)_____

52. How does "for example" relate (D) to (C)?

   _____

   _____

53. How does "instead" relate (G) to (F)?

   _____

   _____

54. How do transitional words and phrases help to relate sentences in a paragraph?

   _____

   _____

   _____

ANSWERS: 51a. for example; 51b. another; 51c. once; 51d. instead; 51e. also; 51f. that is to say; 52. It suggests that this sentence will clarify the idea of the previous sentence by giving a specific example; 53. It suggests a contrast with the meaning of (F); 54. They suggest examples, contrasts, or other relationships between the ideas of sentences which follow each other within a paragraph.

Review of Coherence within the Paragraph

Coherence, the clear connection of sentences within a unified paragraph, is necessary to smooth development. The repetition of key words (John) in some of the sentences assists in making connection; use of key words also keeps the point of view clear from sentence to sentence. In addition, pronouns (he, his, him) which refer to nouns in earlier sentences serve to relate these sentences. Finally, there are transitional words and phrases which also relate sentences which follow each other; a listing of some commonly used transitions follows.

To Show an Addition to Idea in Previous Sentence:

again, also, besides, finally, futhermore, in addition, last, moreover, next, second, similarly, subsequently, too

To Draw a Contrast with Previous Sentence:

but, conversely, however, instead, nevertheless, nor, on the contrary, on the other hand, or, still, yet

To Introduce an Example of Idea in Previous Sentence:

for example, for instance, namely, stated in another way, that is, thus, to clarify

To Make a Conclusion Based on Previous Sentence:

accordingly, as a result, consequently, finally, in conclusion, in other words, then, therefore, thus

Do's and Don't's of Sentence Coherence:

1. Do use pronouns to relate sentences.
2. Do repeat key words to relate sentences.
3. Do use transitional words and phrases to relate sentences.
4. Don't use pronouns to relate sentences unless they refer to specific nouns with clarity.
5. Don't repeat key words too many times or the virtue of repeating for clarity becomes the error of needless repetition.

Some Problems of Paragraphing

Earlier you read that the paragraph is the *smallest unit* which you may use to show the *development* of your thoughts from the general to the specific or from the abstract to the concrete. Unfortunately, writers sometimes forget this important definition, particularly the key words "development of thoughts." Think of what "development" means: "a gradual unfolding or series of progressive changes *from one idea to other ideas.*" Stated in another way, development in paragraphing means the unfolding of the controlling general idea in the topic sentence through the specific sentences in the body or development.

In the simplest of terms, writers recognize that sentences do not make effective paragraphs if these sentences fail to show sufficient development of thought. This applies equally to the generalized topic sentence *used alone as if it were a complete paragraph,* and to specific sentences such as those which belong in the body of a paragraph but which are not unified by a controlling idea. Now, let us look at some samples.

> To understand what an insincere person is, one must, first, explore the meaning of insincere.

55. Is this sample a complete paragraph? _____

56. What does it *seem* to be, a topic sentence or part of paragraph development? _____

57. If you called it a topic sentence, what is the controlling idea? _____

58. Does the writer develop the controlling idea? _____

ANSWERS: 55. no; 56. topic sentence; 57. definition of insincere person; 58. no

Now look at the next sample. Is it like the last one?

> The implication of all this is that an insincere person creates problems for people who know him; I don't like an insincere person.

59. Is this sample a complete paragraph? _____

60. What does it seem to be, a topic sentence or part of paragraph development? _____

61. From what part of a paragraph does it *seem* to be, the beginning or *after* the beginning? _____

_____

62. Write a topic sentence with a controlling idea for which this could be a conclusion.

_____

_____

_____

ANSWERS: 59. no; 60. development; 61. end; 62. To understand what an insincere person is, one must, first, explore the meaning of insincere. (This is the first sample on this page dealing with paragraph problems.)

Let us try another exercise. Look at the lettered descriptions below. Apply the letter from a description to each of the numbered questions which follow.

    a. A complete paragraph
    b. A specific statement; could fit the body of a paragraph
    c. A general statement; could be the topic sentence of a paragraph
    d. Specific statements; controlling idea missing

63. "In fact they would exist more appropriately on a still more distant planet where time—as we know it—creeps and crawls instead of flies from dawn to dusk. Years ago I wrote that sloths reminded me of nothing so much as the wonderful Rath Brother athletes or of a slowed-up moving picture, and I can still think of no better similes."[1]

Identify from descriptions a, b, c, or d. _____

64. "Each generation has its own truth, its own private world, its own way of knowing, and we who are educators would be wise to listen to them for the knowledge they can bring. The young have the supreme advantage of not having been here before; they are not yet settled, they have almost no history and they can consider the world freshly (that is, they can and do when they talk to each other), and they test and retest the ideas that are old and known and reputable. They reject some, they revive and re-create others."[2]

Identify from descriptions a, b, c, or d. _____

65. "The difficulty is that something happens to educators, and to other people, when they think or talk about education." (Harold Taylor)

Identify from descriptions a, b, c, or d. _____

66. "They live apart from us, they hold themselves back, and from the untouchable center of their personal lives they look distantly at our existence and our knowledge as items possessed by beings on a different planet." (Harold Taylor)

Identify from descriptions a, b, c, or d. _____

ANSWERS: 63. d: The controlling idea is "Sloths have no right to be living on the earth today; they would be fitting inhabitants of Mars, where a year is over six hundred days long"; 64. a; 65. c; 66. b

REVIEW OF PARAGRAPH PROBLEMS

1. Don't write a topic sentence alone as if it were a paragraph.
2. Don't organize a group of sentences into a paragraph without providing a controlling idea to unite them.
3. Don't set down in paragraph form a sentence or sentences, however well related, which belong either to the middle or the end of a paragraph and which fail to show the sensible development of a limited subject.

---

1. From *Jungle Days* by William Beebe.
2. From *The Private World of The Man with A Book* by Harold Taylor.

Summary of Paragraphing

A paragraph has two parts, the topic sentence and the body or development. When it is properly structured, its sentences show coherence, a technique used to relate the individual sentences of a paragraph effectively.

The Topic Sentence

1. Is a general statement.
2. Introduces a very limited subject, appropriate to paragraph length.
3. States the limited controlling or central idea of the entire paragraph.
4. Is confined to only one controlling idea.

The Body or Development

1. Contains specific sentences each of which makes a specific different statement to help develop the controlling idea.
2. Shows unity when all sentences deal with the subject introduced in the topic sentence.

The Technique of Coherence

1. Is the means of providing transitions among sentences to effect smooth connections.
2. Shows the repetition of key words as well as the use of pronouns and transitional words and phrases to relate the specific meanings of separate sentences which precede or follow each other.

Read the following selections and answer the questions about each.

STYLE IN SCIENCE
John Rader Platt

All scientists are not alike. Look at any laboratory or university science department. Professor Able is the kind of man who seizes an idea as a dog seizes a stick, all at once. As he talks you can see him stop short, with the chalk in his fingers, and then almost jump with excitement as the insight grips him. His colleague, Baker, on the other hand, is a man who comes to understand an idea as a worm might understand the same stick, digesting it a little at a time, drawing his conclusions cautiously, and tunneling slowly through it from end to end and back again.

Appreciation of Style

1. State the controlling idea of the paragraph.
2. This paragraph is from a longer work. If, however, it appeared as an isolated, complete, short essay, would you consider the controlling idea limited enough to be developed in one paragraph? Defend your answer.
3. Identify some techniques used to achieve coherence.
4. The paragraph shows use of example and contrast. Prove that this is so.
5. Identify figures of speech.

Test Your Comprehension

1. What is the theme of the paragraph? Prove your answer by making specific reference to the text of the paragraph itself.

Vocabulary for Study

insight   colleague

ISHI IN TWO WORLDS
Theodora Kroeber

In 1835, the padre of Mission Santa Barbara transferred the San Nicolas Indians to the mainland. A few minutes after the boat, which was carrying the Indians, had put off from the island, it was found that one baby had been left behind. It is not easy to land a boat on San Nicolas; the captain decided against returning for the baby; the baby's mother jumped overboard, and was last seen swimming toward the island. Half-hearted efforts made to find her in subsequent weeks were unsuccessful: it was believed that she had drowned in the rough surf. In 1853, eighteen years later, seal hunters in the Channel waters reported seeing a woman on San Nicolas, and a boatload of men from Santa Barbara went in search of her. They found her, a last survivor of her tribe. Her baby, as well as all her people who had been removed to the Mission, had died. She lived only a few months after her "rescue" and died without anyone having been able to communicate with her, leaving to posterity this skeletal outline of her grim story, and four words which someone remembered from her lost language and recorded as she said them. It so happens that these four words identify her language as having been Shoshonean, related to Indian languages of the Los Angeles area, not to those of Santa Barbara.

Appreciation of Style

1. What is the controlling idea of this paragraph?
2. A particular noun serves as an important "unifying thread." Which is it? What technique does it show?
3. Each of the eight sentences is related to the one before it. Identify the word or words which relate the sentences in each pair. For example, sentences one and two are related by repetition of "Indians."

   a.   Sentences 2 and 3 by _____

   b.   Sentences 3 and 4 by _____

   c.   Sentences 4 and 5 by_____

   d.   Sentences 5 and 6 by _____

   e.   Sentences 6 and 7 by_____

   f.   Sentences 7 and 8 by_____

4. Are all of the sentences related to the controlling idea? Defend your answer.
5. What style of writing is shown in this paragraph?
6. Identify the author's purpose.

Test Your Comprehension

1. The author "commented" upon relations between the Indians and white men. What theme did she imply? Present evidence to support your statement of theme.

2. The author reported her facts quite objectively. Do you believe she wanted the reader to react objectively?

3. Why is the word "rescue" in quotation marks?

Vocabulary for Study

subsequent   grim   posterity

REVIEW OF PURPOSES AND TECHNIQUES OF EXPOSITION

Purposes: 1. definition, 2. description, 3. narration to show a sequence or process, 4. argumentation, 5. analysis, 6. any appropriate combination

Techniques: 1. emphasis upon concrete vs. abstract, 2. use of example, 3. comparison, 4. contrast, 5. any appropriate combination

THE TRUE BELIEVER
Eric Hoffer

A minority is in a precarious position, however protected it be by law or force. The frustration engendered by the unavoidable sense of insecurity is less intense in a minority intent on preserving its identity than in one bent upon dissolving in and blending with the majority. A minority which preserves its identity is inevitably a compact whole which shelters the individual, gives him a sense of belonging and immunizes him against frustration. On the other hand, in a minority bent on assimilation, the individual stands alone, pitted against prejudice and discrimination. He is also burdened with the sense of guilt, however vague, of a renegade. The orthodox Jew is less frustrated than the emancipated Jew. The segregated Negro in the South is less frustrated than the nonsegregated Negro in the North.

Appreciation of Style

1. State the controlling idea of the paragraph.

2. Identify techniques of coherence used to relate sentences.

3. What purpose does this paragraph serve? Definition? Analysis? Description? Argumentation? More than one?

4. What techniques of development are used in the paragraph? Comparison? Contrast? Example? Anything else? Cite from the selection to prove your answer.

Test Your Comprehension

1. What problem does the author identify?

2. Which does Hoffer prefer, separated or integrated minorities?

Vocabulary for Study

precarious   renegade   prejudice
frustration   engendered
assimilation   emancipated

Writing Sample Eight: Read the paragraph from *Another Country* which follows. Then, write to give your reaction to whatever aspect of the paragraph impressed you most. For example, you could react to the saxophonist, including his behavior, background and need for love. In another vein, you could react to the emotional atmosphere of the setting. *You* decide what your purpose will be and the style and techniques you will use to accomplish your purpose. First, reread the brief review of purposes and techniques of exposition which precedes. Then, read the excerpt from *Another Country*. Finally, read the directions for a critical opinion paper, the sample student critical paper, and the Assignment-Evaluation sheet which follow.

ANOTHER COUNTRY

James Baldwin

There was some pot on the scene and he was a little high. He was feeling great. And, during the last set, he came doubly alive because the saxophone player, who had been way out all night, took off on a terrific solo. He was a kid of about the same age as Rufus, from some insane place like Jersey City or Syracuse, but somewhere along the line he had discovered that he could say it with a saxophone. He had a lot to say. He stood there, wide-legged, humping the air, filling his barrel chest, shivering in the rags of his twenty-odd years, and screaming through the horn *Do you love me? Do you love me? Do you love me?* And, again, *Do you love me? Do you love me? Do you love me?* This, anyway, was the question Rufus heard, the same phrase, unbearably, endlessly, and variously repeated, with all of the force the boy had. The silence of the listeners became strict with abruptly focused attention, cigarettes were unlit, and drinks stayed on the tables; and in all of the faces, even the most ruined and most dull, a curious, wary light appeared. They were being assaulted by the saxophonist who perhaps no longer wanted their love and merely hurled his outrage at them with the same contemptuous, pagan pride with which he humped the air. And yet the question was terrible and real; the boy was blowing with his lungs and guts out of his own short past; somewhere in that past, in the gutters or gang fights of gang shags; in the acrid room, on the sperm-stiffened blanket, behind marijuana or the needle, under the smell of piss in the precinct basement, he had received the blow from which he never would recover and this no one wanted to believe. *Do you love me? Do you love me? Do you love me?* The men on the stand stayed with him, cool and at a little distance, adding and questioning and corroborating, holding it down as well as they could with an ironical self-mockery; but each man knew that the boy was blowing for every one of them. When the set ended they were all soaking. Rufus smelled his odor and the odor of the men around him and "Well, that's it," said the bass man. The crowd was yelling for more but they did their theme song and the lights came on. And he played the last set of his last gig.

Turn to Assignment-Evaluation sheet.

WRITING SAMPLE EIGHT

ASSIGNMENT: A critical opinion based upon a reading selection: *Commenting on an idea from a story*

One of the most common types of student essays is the critical paper. In such a paper, you are asked to select an idea from something you have read and to evaluate it from your own point of view. The idea you select may be as important as an author's theme or something of lesser importance. In essence, you are given freedom of choice to react to something which has interested you.

When writing a critical paper, you are *measuring the worth* of an idea, judging its importance, correctness and/or incorrectness; and your object is to express your own views about it. Therefore, you are obliged to be rational and/or factual in your comments. *You should not expect anyone to accept your unsupported opinion!*

Finally, in criticism, you should be *clear* in showing your agreement, disagreement, or both, with the ideas to which you react and in distinguishing your ideas from those of others.

DIRECTIONS: Write a brief criticism of an idea from an essay, story or poem. Confine your writing to a clear statement of the idea and its source, followed by your own opinions. Present facts and/or reasons to support your opinions and be as specific as possible.

1. Read the selection carefully.
2. Be certain you fully understand the idea which has interested you.
3. List your opinions carefully after phrasing the idea which has interested you in your own words.
4. List the facts and/or reasons which are needed to support your opinions, including, if necessary, brief quotations from the original.
5. Study the sample critical paper which follows.
6. Review the Assignment-Evaluation sheet which follows the critical paper to be certain you understand the criteria for contents.
7. Arrange your opinions and facts carefully.
8. Write a rough draft of your paper.
9. Compare your rough draft with the criteria.
10. Rewrite as many times as necessary to correct your paper for contents and mechanics before you hand it in.

SAMPLE STUDENT CRITICAL OPINION

The following sample paper is based upon the short story, "Young Man Axelbrod," which appears in Chapter 3 of this textbook.

AXELBROD AND HIGHER EDUCATION

Sinclair Lewis used his short story, "Young Man Axel-brod," to criticize higher education; he accomplished this by showing college through Knute Axelbrod's eyes.

Knute Axelbrod was very interested in education and wanted to be a scholar when he was young. However, he had to set aside his dreams when he was eighteen to work his farm. He married early, and he and his wife started having children right away.

Nevertheless, during the long years of his family responsibilities, Knute Axelbrod never lost his taste for learning, for he read as much as he could find the time to do so. Finally, at the age of sixty-four, with his wife dead and his children mature and independent, Knute Axelbrod decided to go to college. To accomplish his goal, Axelbrod studied hard, took entrance examinations and was admitted to Yale University.

Yale was a great disappointment to Knute Axelbrod. He had imagined a college as a place full of special people who really desired to learn everything they possibly could. He realized, though, that most of the people there were seeking college degrees just so they could get higher-paying jobs.

Sinclair Lewis gave me the impression that, like Axelbrod, he thought college should be a place of serious learning, not somewhere to go just to increase wages. For example, Lewis showed that too many students do not take their work seriously. In one of Axelbrod's classes, the old man ". . . became aware that certain lewd fellows of the lesser sort were playing poker just behind him." The author, furthermore, called these boys "mockers of sound learning," giving other examples of boys who read newspapers and kicked each other in class.

Lewis also gave me the impression that he didn't think too highly of some professors either. For example, "Knute tried not to miss one of (Professor) Blevins' sardonic proofs that the correct date of the second marriage of Themistocles was two years and seven days later than the date assigned by that illiterate ass, Frutari of Padua." So what!

I think that Lewis' intention in this example was to emphasize how some professors spend too much time on "little things," instead of teaching their students how to appreciate the beauty and importance of life. As a result, I believe that Lewis felt, as I feel, that higher education is often focused upon the wrong things. Furthermore, it is often totally ignored by the students who may, perhaps, need it most.

Student writes his own title

Student describes the work he is criticizing and states his controlling idea

Student gives just enough information about the story to make his critical opinion clear to the reader

Student restates the controlling idea briefly and presents general evidence to support it

Student relates general idea to author as well as to a character in the story

Student presents concrete evidence from the story to support the controlling idea; emphasizes the poor qualities of students

Student offers additional evidence from the story to show weaknesses of subject matter and the professors

Student emphasizes and restates his criticism by generalizing from the evidence he presented; an appropriate form of termination

---

Study the Assignment-Evaluation sheet next
before you try to do your paper on the excerpt
from <u>Another Country</u>.

WRITING SAMPLE 8—EVALUATION

Write a critical opinion of some aspect of James Baldwin's excerpt from *Another Country*.
Length: (select your own length)

Required in Contents	Full	Earned	For Study
1. Show a clear purpose for your criticism _____	25		
2. Make a clear statement of your controlling idea	25		
3. Give enough information about the selection so your reader can understand your comments	25		
4. Develop your controlling idea in concrete words and specific detail	25		
PROOFREAD YOUR WORK CAREFULLY!			
TOTAL	100		

Instructor's Comments:

ENGLISH MECHANICS: Instructor Assigns Values for Criteria

Content Areas	Full	Earned	For Study
ORGANIZATION: Introduction Chronological Organization Topical Organization Rational Organization Smooth Development Termination	——— ——— ——— ——— ——— ———		Chapter 13 Chapter 15 Chapter 16 Chapter 17 Chapter 14 Chapter 18
PARAGRAPHING: Introduction Development (unity) Development (coherence)	——— ——— ———		Page 163 Page 165 Page 168
SENTENCES: completeness; variety; economy; use of modifiers; pronouns; agreement; use of verbs, phrases, clauses	———		
USE OF LANGUAGE: Level of usage Idiomatic usage Vividness	———		Chapter 8
PUNCTUATION AND CAPITALIZATION and related graphics: Quotation marks	———		Chapter 7
SPELLING:			
TOTAL	100		

Mechanics not in this text are assigned in supplementary text.

Figure 14. Where do I begin? By Schain.

The Essay: **13**
How It Is Introduced

The essay is a well-organized expression of thought, ranging in length from the single paragraph to the full-length book. It may be formal or informal, objective or personal, serious or humorous. Essay organization, similarly, shows variation: it may be chronological, topical, rational or logical; or it may involve combinations of these approaches. The essay, furthermore, may be used for the various purposes identified in the chapter on paragraphing: analysis, argumentation, description and/or definition; and it may be written in any combination of expository and narrative styles, depending upon the writer's purpose.

Skillful writers follow some similar basic practices, no matter what the length, tone, language, organization, or purpose of their work. First, they identify, define, and limit their essay topics to what they actually plan to accomplish. Second, they develop their ideas with care to clarify *their subjects*. Third, during the development of their subjects, they use a variety of techniques to assure clarity, including specific lively detail, definition of unfamiliar terms, comparison, contrast, and example. Fourth, they terminate their work in a manner best suited to the subject: they may summarize, recommend, form conclusions, or combine methods of termination. Finally, the *concerned* writer always asks himself this most important question: Am I fulfilling my purpose and communicating my ideas to the reader?

Introduction to an Essay

The introduction to an essay is very similar to the topic sentence in a paragraph, for it states the subject and controlling idea. The length of an introduction, of course, varies with the complexity of the subject and the planned length of the completed essay. For example, in a short essay, the introduction may be one short paragraph or only the first sentence of the first paragraph. On the other hand, in an essay of thousands of words in length, the introduction may be many paragraphs or pages, even a complete chapter in a book. The point is that an introduction should *prepare the reader for what follows as specifically and clearly as possible.*

Now examine the following introductions to some short essays. Try to identify the general subjects and controlling or central ideas. You can see if these ideas are properly developed by reading the complete essays at the end of this chapter. See page 185 for answers.

CRIME AND BARBARIC PUNISHMENT
Harry Golden

The British House of Commons has voted to abolish capital punishment. Up in Massachusetts, that noble lady, Mrs. Herbert Ehrmann (head of the Society for the Abolition of Capital Punishment) has victory within her grasp. She has worked unceasingly over the years with what is practically a one-woman organization.

1. Write the subject and controlling idea in your own words.

_____

_____

_____

WEATHER RECORDS
Robert Benchley

Whatever else this year of grace goes down in the history books, it certainly has gone hog-wild on weather records.

2. Write the subject and controlling idea in your own words.

_____

_____

_____

IT'S HARD FOR COLLEGIANS TO LIVE UP TO ROLES
Art Buchwald

It's very hard for many college students to live up to the roles they have been given by the mass media. What newspapers, magazines, and television networks expect from students is more than most of them can deliver. I discovered this when I was speaking at a Midwestern campus the other day.

3. Write the subject and controlling idea in your own words.

_____

_____

_____

EDISON: INVENTOR OF INVENTION

Walter Lippman

It is impossible to measure the importance of Edison by adding up the specific inventions with which his name is associated. Far-reaching as many of them have been in their effect on modern civilization, the total effect of Edison's career surpasses the sum of them all. He did not merely make the incandescent lamp and the phonograph and innumerable other devices practicable for general use; it was given to him to demonstrate the power of applied science so concretely, so understandably, so convincingly that he altered the mentality of mankind. In his lifetime, largely because of his successes, there came into widest acceptance the revolutionary conception that man could by the use of his intelligence invent a new mode of living on his planet; the human spirit, which in all previous ages had regarded the conditions of life as essentially unchanging and beyond man's control, confidently, and perhaps somewhat naively, adopted the conviction that anything could be changed and everything could be controlled.

4. Write the subject and controlling idea in your own words.

_____

_____

_____

After reviewing the answers to questions 1-4 below, read the four short essays at the end of this chapter to see how the introductions to these essays were developed.

ANSWERS TO QUESTIONS 1-4 ON PAGES 184-185:

1. The subject is capital punishment. Golden is against it and believes it may soon be discontinued in Massachusetts through the efforts of largely one woman.
2. The subject is weather records and the year in which the essay was written broke many. "Hog-wild" suggests humor.
3. The subject is the difference between college student behavior and how mass media report their behavior. Most students can't live up to the reports of mass media.
4. The subject is the impact Edison's amazing inventiveness had upon our culture. Edison convinced us that man could do amazing things to influence his mode of living on his world.

CRIME AND BARBARIC PUNISHMENT

Harry Golden

The British House of Commons has voted to abolish capital punishment. Up in Massachusetts, that noble lady, Mrs. Herbert Ehrmann (head of the Society for the Abolition of Capital Punishment) has victory within her grasp. She has worked unceasingly over the years with what is practically a one-woman organization.

North Carolina, which has shown itself capable of true greatness on many occasions, has all but followed the Mother Country in the final elimination of the act of legal barbarism. By two amendments in the Legislature, mandatory death sentences have been removed for conviction in crimes of burglary, arson, murder, and rape. A defendant who pleads guilty to first-degree murder is automatically subject to a life sentence. *For a Southern state this is a remarkable development, and the manner in which it was handled is worthy of careful study throughout the country.*

The abolition of capital punishment is not a "public opinion" project. Contrary to the fairy tale of the wisdom of the taxi driver and the man-in-the-street, let us face the fact that the taxi driver and the man-in-the-street are hanging jurors. In every capital case from Socrates to Vanzetti, they have said the same thing: "I say, let's hang 'em." This requires tactful handling—the constant attempt to "communicate" through a few key people, the few people who really mold public opinion.

But, while progress is being made here in North Carolina, things are not so hopeful everywhere.

Up in New York, for instance, John O'Donnell of the *Daily News* (he who peddled the story of the Wacs and contraceptives during the war) wrote a column in which he recommended a system of prolonged torture for convicted kidnapers and murderers. He writes, "... [let us] inflict unusual punishment... [as] prolonged as medical science can accomplish ... as merciless ... as ancient torture ... [all this] ... to be imposed publicly in the Yankee Stadium before television cameras. . ."

If Mr. O'Donnell's system of prolonged torture is calculated to *punish* the criminal, he is wrong. No matter how "prolonged" the torture may be, we now know that it has no punitive effect beyond the first serious blow. Almost at once there is a complete paralysis of the nerve centers which renders the subject insensible to pain. Often this paralysis sets in even before the first blow is actually struck. In nine cases out of ten the mere opening of the cell door is enough to destroy all contact with reality. The march to the electric chair and the sitting down are purely mechanical. Even the outcry of the one being tortured is psychological, merely an association of ideas between the raising of the bludgeon or whip and his memory of pain. In one area of this highly enlightened O'Donnell thesis, he appears to be on solid ground. The public torture of a criminal would be a wonderful therapy for many of those who viewed it, but not in the way Mr. O'Donnell thinks. The folks used to bring their picnic baskets to all public hangings. But for public torture they really went to town. The emperor of Rome came out with thousands of cheering onlookers, who felt quite *spent* when the fun was over. For the sexually impotent particularly, public torture is a joy beyond words.

If Mr. O'Donnell's public torture idea was calculated to serve as a warning to others, we enter into a highly controversial area in the history of human behavior. The findings would seem to indicate that *punishment is not a deterrent to crime.* A murder was once committed outside the death house at Sing Sing, and the murderer was the trusty who polished the electric chair before each execution. William E.H. Lecky, in his *History of European Morals*, writes that in old England when they hanged pickpockets, all the pickpockets of the country would come to ply their trade among the folks whose attention was diverted.

Where we have fallen down in our handling of kidnapers, sex criminals, and murderers of children is in our lack of scientific preventive measures. The great criminologist, Dr. Frederic Wertham, knows what he is talking about when he says that over half the criminals charged with such offenses had already given society ample warning—they had previously been in the toils of the law, or in mental institutions, or in clinics under observation, time and time again. It is here that our law and criminal procedure have been wholly inadequate to keep these people isolated, and in other ways protect society from them.

Yet, the legalized murder continues.

In North Carolina we use gas to carry out the sentence of death. New York and many other states use the electric chair; others continue the old-fashioned method of hanging, and one state (Utah) gives the doomed man or woman a choice between hanging and shooting. Which is the most humane?

In the gas chamber a man sits in a chair with mighty leather tentacles hugging him close. Beneath the chair there is a jar containing acid. Above the jar there is a tiny chute in which, behind a little gate, are several lumps of egg-shaped pellets. There is a stethoscope fastened with tape over the doomed man's heart, connected to a long tube which comes through the wall. A cord is pulled, the little gate opens, and a pellet flops into the acid. There is a little bubbling, the doctor listens to the stethoscope. It's like a game. The man in the chair in the sealed room trembles. His face flushes, then turns purple. His eyes roll—he coughs and coughs, then a gasp, and it's the end. They say that sometimes there are convulsions for at least two minutes while he is choking to death. Seldom does the heart stop pounding before five minutes.

In the electric chair the convicted felon is strapped tightly, with a hood over his head containing an electrode. There's a small sponge placed between his head and the electrode to carry the power. The spot on the head where the wet electrode rests has been shaved. Another electrode is attached with a small wet sponge to the right leg below the knee. The warden gives the signal and the switch is thrown. The man in the chair lurches forward violently. The smell of burning flesh fills the room. As the current is reduced the doomed man relaxes a bit as the air is expelled from his lungs. Sometimes a second shock is necessary. Once in New York three shocks were required to put a man to death. Even at that, the rumor persists that it is the autopsy which follows that really finishes him. That, I wouldn't know. Electrical engineers would know more about that.

The states which hang their murderers say that their method is the most humane. If the hangman knows his business and puts the knot in the proper place the trap will break the man's neck quickly—say in about one minute.

The elimination of capital punishment will someday mark the end of a criminal code which was once the most ferocious in the world. Two centuries ago England executed little children. After hanging, the body was cut in quarters, salted down (they called it "atomizing"), and delivered to the relatives; all except the head. In the history of Dr. Ford, England's famous hangman, we find that in the year 1807 a crowd of eighty thousand gathered to witness the hanging of two murderers. Twenty-eight people were trampled to death in the crowd. For well over a century the position of official hangman really was a "concession." He received no pay, but he made a good living by selling pieces of the rope for a shilling. Often a few chiselers would be selling bootleg rope, and on one occasion one such chiseler was beaten to death when the people discovered that they had been *cheated* and had bought pieces of *unused* rope.

Many more legislative steps still remain to be taken in, affirming the sanctity of human life and the futility of killing by the state.

Appreciation of Style

1. Why does Golden make frequent use of concrete examples in the development of his essay?
2. Identify the controlling idea of the essay.
3. What is the tone of the essay?

Test Your Comprehension

1. List several reasons Golden gives for opposing "barbaric punishment."
2. Why would "prolonged torture" be ineffective punishment for criminals?
3. Is there evidence that people enjoy the sight of suffering?
4. If you were writing a critical opinion of this essay, to what would you react?

Vocabulary for Study

tactful	criminologist	stethoscope
calculated	insensible	

WEATHER RECORDS
Robert Benchley

Whatever else this year of grace goes down for in the history books, it certainly has gone hog-wild on weather records.

You couldn't walk around the weather bureau for the broken heat and cold records. Sometimes they even broke a record for medium temperature just to keep the ball rolling.

Of course, when you come to think of it, it isn't so much of a stunt to break a weather record. When you really come to think of it, you might go crazy trying not to break one. The wonder is that a record isn't broken every day. (Meterological note: As a matter of fact, one is broken every day, if you know where to look.)

In the first place, there are 1,460 major records each year, all aching to be broken. There is a heat, cold, rain-precipitation and snowfall record for each day in the year. Then there are the number of years the weather bureau has been keeping records, and the number of weather bureaus—Give up?

There is always a slightly cocky note in the weather bureau's announcement that "yesterday was the hottest May 27th since 1899, on which date the thermometer registered 91 degrees." On reading it you fall over forward in a belated sunstroke.

But they don't say anything about the fact that on May 26th of last year the temperature may have been 92 degrees. They don't say "yesterday was the hottest May 27th since May 26, 1933." Oh, no! They've got to have that record, sleazy as it is.

Why not get right down to really unimportant details and say "3 p.m. yesterday was the hottest overcast 3 p.m. on a May 27th to fall on a Sunday since 1887," or "more snow was tracked into the vestibule of the Weather Bureau yesterday between 9 a.m. and noon than on any previous day in its fifty years of existence." Statements like this would lend variety to weather reports, besides building up the supply of record-breaking days.

It would also be fun for the citizenry itself to send in little personal weather record-breakers, for publication just underneath the official statement:

"At 11:30 last night all heat records for the guest room of Mrs. Albert J. Arnkle at Bellclapper, Long Island, were broken when the thermometer registered a flat 96. The highest previous mark set by this guest room was 94 on the night of July 4, 1911. By an odd coincidence, Mr. George Losh was the guest occupying the room on both nights, so he can vouch for the figures being accurate."

"Yesterday, besides being the hottest Sunday since Friday, June 16th, 1929, found Mr. Larz Swamberg, of 486 Oakroot St., in the oddest assortment of clothing since he last wore diapers on June 11, 1890. He appeared at 10 a.m. wearing a Swiss Alpine coat of some crash material, pyjama pants and a pair of felt slippers. Later in the day he substituted a sleeveless jersey for the crash coat and replaced the slippers with a pair of rope *espadrilles*. At 4 p.m., when the thermometer reached its peak, Mr. Swamberg also established an all-time record for the household by discarding everything but a Panama hat and sitting in the bathtub. Mr. Swamberg feels the heat."

There is no reason why the Weather Bureau should get all the credit for record-breaking weather. We can all do our part.

Appreciation of Style

1. Give the controlling idea of the essay. Cite data which support the controlling idea.
2. Which style is emphasized, exposition or narration?
3. What is Benchley's tone?
4. Identify the transitional word in the eighth paragraph, beginning with "It."
5. Identify the topic sentence in the second last paragraph, beginning with "Yesterday."

Test Your Comprehension

1. Identify Benchley's theme in this essay. Did he communicate some serious intent?
2. What was Benchley's purpose for writing this essay?

Vocabulary for Study

meteorological	precipitation	sleazy	vestibule

IT'S HARD FOR COLLEGIANS TO LIVE UP TO ROLES

Art Buchwald

It's very hard for many college students to live up to the roles they have been given by the mass media. What newspapers, magazines and television networks expect from students is more than most of them can deliver. I discovered this when I was speaking at a Midwestern campus the other day.

A student, whom I shall call Ronald Hoffman, seemed very troubled and I asked him what the problem was.

"My parents are coming up next week, and I don't know what to do."

"Why?"

"Well, you see, I told them I was living off campus with this coed in an apartment. But the truth is that I'm living in the dormitory."

"That shouldn't really disturb them."

"Oh, but it will. They're very proud of me, and they think I should have a mind of my own. When my Dad heard I was living off campus with a coed, he doubled my allowance because, as he put it, 'Anyone who is willing to spit in the eye of conformity deserves his father's support.' I don't know what he's going to say when he finds out I used the money to buy books."

"It'll hurt him," I agreed. "What will your mother say?"

"I don't know. She's been crying a lot since I wrote her about living with this coed, and Dad's been arguing with her that her trouble is she doesn't understand youth. Mom's likely to get pretty sore when she discovers she's been crying for nothing."

"Not to mention how silly your father will look for making her cry."

Ronald shook his head sadly. "The trouble with parents these days is they believe everything they read. 'Life' magazine, in a 'Sex on the Campus' article, made it sound so easy to find a coed to live with. Well, let me tell you, for every Linda le Clair of Barnard who's playing house with a male college student, there're a million coeds who won't even do the dishes."

"Then all this talk of students living out of wedlock is exaggerated?"

"Exaggerated? When I got here I asked ten girls if they wanted to live with me. The first one said she didn't come to college to iron shirts for the wrong guy, four told me frankly that it would hurt their chances of finding a husband, four told me to drop dead and one reported me to the campus police. I was lucky to get a room in the dormitory."

"I guess it's no fun for a young man to pretend he's a swinger."

"You can say that again. Every time I go home, everybody wants to know about the pot parties and orgies I go to at school. The only thing that's saved me is that I've seen 'La Dolce Vita' twice."

"You have to depend on your imagination?"

"What college boy doesn't?" Ronald asked. "There are more conscientious objectors amongst coeds in the Sexual Revolution than any modern sociologist would dare admit."

"Believe me, son—whatever it is you have been trying to prove—I would say you've proved it!"

Figure 15. Berry's World by Jim Berry. Reprinted by permission of Newspaper Enterprise Association, Inc.

"It's enough to destroy your faith in Hugh Hefner," I said.

"Look, I'm not complaining," Ronald said. "I'm just trying to figure out how to explain it to my father. He's living his fantasies through me and I hate to let him down."

"Why don't you tell him the reason you can't introduce the coed you're living with is that she's going to have a baby?"

"Hey," Ronald said, "that's a great idea. It might cause Mom to cry again, but it will make Dad awfully proud."

Appreciation of Style

1. Identify Buchwald's tone in this essay.

2. Is this selection narrative or expository? Support your answer.

3. Identify the point of view of the essay.

Test Your Comprehension

1. This essay is satirical; that is, the author dealt with a serious subject in a humorous way. Prove this statement by contrasting the tone of the language and the meaning of the essay.

2. If you were asked to write a critical opinion of this essay, what aspect of the contents would interest you most?

Vocabulary for Study

conformity   fantasies   conscientious objector   sociologist

EDISON: INVENTOR OF INVENTION

Walter Lippmann

It is impossible to measure the importance of Edison by adding up the specific inventions with which his name is associated. Far-reaching as many of them have been in their effect on modern civilization, the total effect of Edison's career surpasses the sum of them all. He did not merely make the incandescent lamp and the phonograph and innumerable other devices practicable for general use; it was given to him to demonstrate the power of applied science so concretely, so understandably, so convincingly that he altered the mentality of mankind. In his lifetime, largely because of his successes, there came into widest acceptance the revolutionary conception that man could by the use of his intelligence invent a new mode of living on his planet; the human spirit, which in all previous ages had regarded the conditions of life as essentially unchanging and beyond man's control, confidently, and perhaps somewhat naively, adopted the conviction that anything could be changed and everything could be controlled.

The idea of progress is in the scale of history a very new idea. It seems first to have taken possession of a few minds in the seventeenth and eighteenth centuries as an accompaniment of the great advances in pure science. It gained greater currency in the first half of the nineteenth century when industrial civilization began to be transformed by the application of steam power. But these changes, impressive as they were, created so much human misery by the crude and cruel manner in which they were exploited that all through the century men instinctively feared and opposed the progress of machines, and of the sciences on which they rested. It was only at the end of the century, with the perfecting of the electric light bulb, the telephone, the phonograph, and the like, that the ordinary man began to feel that science could actually benefit him. Edison supplied the homely demonstrations which insured the popular acceptance of science, and clinched the popular argument, which had begun with Darwin, about the place of science in man's outlook on life.

Thus he became the supreme propagandist of science and his name the great symbol of an almost blind faith in its possibilities. Thirty years ago, when I was a schoolboy, the ancient conservatism of man was still the normal inheritance of every child. We began to have electric lights, and telephones, and to see horseless carriages, but our attitude was a mixture of wonder, fear, and doubt. Perhaps these things would work. Perhaps they would not explode. Today every schoolboy not only takes all the existing inventions as much for granted as we took horses and dogs for granted, but, also, he is entirely convinced that all other desirable things can and will be invented. In my youth the lonely inventor who could not obtain a hearing was still the stock figure of the imagination. Today the only people who are not absolutely sure that television is perfected are the inventors themselves. No other person played so great a part as Edison in this change in human expectation, and, finally, by the cumulative effect of his widely distributed inventions plus a combination of the modern publicity technique and the ancient myth-making faculty of men, he was lifted in the popular imagination to a place where he was looked upon not only as the symbol but the creator of a new age.

In strict truth an invention is almost never the sole product of any one mind. The actual inventor is almost invariably the man who succeeds in combining and perfecting previous discoveries in such a way as to make them convenient and profitable. Edison had a peculiar genius for carrying existing discoveries to the point where they could be converted into practicable devices, and it would be no service to his memory, or to the cause of science which he serves so splendidly, to pretend that he invented by performing solitary miracles. The light which was born in his laboratory at Menlo Park fifty-two years ago was conceived in the antecedent experiments of many men in many countries over a period of nearly forty years, and these experiments in their turn were conceivable only because of the progress of the mathematical and physical sciences in the preceding two centuries.

The success which Edison finally achieved in his specific inventions demonstrated the possibility of invention as a continuing art. Mr. Hoover, in his tribute printed yesterday, pointed directly to this fact as constituting the historic importance of the man, when he said that Edison "did more than any other American to place invention on an organized basis of the utilization of the raw materials of pure science and discovery." Because of Edison, more than of any other man, scientific research has an established place in our society; because of the demonstrations he made, the money of taxpayers and stockholders has become available for studies the nature of which they do not often understand, though they appreciate their value and anticipate their ultimate pecuniary benefits.

It would be a shallow kind of optimism to assume that the introduction of the art of inventing has been an immediate and unmixed blessing to mankind. It is rather the most disturbing element in civilization, the most profoundly revolutionary thing which has ever been let loose in the world. For the whole ancient wisdom of man is founded upon the conception of a life which in its fundamentals changes imperceptibly if at all. The effect of organized, subsidized invention, stimulated by tremendous incentives of profit, and encouraged by an insatiable popular appetite for change, is to set all the relations of men in violent motion, and to create overpowering problems faster than human wisdom has as yet been able to assimilate them. Thus the age we live in offers little prospect of outward stability, and only those who by an inner serenity and disentanglement have learned how to deal with the continually unexpected can be at home in it. It may be that in time we shall become used to change as in our older wisdom we had become used to the unchanging. But such wisdom it is impossible to invent or to make widely and quickly available by mass production and salesmanship. It will, therefore, grow much more slowly than the inventions which ultimately it must learn to master.

Appreciation of Style

1. Identify the controlling idea.
2. Select some statements from the essay which clearly support the controlling idea.
3. Describe the author's tone.

Test Your Comprehension

1. Why is the idea of continuing progress a recent development in human history?
2. Why did Lippmann say that the total of Edison's influence on civilization was greater than the inventions he produced?
3. How do you know that this essay was not written recently?
4. Did Lippmann have mixed feelings about the influence of Edison's contributions on society?
5. Identify the author's purpose in this essay.

Vocabulary for Study

cumulative	pecuniary	imperceptibly
antecedent	innumerable	insatiable
profoundly	propaganda	disentanglement

Writing Sample Nine: Write a summary of the important ideas in one of the four essays you have just read. *First,* study the instructions for the assignment and the Model Student Summary which follow. Then review the Assignment-Evaluation sheet which follows the Model.

WRITING SAMPLE NINE

ASSIGNMENT: A summary of a writer's work

A summary is a greatly shortened version of a piece of writing. It presents enough information to inform the reader of the general characteristics and some important details of the original. Your purpose in writing a summary is to *sample* an author's writing carefully and clearly so that your reader knows what the writing is and something of what it contains. You should write a summary as briefly as possible and *in your own words.*

A summary of a story, fact or fiction, usually deals with character(s) and experience. On the other hand, a brief version of an essay is usually limited to a general description followed by some of the important details. Both, furthermore, are most easily handled through imitating the organization of the original.

DIRECTIONS: Write a brief summary of an essay or story. Confine your writing to an introductory description followed by a careful selection of *typical* important details from the original. Use your own words with the possible exception of brief quotes.

1. Read the original carefully.
2. Make a brief introductory description of the contents: author, type of writing, etc.
3. List some typical important details from the original.
4. Study the sample summary paper which follows.
5. Review the Assignment-Evaluation sheet which follows the sample paper to learn the criteria for contents.
6. Arrange your ideas for the paper in outline form.
7. Write a rough draft from your outline.
8. Compare your rough draft with the criteria.
9. Rewrite as many times as necessary to correct your paper for contents and English mechanics.

SAMPLE STUDENT SUMMARY

The following sample paper is based upon the autobiographical essay, "Wallace," which appears in Chapter 14, page 201, of this textbook.

A FRIEND IN NEED

The mature man, Richard Rovere, wrote the autobiographical essay, "Wallace," to show his appreciation for a friend, Wallace Duckworth, who had helped him to adjust in school many years earlier. The essay was written as a narrative.

The young Rovere's teachers did not like him. For example, one threw a textbook at him and another addressed him by a sarcastic name, both after only a few minutes of acquaintance. There was something in Rovere's manner or appearance—the way he sat or his facial expression—which attracted their anger. As a result, Rovere was an unhappy boy, for he believed that the teachers with their maturity and wisdom must be correct and that he was, indeed, worthless. In despair, Rovere believed that he must be a failure in school, and became apathetic.

Things changed when Rovere was fourteen, after Wallace Duckworth's enrollment at the preparatory school. Wallace, a brilliant boy, hated school and teachers; but, unlike Rovere, he didn't mind being a failure and he showed his dislike actively. Wallace played pranks to make himself look clever and his teachers look foolish. For example, one day Wallace came to his algebra class with some wire sticking out of his shirt sleeve, and played with the wire, ignoring the lesson. Mr. Potter, his teacher, saw this and demanded that Wallace hand him the wire. Wallace extended his arm and Mr. Potter tried to grab the wire away. However, the wire had much tension and seemed endless as Mr. Potter tugged foot after foot out of Wallace's sleeve, becoming angrier and angrier. Finally, Wallace released all the wire suddenly, and Mr. Potter, all tension removed from the wire, fell to the floor in a tangle of the metal.

Student's own title

Student describes the work he is summarizing including title and author; he gives controlling idea also

Student gives Rovere's childhood problem, including some typical specific detail, following Rovere's own organization

Student introduces Rovere's friend and gives the process which helped Rovere

Student gives specific example of how Wallace made teachers look foolish and, thus, human

It was pranks such as these, humanizing teachers in Rovere's eyes, which led Rovere to change his opinion of the infallibility of teachers. He realized that if teachers had weaknesses themselves, perhaps they could also be wrong in judging his worth as a human being.

Student shows how Wallace's pranks helped Rovere

Wallace's stay at Rovere's school was short. He was expelled, but not before his influence upon Rovere had been strongly implanted. Wallace's actions served not only to humanize teachers in Rovere's eyes but also to convince Rovere that he was capable of succeeding in his school work. Remarkably, while failing his own work intentionally, Wallace helped Rovere with his work which helped Rovere to develop confidence in his own ability.

Summary is developed chronologically to follow the sequence of the narrative

Student shows the other way Wallace helped Rovere; student never expresses his own opinion in the summary

Rovere never forgot the help his friend gave him and wrote this essay to tell the story of his "genius friend" for all to know.

Student terminates essay with author's own conclusion restated

Study the Assignment-Evaluation sheet on the next page before you proceed further in your work.

EVALUATION SHEET FOR SUMMARY (SAMPLE 9)

Write a brief summary of an essay or story of your own choice.
Length: optional but related to the length of original

Required in Contents	Full	Earned	For Study
1. Make brief introductory description, including author, title, type of writing	15		
2. Give *typical* important details from the original	35		
3. Imitate organization of the original	15		
4. Adopt the same tone as the original	15		
5. Avoid expressing your own opinion	10		
6. Be as brief as possible	10		
PROOFREAD YOUR WORK CAREFULLY!	0		
TOTAL	100		

Instructor's Comments:

ENGLISH MECHANICS: Instructor Assigns Values for Criteria

Content Areas	Full	Earned	For Study
ORGANIZATION: Introduction Chronological Organization Topical Organization Rational Organization Smooth Development Termination	——— ——— ——— ——— ——— ———		Chapter 13 Chapter 15 Chapter 16 Chapter 17 Chapter 14 Chapter 18
PARAGRAPHING: Introduction Development (unity) Development (coherence)	——— ——— ———		Page 163 Page 165 Page 168
SENTENCES: completeness; variety; economy; use of modifiers; pronouns; agreement; use of verbs, phrases, clauses	———		
USE OF LANGUAGE: Level of usage Idiomatic usage Vividness	———		Chapter 8
PUNCTUATION AND CAPITALIZATION and related graphics: Quotation marks	———		Chapter 7
SPELLING:			
TOTAL	100		

Mechanics not in this text are assigned in supplementary text.

The Essay: Smooth Development

The development of an essay may be compared with the development of a paragraph, for both develop the subject and controlling or central idea in unified fashion and through specific detail. Both show the quality of coherence or transition which is essential to the smooth connection of individual elements, whether the elements are sentences or paragraphs.

Paragraphs, specific elements of an essay, must be effectively related just as sentences within a paragraph are related. The techniques of doing so are similar: the use of transitional words and phrases, repetition of key words, and clear use of pronouns.

Paragraph Transition

Study the pairs of paragraphs below and identify the technique of transition which is used to relate them.

WALLACE
Richard Rovere

The aversion I inspired in teachers might under certain circumstances have been turned to good account. It might have stimulated me to industry; it might have made me get high marks, just so I could prove to the world that my persecutors were motivated by prejudice and perhaps by a touch of envy; or it might have bred a monumental rebelliousness in me, a contempt for all authority, that could have become the foundation of a career as the leader of some great movement against all tyranny and oppression.

It did none of these things. Instead, I became, so far as my school life was concerned, a thoroughly browbeaten boy, and I accepted the hostility of my teachers as an inescapable condition of life. In fact, I took the absolutely disastrous view that my teachers were unquestionably right in their estimate of me as a dense and altogether noxious creature who deserved, if anything, worse than he got. . . .

1. Identify the transitional wording which relates the paragraphs. ⎯⎯⎯⎯⎯⎯⎯⎯⎯⎯⎯

2. Which technique of transition is shown?
   a. Key word(s)
   b. Transitional word(s)
   c. Pronoun

3. To what word(s) in the first paragraph does the transition in the second paragraph relate?

ANSWERS: 1. "It did none of these things." (the whole sentence); 2. c; 3. aversion

WALLACE

I was freshly reminded of my debt to Wallace not long ago when my mother happened to come across a packet of letters I had written to her and my father during my first two years in a boarding school on Long Island. In one of these, I reported that "There's a new kid in school who's supposed to be a scientifical genius." Wallace was this genius. In a series of intelligence and aptitude tests we all took in the opening week, he achieved some incredible score, a mark that, according to the people who made up the tests, certified him as a genius and absolutely guaranteed that in later life he would join the company of Einstein, Steinmetz, and Edison. Naturally, his teachers were thrilled—but not for long.

Within a matter of weeks it became clear that although Wallace was unquestionably a genius, or at least an exceptionally bright boy, he was disposed to use his considerable gifts not to equip himself for a career in the service of mankind but for purely anti-social undertakings. Far from making the distinguished scholastic record everyone expected of him, he made an altogether deplorable one. . . .

4. Identify the transitional wording. _____

---

5. Which technique(s) is shown?
   a. Key word(s)
   b. Transitional word(s)
   c. Noun

6. To what does the transition relate in the first paragraph?

ANSWERS: 4. "but not for long" (end of one paragraph) *and* "within a matter of weeks" (beginning of next paragraph) *and* repetition of "Wallace"; 5. b and a; 6. "not for long" and "Wallace"

WALLACE

Church began as usual that Sunday morning. The headmaster delivered the invocation and then announced the number and title of the first hymn. He held up his hymnal and gave the genteel, throat-clearing cough that was his customary signal to the organist to get going. The organist came down on the keys but not a peep sounded from the pipes. He tried again. Nothing but a click.

When the headmaster realized that the organ wasn't working, he walked quickly to the rear and consulted in whispers with the organist. Together they made a hurried inspection of the instrument, peering inside it, snapping the electric switch back and forth, and reaching to the base plug to make certain the juice was on. Everything seemed all right, yet the organ wouldn't sound a note.

7. Identify the transitional wording. _____

8. Which technique of transition is shown?
   a. Key word(s)
   b. Transitional word(s)
   c. Pronoun

9. Smooth development of an essay depends in part upon _____transition.

10. Define transition among the paragraphs of an essay.

_____

_____

ANSWERS: 7. when, headmaster, organ; 8. a (headmaster) and b (*when* is transitional because it shows a time relationship); 9. paragraph; 10. Transition among paragraphs in an essay depends upon relating them smoothly through repetition of key words, use of transitional words and phrases and clear reference of pronouns

Now, read the autobiographical essay, "Wallace."

WALLACE[*]
Richard H. Rovere

As a schoolboy, my relations with teachers were almost always tense and hostile. I disliked my studies and did very badly in them. There are, I have heard, inept students who bring out the best in teachers, who challenge their skill and move them to sympathy and affection. I seemed to bring out the worst in them. I think my personality had more to do with this than my poor classroom work. Anyway, something about me was deeply offensive to the pedagogic temperament.

Often, it took a teacher no more than a few minutes to conceive a raging dislike for me. I recall an instructor in elementary French who shied a textbook at my head the very first day I attended his class. We had never laid eyes on each other until fifteen or twenty minutes before he assaulted me. I no longer remember what, if anything, provoked him to violence. It is possible that I said something that was either insolent or intolerably stupid. I guess I often did. It is also possible that I said nothing at all. Even my silence, my humility, my acquiescence, could annoy my teachers. The very sight of me, the mere awareness of my existence on earth, could be unendurably irritating to them.

This was the case with my fourth-grade teacher, Miss Purdy. In order to make the acquaintance of her new students on the opening day of school, she had each one rise and give his name and address as she called the roll. Her voice was soft and gentle, her manner sympathetic, until she

_____

[*]Reprinted by permission; copyright © 1950, *The New Yorker* Magazine, Inc.

Figure 16. By Schain.

came to me. Indeed, up to then I had been dreamily entertaining the hope that I was at last about to enjoy a happy association with a teacher. When Miss Purdy's eye fell on me, however, her face suddenly twisted and darkened with revulsion. She hesitated for a few moments while she looked me up and down and thought of a suitable comment on what she saw. "Aha!" she finally said, addressing not me but my new classmates, in a voice that was now coarse and cruel. "I don't have to ask *his* name. There, boys and girls, is Mr. J. Pierpont Morgan, lounging back in his mahogany-lined office." She held each syllable of the financier's name on her lips as long as she was able to, so that my fellow-students could savor the full irony of it. I imagine my posture was a bit relaxed for the occasion, but I know well that she would not have resented anyone else's sprawl as much as she did mine. I can even hear her making some friendly, schoolmarmish quip about too much summer vacation to any other pupil. Friendly quips were never for me. In some unfortunate and mysterious fashion, my entire being rubbed Miss Purdy and all her breed the wrong way. Throughout the fourth grade, she persisted in tormenting me with her idiotic Morgan joke. "And perhaps Mr. J.P. Revere can tell us all about Vasco da Gama this morning," she would say, throwing in a little added insult by mispronouncing my surname.

The aversion I inspired in teachers might under certain circumstances have been turned to good account. It might have stimulated me to industry; it might have made me get high marks, just so I could prove to the world that my persecutors were motivated by prejudice and perhaps by a touch of envy; or it might have bred a monumental rebelliousness in me, a contempt for all authority, that could have become the foundation of a career as the leader of some great movement against all tyranny and oppression.

It did none of these things. Instead, I became, so far as my school life was concerned, a thoroughly browbeaten boy, and I accepted the hostility of my teachers as an inescapable condition of life. In fact, I took the absolutely disastrous view that my teachers were unquestionably right in their estimate of me as a dense and altogether noxious creature who deserved, if anything, worse than he got. These teachers were, after all, men and women who had mastered the parts of speech, the multiplication tables, and a simply staggering number of imports and exports in a staggering number of countries. They could add up columns of figures the very sight of which made me dizzy and sick to the stomach. They could read "As You Like It" with pleasure—so they said, anyway, and I believed everything they said. I felt that if such knowledgeable people told me that I was stupid, they certainly must know what they were talking about. In consequence, my grades sank lower and lower, my face became more noticeably blank, my manner more mulish, and my presence in the classroom more aggravating to whoever presided over it. To be sure, I hated my teachers for their hatred of me, and I missed no chance to abuse them behind their backs, but fundamentally I shared with them the view that I was a worthless and despicable boy, as undeserving of an education as I was incapable of absorbing one. Often, on school days, I wished that I were dead.

This was my attitude, at least, until my second year in preparatory school, when, at fourteen, I fell under the exhilarating, regenerative influence of my friend Wallace Duckworth. Wallace changed my whole outlook on life. It was he who freed me from my terrible awe of teachers; it was he who showed me that they could be brought to book and made fools of as easily as I could be; it was he who showed me that the gap between their knowledge and mine was not unbridgeable. Sometimes I think that I should like to become a famous man, a United States Senator or something of that sort, just to be able to repay my debt to Wallace. I should like to be so important that people would inquire into the early influences on my life and I would be able to tell them about Wallace.

I was freshly reminded of my debt to Wallace not long ago when my mother happened to come across a packet of letters I had written to her and my father during my first two years in a boarding school on Long Island. In one of these, I reported that "There's a new kid in school who's supposed to be a scientific genius." Wallace was this genius. In a series of intelligence and aptitude tests we all took in the opening week, he achieved some incredible score, a mark that, according to the people who made up the tests, certified him as a genius and absolutely guaranteed that in later life he would join the company of Einstein, Steinmetz, and Edison. Naturally, his teachers were thrilled—but not for long.

Within a matter of weeks it became clear that although Wallace was unquestionably a genius, or at least an exceptionally bright boy, he was disposed to use his considerable gifts not to equip himself for a career in the service of mankind but for purely anti-social undertakings. Far from making the distinguished scholastic record everyone expected of him, he made an altogether deplorable one. He never did a lick of school work. He had picked up his scientific knowledge somewhere but evidently not from teachers. I am not sure about this, but I think Wallace's record, as long as he was in school, was even worse than mine. In my mind's eye there is a picture of the sheet of monthly averages thumbtacked to the bulletin board across the hall from the school post office; my name is one from the bottom, the bottom name being Wallace's.

As a matter of fact, one look at Wallace should have been enough to tell the teachers what sort of genius he was. At fourteen, he was somewhat shorter than he should have been and a good deal stouter. His face was round, owlish, and dirty. He had big, dark eyes, and his black hair, which hardly ever got cut, was arranged on his head as the four winds wanted it. He had been outfitted with attractive and fairly expensive clothes, but he changed from one suit to another only when his parents came to call on him and ordered him to get out of what he had on.

The two most impressive things about him were his mouth and the pockets of his jacket. By looking at his mouth, one could tell whether he was plotting evil or had recently accomplished it. If he was bent upon malevolence, his lips were all puckered up, like those of a billiard player about to make a difficult shot. After the deed was done, the pucker was replaced by a delicate, unearthly smile. How a teacher who knew anything about boys could miss the fact that both expressions were masks of Satan I'm sure I don't know. Wallace's pockets were less interesting than his mouth, perhaps, but more spectacular in a way. The side pockets of his jacket bulged out over his pudgy haunches like burro hampers. They were filled with tools—screwdrivers, pliers, files, wrenches, wire cutters, nail sets, and I don't know what else. In addition to all this, one pocket always contained a rolled-up copy of *Popular Mechanics*, while from the top of the other protruded *Scientific American* or some other such magazine. His breast pocket contained, besides a large collection of fountain pens and mechanical pencils, a picket fence of drill bits, gimlets, kitchen knives, and other pointed instruments. When he walked, he clinked and jangled and pealed.

Wallace lived just down the hall from me, and I got to know him one afternoon, a week or so after school started, when I was wrestling with an algebra lesson. I was really trying to get good marks at the time, for my father had threatened me with unpleasant reprisals if my grades did not show early improvement. I could make no sense of the algebra, though, and I thought that the scientific genius, who had not as yet been unmasked, might be generous enough to lend me a hand.

It was a study period, but I found Wallace stretched out on the floor working away at something he was learning to make from *Popular Mechanics*. He received me with courtesy, but after hearing my request he went immediately back to his tinkering. "I could do that algebra all right," he said, "but I can't be bothered with it. Got to get this dingbat going this afternoon. Anyway, I don't care about algebra. It's too twitchy. Real engineers never do any of that stuff. It's too twitchy for them." I soon learned that "twitch" was an all-purpose word of Wallace's. It turned up in one form or another, in about every third sentence he spoke. It did duty as a noun, an adjective, a verb, and an adverb.

I was disappointed by his refusal of help but fascinated by what he was doing. I stayed on and watched him as he deftly cut and spliced wires, removed and replaced screws, referring, every so often, to his magazine for further instruction. He worked silently, lips fiendishly puckered, for some time, then looked up at me and said, "Say, you know anything about that organ in the chapel?"

"What about it?" I asked.

"I mean do you know anything about how it works?"

"No," I said. "I don't know anything about that."

"Too bad," Wallace said, reaching for a pair of pliers. "I had a really twitchy idea." He worked at his wires and screws for quite a while. After perhaps ten minutes, he looked up again. "Well, anyhow," he said, "maybe you know how to get in the chapel and have a look at the organ?"

"Sure, that's easy," I said. "Just walk in. The chapel's always open. They keep it open so you can go in and pray if you want to, and things like that."

"Oh" was Wallace's only comment.

I didn't at all grasp what he had in mind until church time the following Sunday. At about six o'clock that morning, several hours before the service, he tip-toed into my room and shook me from sleep. "Hey, get dressed," he said. "Let's you and I twitch over to the chapel and have a look at the organ."

Game for any form of amusement, I got up and went along. In the bright, not quite frosty October morning, we scurried over the lawns to the handsome Georgian chapel. It was an hour before the rising bell.

Wallace had brought along a flashlight as well as his usual collection of hardware. We went to the rear of the chancel, where the organ was, and he poked the light underneath the thing and inside it for a few minutes. Then he got out his pliers and screwdrivers and performed some operations that I could neither see nor understand. We were in the chapel for only a few minutes. "There," Wallace said as he came up from under the keyboard. "I guess I got her twitched up just about right. Let's go." Back in my room, we talked softly until the rest of the school began to stir. I asked Wallace what, precisely, he had done to the organ. "You'll see," he said, with that faint, faraway smile where the pucker had been. Using my commonplace imagination, I guessed that he had fixed the organ so it would give out peculiar noises or something like that. I didn't realize then that Wallace's tricks were seldom commonplace.

Church began as usual that Sunday morning. The headmaster delivered the invocation and then announced the number and title of the first hymn. He held up his hymnal and gave the genteel, throat-clearing cough that was his customary signal to the organist to get going. The organist came down on the keys but not a peep sounded from the pipes. He tried again. Nothing but a click.

When the headmaster realized that the organ wasn't working, he walked quickly to the rear and consulted in whispers with the organist. Together they made a hurried inspection of the instrument, peering inside it, snapping the electric switch back and forth, and reaching to the base plug to make certain the juice was on. Everything seemed all right, yet the organ wouldn't sound a note.

"Something appears to be wrong with our organ," the headmaster said when he returned to the lectern. "I regret to say that for this morning's services we shall have to—"

At the first word of the announcement, Wallace, who was next to me in one of the rear pews, slid out of his seat and bustled noisily down the middle aisle. It was highly unusual conduct, and every eye was on him. His gaudy magazines flapped from his pockets, his portable workshop clattered and clanked as he strode importantly to the chancel and rose on tiptoe to reach the ear of the astonished headmaster. He spoke in a stage whisper that could be heard everywhere in the chapel. "Worked around organs quite a bit, sir," he said. "Think I can get this one going in a jiffy."

Given the chance, the headmaster would undoubtedly have declined Wallace's kind offer. Wallace didn't give him the chance. He scooted for the organ. For perhaps a minute, he worked on it, hands flying, tools tinkling.

Then, stuffing the tools back into his pockets, he returned to the headmaster. "There you are, sir," he said, smiling up at him. "Think she'll go all right now." The headmaster, with great doubt in his heart, I am sure, nodded to the organist to try again. Wallace stood by, looking rather like the inventor of a new kind of airplane waiting to see his brain child take flight. He faked a look of deep anxiety, which, when a fine, clear swell came from the pipes, was replaced by a faint smile of relief, also faked. On the second or third chord, he bustled back down the aisle, looking very solemn and businesslike and ready for serious worship.

It was a fine performance, particularly brilliant in its timing. If Wallace had had to stay at the organ even a few seconds longer—that is, if he had done a slightly more elaborate job of twitching it in the first place—he would have been ordered back to his pew before he had got done with the repairs. Moreover, someone would probably have guessed that it was he who had put it on the fritz in the first place. But no one did guess it. Not then, anyway. For weeks after that, Wallace's prestige in the school was enormous. Everyone had had from the beginning a sense of honor and pride at having a genius around, but no one up to then had realized how useful a genius could be. Wallace let on after church that Sunday that he was well up on the workings not merely of organs but also of heating and plumbing systems, automobiles, radios, washing machines, and just about everything else. He said he would be pleased to help out in any emergency. Everyone thought he was wonderful.

"That was a real good twitch, wasn't it?" he said to me when we were by ourselves. I said that it certainly was.

From that time on, I was proud and happy to be Wallace's cupbearer. I find it hard now to explain exactly what his victory with the organ, and all his later victories over authority, meant to me, but I do know that they meant a very great deal. Partly, I guess, it was just the knowledge that he enjoyed my company. I was an authentic, certified dunce and he was an acknowledged genius, yet he liked being with me. Better yet was my discovery that this super-brain disliked schoolwork every bit as much as I did. He was bored silly, as I was, by "Il Penseroso" and completely unable to stir up any enthusiasm for "Silas Marner" and all the foolish goings on over Eppie. Finally, and this perhaps was what made me love him most, he had it in his power to humiliate and bring low the very people who had so often humiliated me and brought me low.

As I spent the long fall and winter afternoons with Wallace, being introduced by him to the early novels of H.G. Wells, which he admired extravagantly, and watching him make crystal sets, window-cleaning machines, automatic chair-rockers, and miniature steam turbines from plans in *Popular Mechanics*, I gradually absorbed bits of his liberating philosophy. "If I were you," he used to say, "I wouldn't be scared by those teachers. They don't know anything. They're twitches, those teachers, real twerpy, twitchy twitches." "Twerpy" was an adjective often used by Wallace to modify "twitch." It added several degrees of twitchiness to anything twitchy.

Although Wallace had refused at first to help me with my lessons, he later gave freely of his assistance. I explained to him that my father was greatly distressed about my work and that I really wanted to make him happier. Wallace was moved by this. He would read along in my Latin grammar, study out algebra problems with me, and explain things in language that seemed a lot more lucid than that of my teachers. Before long, I began to understand that half my trouble lay in my fear of my studies, my teachers, and myself. "Don't know why you get so twitched up over this stuff," Wallace would say a trifle impatiently as he helped me get the gist of a speech in "As You Like It." "There isn't anything hard about this. Fact, it's pretty good right in here. It's just those teachers who twitch it all up, I wish they'd all go soak their heads."

Wallace rode along for quite a while on the strength of his intelligence tests and his organ fixing, but in time it became obvious that his disappointing classroom performance was not so much the result of failure to adjust to a new environment (as a genius, he received more tolerance in this respect than non-geniuses) as of out-and-out refusal to cooperate with the efforts being made to educate him. Even when he had learned a lesson in the course of helping me with it, he wouldn't give the teachers the satisfaction of thinking he had learned anything in their classes. Then, too, his pranks began to catch up with him. Some of them, he made no effort to conceal.

He was easily the greatest teacher-baiter I have ever known. His masterpiece, I think, was one he thought up for our algebra class. "Hey, you twitch," he called to me one day as I was passing his room on my way to the daily ordeal of "x"s and "y"s. "I got a good one for old twitch

Potter." I went into his room, and he took down from his closet shelf a spool of shiny copper wire. "Now, watch this," he said. He took the free end of the wire and drew it up through the left sleeve of his shirt. Then he brought it across his chest, underneath the shirt, and ran it down the right sleeve. He closed his left fist over the spool and held the free end of the wire between right thumb and forefinger. "Let's get over to that dopey class," he said, and we went.

When the lesson was well started, Wallace leaned back in his seat and began to play in a languorous but ostentatious manner with the wire. It glistened brightly in the strong classroom light, and it took Mr. Potter, the teacher, only a few seconds to notice that Wallace was paying no mind to the blackboard equations but was, instead, completely absorbed in the business of fingering the wire.

"Wallace Duckworth, what's that you're fiddling with?" Mr. Potter said.

"Piece of wire, sir."

"Give it to me this instant."

"Yes, sir," Wallace said, extending his hand.

Mr. Potter had, no doubt, bargained on getting a stray piece of wire that he could unceremoniously pitch into the wastebasket. Wallace handed him about eighteen inches of it. As Mr. Potter took it, Wallace released several inches more.

"I want *all* that wire, Wallace," Mr. Potter said.

"I'm giving it to you, sir," Wallace answered. He let go of about two feet more. Mr. Potter kept pulling. His rage so far overcame his reason that he couldn't figure out what Wallace was doing. As he pulled, Wallace fed him more and more wire, and the stuff began to coil up on the floor around his feet. Guiding the wire with the fingers of his right hand, Wallace created quite a bit of tension, so that eventually Mr. Potter was pulling hand over hand, like a sailor tightening lines in a high sea. When he thought the tension was great enough, Wallace let two or three feet slip quickly through his hands, and Mr. Potter toppled to the floor, landing in a terrible tangle of wire.

I no longer remember all of Wallace's inventions in detail. Once, I recall, he made, in the chemistry laboratory, some kind of invisible paint—a sort of shellac, I suppose—and covered every blackboard in the school with it. The next day, chalk skidded along the slate and left about as much impression as it would have made on a cake of ice. The dormitory he and I lived in was an old one of frame construction, and when we had fire drills, we had to climb down outside fire escapes. One night, Wallace tied a piece of flypaper securely around each rung of each ladder in the building, then rang the fire alarm. Still another time, he went back to his first love, the organ, and put several pounds of flour in the pipes, so that when the organist turned on the pumps, a cloud of flour filled the chapel. One of his favorite tricks was to take the dust jacket from a novel and wrap it around a textbook. In a Latin class, then, he would appear to be reading "Black April" when he should have been reading about the campaigns in Gaul. After several of his teachers had discovered that he had the right book in the wrong cover (he piously explained that he put the covers on to keep his books clean), he felt free to remove the textbook and really read a novel in class.

Wallace was expelled shortly before the Easter vacation. As the winter had drawn on, life had become duller and duller for him, and to brighten things up he had resorted to pranks of larger conception and of an increasingly anti-social character. He poured five pounds of sugar into the gasoline tank of the basketball coach's car just before the coach was to start out, with two or three of the team's best players in his car, for a game with a school about twenty-five miles away. The engine functioned adequately until the car hit an isolated spot on the highway, miles from any service place. Then it gummed up completely. The coach and the players riding with him came close to frostbite, and the game had to be called off. The adventure cost Wallace's parents a couple of hundred dollars for automobile repairs. Accused of the prank, which clearly bore his trademark, Wallace had freely admitted his guilt. It was explained to his parents that he would be given one more chance in school; another trick of any sort and he would be packed off on the first train.

Later, trying to justify himself to me, he said, "You don't like that coach either, do you? He's the twerpiest twitch here. All teachers are twitchy, but coaches are the worst ones of all."

I don't recall what I said. Wallace had not consulted me about several of his recent escapades, and although I was still loyal to him, I was beginning to have misgivings about some of them.

As I recall it, the affair that led directly to his expulsion was a relatively trifling one, something to do with blown fuses or short circuits. At any rate, Wallace's parents had to come and fetch him home. It was a sad occasion for me, for Wallace had built in me the foundations for a sense of security. My marks were improving, my father was happier, and I no longer cringed at the sight of a teacher. I feared, though, that without Wallace standing behind me and giving me courage, I might slip back into the old ways. I was very near to tears as I helped him pack up his turbines, his tools, and his stacks of magazines. He, however, was quite cheerful. "I suppose my Pop will put me in another one of these places, and I'll have to twitch my way out of it all over again," he said.

"Just remember how dumb all those teachers are," he said to me a few moments before he got into his parents' car. "They're so twitchy dumb they can't even tell if anyone else is dumb." It was rather a sweeping generalization, I later learned, but it served me well for a number of years. Whenever I was belabored by a teacher, I remembered my grimy genius friend and his reassurances. I got through school somehow or other. I still cower a bit when I find that someone I've met is a schoolteacher, but things aren't too bad and I am on reasonably civil terms with a number of teachers, and even a few professors.

Appreciation of Style

1. Give some examples of how Rovere supported general statements with specific details.
2. Identify the style of the essay.
3. Which is the strongest element in the essay: setting, plot, characterization, or theme? Support your choice.
4. Identify the mature Rovere's tone.

Test Your Comprehension

1. Why was Rovere such a dismal failure in school?
2. Why was Wallace such a dismal failure in school?
3. Contrast the two moods of the young Rovere, before and after he came to know Wallace.
4. Identify Rovere's purpose for writing this essay.

Vocabulary for Study

inept	aversion	exhilarating
pedagogic	mulish	regenerative
irony	despicable	malevolence

Writing Sample Ten: Write a statement of theme and support it by reference to the text. Use any essay or story you have read in this text. Refer to the instructions for the assignment and the model student theme paper, as well as the Assignment-Evaluation sheet, which follow.

WRITING SAMPLE TEN

ASSIGNMENT: A statement of theme with support from the original work to support the statement

One of the important skills of reading is the ability to recognize an author's theme or "big idea." In a sense, the theme is the generalization you can draw from the details or events of an essay or story. Sometimes an author states his theme himself or at least he suggests it in a fairly obvious manner; sometimes you must conclude the theme from what is implied in the author's details. Whenever you proceed to identify a theme, if you apply the following questions to the job, you may be helped.

1. If you read a story, you might ask, "What is the *meaning* of the experience which the author showed?"
2. If you read an essay, expository in style, you might ask, "What did the author try to teach me or to persuade me to believe?"

Once you think you have extracted the theme, you should test your judgment by applying two additional questions.

1. Does this theme account for or apply to the experiences about which I read in this story?
2. Does this theme fit the facts and/or reasons which I observed in this essay?

Perhaps an example of a relatively simple fable by the ancient Greek, Aesop, may help to clarify the problem of theme selection further.

THE DISCONTENTED DONKEY

One cold winter day a donkey stood in a nice, cozy barn. He had plenty of good hay to eat; and no work to do. But he was not happy.

"Ho-hum!" he said to himself. "Ho-hum! I wish I were out in a green field, on a spring day, with the warm air all around and fresh new grass to eat."

By and by the spring days came. He played in the green field and ate the fresh grass. But sometimes his master hitched him to a cart and made him help with the spring chores.

"Ohh!" sighed the donkey. "Ohh, I am so tired! I wish it were summer. All these spring chores would be done and I could lie down in the meadow all day."

By and by the summer days came; and he could lie down in the sun. But sometimes the donkey had to work, carrying hay from the meadow to the barn.

"Ahh!" groaned the donkey. "Ahh. I am DISGUSTED! I wish it was autumn. I could be in the garden."

By and by the autumn days came; but the donkey had to do his share of the work, carrying vegetables from the garden up to the house, to be stored in the farmer's cellar.

"Oh dear, oh dear," moaned the donkey. "Oh dear, I wish it was winter. And I wish I was standing in my nice, cozy barn, doing nothing all day. And I wish I was eating that good hay from the meadow."

By and by the winter days came, and the donkey was standing in his nice, cozy barn, and he was eating that good hay from the meadow.

Bearing in mind that a fable by Aesop used characters which were animals to symbolize people and served the purpose of making a significant statement about people, what is the theme of "The Discontented Donkey"? Write and support it.

_____

_____

_____

ANSWER: *Theme:* There are some people who are never satisfied. *Evidence:* The donkey, symbolizing a human, was never content with what he had. When he had hay, he wanted grass; when in the barn, he wanted to be in the meadow, and so on.

Let us review a few important points now. After you have made a selection of theme, your job in a "theme" paper is to prove that you have shown good judgment by using some important details from the original work as evidence. This procedure is a form of inductive reasoning which means using specific details to arrive at a general conclusion (see Chapter 17 for more information about inductive reasoning). Now, proceed to the directions for the assignment.

DIRECTIONS: In your own words, write a 300-word paper to identify the theme of an essay or story. Support your identification by referring to important details from the original.

1. Read the original carefully.
2. Conclude the theme.
3. List the details from the original which support your statement of theme.
4. Study the sample theme paper which follows to learn the form for such an assignment.
5. Review the Assignment-Evaluation sheet which follows the sample paper to learn the criteria for contents.
6. Arrange the ideas for your paper in an outline form.
7. Write a rough draft of your paper.
8. Compare your rough draft with the criteria.
9. Rewrite as many times as necessary to correct your paper for contents and English mechanics.

SAMPLE STUDENT STATEMENT OF THEME

The following sample paper is based upon the autobiographical essay, "Wallace," which began on page 201 of the text.

JUDGE PEOPLE BY THEIR MERITS

Student's own title

Richard Rovere's purpose for writing the autobiographical essay, "Wallace," was to express his gratitude to his old school chum, Wallace Duckworth. Wallace made the young Rovere realize that not all people are what they appear to be. People should

Student identifies work, author, purpose and theme; the theme is controlling idea of the student's paper

be judged on their merits, not on their positions or titles; this is the theme of the essay and the insight Rovere learned in his youth.

Rovere had a bad time during his school years. His teachers despised him although he never consciously did bad things. Rovere was quiet but his teachers, nevertheless, ridiculed, tormented, and belittled him. He accepted this treatment without complaint because he felt they were well-qualified to judge. As a result, the young boy lacked self-confidence and greatly feared his teachers.

While Rovere was suffering his rejections and fears, Wallace Duckworth enrolled in the school. Although Wallace had tested at the level of genius, and the teachers expected much of him, he did poorly in his classes. Wallace resented authority and feared nothing.

The two boys became close friends. Rovere watched his friend play practical jokes on his teachers, making them appear foolish and getting little or no punishment for his acts. As a contrast, Rovere, who was too frightened to do anything, received much abuse. Soon, Rovere realized that his teachers were not expert judges of character. This insight gave him confidence, and he began improving in his schoolwork.

As time went on, Rovere's belief that his teachers knew everything and he knew nothing gradually disappeared. He learned that all people had good and bad qualities and that they should be judged on their merits—not appearance. This knowledge changed his life for the better.

Student supports his statement of theme (an argument) by providing facts from the original:

The shy, fearful Rovere was abused "unjustly" while the aggressive Wallace often was unpunished

Rovere, seeing the teachers as less than perfect for the first time, changed his opinion of them and of himself

Student confines his paper to the introduction of evidence from the original; no expression of opinion

Termination is restatement of theme

EVALUATION SHEET FOR THEME (SAMPLE 10)

Write a statement of the theme of an essay or story of your own choice. Support your selection of theme by making reference to the original work.

Length: optional but be as brief as possible

Required in Contents	Full	Earned	For Study
1. Make a brief introductory description, including author, title, type of writing	30		
2. State the theme as clearly and specifically as possible	30		
3. Present specific evidence from the original to support your selection of the theme. Be certain you show a clear connection between the theme and the evidence you give.	30		
4. Avoid expressing your own opinion	10		
PROOFREAD YOUR WORK CAREFULLY!	0		
TOTAL	100		

Instructor's Comments:

ENGLISH MECHANICS: Instructor Assigns Values for Criteria

Content Areas	Full	Earned	For Study
ORGANIZATION: Introduction	————		Chapter 13
Chronological Organization	————		Chapter 15
Topical Organization	————		Chapter 16
Rational Organization	————		Chapter 17
Smooth Development	————		Chapter 14
Termination	————		Chapter 18
PARAGRAPHING: Introduction	————		Page 163
Development (unity)	————		Page 165
Development (coherence)	————		Page 168
SENTENCES: completeness; variety; economy; use of modifiers; pronouns; agreement; use of verbs, phrases, clauses	————		
USE OF LANGUAGE: Level of usage Idiomatic usage Vividness	————		Chapter 8
PUNCTUATION AND CAPITALIZATION and related graphics: Quotation marks	————		Chapter 7
SPELLING:			
TOTAL	100		

Mechanics not in this text are assigned in supplementary text.

Figure 17. What Happened to My Time Sequence? By Schain.

The Essay: Chronological Organization

Beyond smooth development in an essay is the additional consideration of what *type* of development to use, whether chronological, topical, rational (logical), or some combination. Generally, whichever method a writer uses depends upon the nature of his subject and his own purpose for writing.

In earlier chapters, the purposes of exposition were explained, including analysis, argument, definition, description, and showing a process. In this chapter and later ones, the methods of development are shown, with treatment of chronological organization first.

Do you remember the "moments of experience" papers which you wrote earlier? How did you arrange your ideas in them? Didn't you start your papers at the *beginning* of your experiences and present the incidents as they occurred *in time*? How about the autobiographical essay, "Wallace," which you read in the last chapter? Wasn't it arranged, also, in a chronological way? In essence, then, chronological organization, whether in an essay or a story, emphasizes *time of occurrence* as the major technique for arranging ideas.

Study the essay by Claude Bernard which follows. Although it is designed by the author mainly to report, *to tell* about a scientific study he made, note how he used narrative style and arranged his ideas in order of time. Look for evidence of chronological treatment: actual dates and a sequence of events as they occurred. Finally, study the notes placed in the margin alongside Bernard's text, for they describe the development as it occurs.

CARBON MONOXIDE POISONING
Claude Bernard

About 1846, I wished to make experiments on the cause of poisoning with carbon monoxide. I knew that this gas had been described as toxic, but I knew literally nothing about the mechanism of its poisoning; I therefore could not have a preconceived opinion. What, then, was to be done? I must bring to birth an idea by making a fact appear, i.e., make another experiment to see. In fact I poisoned a dog by making him breathe carbon monoxide and after death I at once opened his body. I looked at

Bernard gives the subject: carbon monoxide poisoning; his controlling idea is to follow the process of experimentation to find the cause; he begins reporting the process step-by-step

the state of the organs and fluids. What caught my attention at once was that its blood was scarlet in all the vessels, in the veins as well as the arteries, in the right heart as well as in the left. I repeated the experiment on rabbits, birds and frogs, and everywhere I found the same scarlet coloring of the blood. But I was diverted from continuing this investigation, and I kept this observation a long time unused except for quoting it in my course *a propos* of the coloring of blood.

In 1856, no one had carried the experimental question further, and in my course at the College de France on toxic and medicinal substances, I again took up the study of poisoning by carbon monoxide which I had begun in 1846. I found myself then in a confused situation, for at this time I already knew that poisoning with carbon monoxide makes the blood scarlet in the whole circulatory system. I had to make hypotheses, and establish a preconceived idea about my first observation, so as to go ahead. Now, reflecting on the fact of scarlet blood, I tried to interpret it by my earlier knowledge as to the cause of the color of blood. Whereupon all the following reflections presented themselves to my mind. The scarlet color, said I, is peculiar to arterial blood and connected with the presence of a large proportion of oxygen, while dark coloring belongs with absence of oxygen and presence of a larger proportion of carbonic acid; so the idea occurred to me that carbon monoxide, by keeping venous blood scarlet, might perhaps have prevented the oxygen from changing into carbonic acid in the capillaries. Yet it seemed hard to understand how that could be the cause of death. But still keeping on with my inner preconceived reasoning, I added: If that is true, blood taken from the veins of animals poisoned with carbon monoxide should be like arterial blood in containing oxygen; we must see if that is the fact.

He continues his experimenting ten years later, still reporting the process step-by-step

Following this reasoning, based on interpretation of my observation, I tried an experiment to verify my hypothesis as to the persistence of oxygen in the venous blood. I passed a current of hydrogen through scarlet venous blood taken from an animal poisoned with carbon monoxide, but I could not liberate the oxygen as usual. I tried to do the same with arterial blood; I had no greater success. My preconceived idea was therefore false. But the impossibility of getting oxygen from the blood of a dog poisoned with carbon monoxide was a second observation which suggested a fresh hypothesis. What could have become of the oxygen in the blood? It had not changed with carbonic acid, because I had not set free large quantities of that gas in passing a current of hydrogen through the blood of the poisoned animals. Moreover, that hypothesis was contrary to the color of the blood. I exhausted myself in conjectures about how carbon monoxide could cause the oxygen to disappear from the blood; and as gases displace one another I naturally thought that the carbon monoxide might have displaced the oxygen and driven it out of the blood. To learn this, I decided to vary my experimentation by putting the blood in artificial conditions that would allow me to

Finally, Bernard finishes the process of experimentation, summarizes the data he collected, and reports his conclusions.

Note how he is always trying to interpret his evidence in order to plan new experiments

recover the displaced oxygen. So I studied the action of carbon monoxide on blood experimentally. For this purpose I took a certain amount of arterial blood from a healthy animal; I put this blood on the mercury in an inverted test tube containing carbon monoxide; I then shook the whole thing so as to poison the blood sheltered from contact with the outer air. Then, after an interval, I examined whether the air in the test tube in contact with the poisoned blood had been changed, and I noted that the air thus in contact with the blood had been remarkably enriched with oxygen, while the proportion of carbon monoxide was lessened. Repeated in the same conditions, these experiments taught me that what had occurred was an exchange, volume by volume, between the carbon monoxide and the oxygen of the blood. But the carbon monoxide, in displacing the oxygen that it had expelled from the blood, remained chemically combined in the blood and could no longer be displaced either by oxygen or by other gases. So that death came through death of the molecules of blood, or in other words by stopping their exercises of a physiological property essential to life.

This last example, which I have very briefly described, is complete; it shows from one end to the other, how we proceed with the experimental method and succeed in learning the immediate cause of phenomena. To begin with I knew literally nothing about the mechanism of the phenomenon of poisoning with carbon monoxide. I undertook an experiment to see, i.e., to observe. I made a preliminary observation of a special change in the coloring of blood. I interpreted this observation, and I made an hypothesis which proved false. But the experiment provided me with a second observation about which I reasoned anew, using it as a starting point for making a new hypothesis as to the mechanism, by which the oxygen in the blood was removed. By building up hypotheses, one by one, about the facts as I observed them, I finally succeeded in showing that carbon monoxide replaces oxygen in a molecule of blood, by combining with the substance of the molecule. Experimental analysis, here, has reached its goal. This is one of the cases, rare in physiology, which I am happy to be able to quote. Here the immediate cause of the phenomenon of poisoning is found and is translated into a theory which accounts for all the facts and at the same time includes all the observations and experiments. Formulated as follows, the theory posits the main facts from which all the rest are deducted: Carbon monoxide combines more intimately than oxygen with the hemoglobin in a molecule of blood. It has quite recently been proved that carbon monoxide forms a definite combination with hemoglobin. So that the molecule of blood, as if petrified by the stability of the combination, loses its vital properties. Hence everything is logically deduced: because of its property of more intimate combination, carbon monoxide drives out of the blood the oxygen essential to life; the molecules of blood become inert, and the animal dies, with symptoms of hemorrhage, from true paralysis of the molecules.

Bernard's conclusions are reached rationally or logically from the process of experimentation; the essay, therefore, shows the use of reason or logic which is based upon chronological reporting (See Chapters 17 and 18 for further detail)

Appreciation of Style

1. The overall structure of Bernard's essay is chronological. Prove this statement.
2. Show that Bernard makes use of specific detail to develop his controlling idea.
3. Identify the dominant point of view and tone.

Test Your Comprehension

1. Specifically, how does carbon monoxide poison animal life?
2. Is there an application of Bernard's findings today?

Vocabulary for Study

toxic	scarlet	persistence
inert	deduced	preconceived
petrified	hypothesis	

ADDITIONAL REVIEW QUESTIONS

1. Chronological organization emphasizes_____as a method of development.

2. A sequence of events is_____arranged.

3. A subject such as "The History of Baseball" would be arranged_____.

4. A subject such as "The Time I Visited Yosemite Park" could be arranged_____.

5. Define chronological organization: _____

_____

_____

ANSWERS: 1. time; 2. chronologically; 3. chronologically; 4. chronologically; 5. arrangement of
ideas in a sequence, according to time

*Now, read the following essays as additional examples
of chronological organization.*

DO INSECTS THINK?

Robert Benchley

In a recent book entitled *The Psychic Life of Insects*, Professor Bouvier says that we must be careful not to credit the little winged fellows with intelligence when they behave in what seems like an intelligent manner. They may be only reacting. I would like to confront the Professor with an instance of reasoning power on the part of an insect which can not be explained away in any such manner.

During the summer of 1899, while I was at work on my treatise *Do Larvae Laugh?* we kept a female wasp at our cottage in the Adirondacks. It really was more like a child of our own than a wasp, except that it *looked* more like a wasp than a child of our own. That was one of the ways we told the difference.

It was still a young wasp when we got it (thirteen or fourteen years old) and for some time we could not get it to eat or drink, it was so shy. Since it was a female, we decided to call it Miriam, but soon the children's nickname for it—"Pudge"—became a fixture, and "Pudge" it was from that time on.

One evening I had been working late in my laboratory fooling round with some gin and other chemicals, and in leaving the room I tripped over a nine of diamonds which someone had left lying on the floor and knocked over my card catalogue containing the names and addresses of all the larvae worth knowing in North America. The cards went everywhere.

I was too tired to stop to pick them up that night, and went sobbing to bed, just as mad as I could be. As I went, however, I noticed the wasp flying about in circles over the scattered cards. "Maybe Pudge will pick them up," I said half-laughingly to myself, never thinking for one moment that such would be the case.

When I came down the next morning Pudge was still asleep over in her box, evidently tired out. And well she might have been. For there on the floor lay the cards scattered all about just as I had left them the night before. The faithful little insect had buzzed about all night trying to come to some decision about picking them up and arranging them in the catalogue box, and then, figuring out for herself that, as she knew practically nothing about larvae of any sort except wasp-larvae, she would probably make more of a mess of rearranging them than as if she left them on the floor for me to fix. It was just too much for her to tackle, and, discouraged, she went over and lay down in her box, where she cried herself to sleep.

If this is not an answer to Professor Bouvier's statement that insects have no reasoning power, I do not know what is.

Appreciation of Style

1. This essay, humorous and nonsensical in intent, emphasizes chronological organization. Prove this statement.
2. Which style is emphasized more, exposition or narration? Why?
3. Identify the transitional word in the last paragraph.

Test Your Comprehension

1. What main idea does Benchley *seem* to advocate?
2. Does Benchley want his readers to take him seriously? Explain.

Vocabulary for Study

psychic

UNIVERSITY DAYS

James Thurber

I passed all the other courses that I took at my University, but I could never pass botany. This was because all botany students had to spend several hours a week in a laboratory looking through a microscope at plant cells, and I could never see through a microscope. I never once saw a cell through a microscope. This used to enrage my instructor. He would wander around the laboratory pleased with the progress all the students were making in drawing the involved and, so I am told, interesting structure of flower cells, until he came to me. I would just be standing there. "I can't see anything," I would say. He would begin patiently enough, explaining how anybody can see through a microscope, but he would always end up in a fury, claiming that I could *too* see through a microscope but just pretended that I couldn't. "It takes away from the beauty of flowers anyway," I used to tell him. "We are not concerned with beauty in this course," he would say. "We are concerned solely with what I may call the *mechanics* of flars." "Well," I'd say, "I can't see anything." "Try it just once again," he'd say, and I would put my eye to the microscope and see nothing at all, except now and again, a nebulous milky substance—a phenomenon of maladjustment. You were supposed to see a vivid, restless clockwork of sharply defined plant cells. "I see what looks like a lot of milk," I would tell him. This, he claimed, was the result of my not having adjusted the microscope properly; so he would readjust it for me, or rather, for himself. And I would look again and see milk.

I finally took a deferred pass, as they called it, and waited a year and tried again. (You had to pass one of the biological sciences or you couldn't graduate.) The professor had come back from vacation brown as a berry, bright-eyed, and eager to explain cell-structure again to his classes. "Well," he said to me, cheerily, when we met in the first laboratory hour of the semester, "we're going to see cells this time, aren't we?" "Yes, sir," I said. Students to right of me and to left of me and in front of me were seeing cells; what's more, they were quietly drawing pictures of them in their notebooks. Of course, I didn't see anything.

"We'll try it," the professor said to me, grimly, "with every adjustment of the microscope known to man. As God is my witness, I'll arrange this glass so that you see cells through it or I'll give up teaching. In twenty-two years of botany, I—" He cut off abruptly for he was beginning to quiver all over, like Lionel Barrymore, and he genuinely wished to hold onto his temper; his scenes with me had taken a great deal out of him.

So we tried it with every adjustment of the microscope known to man. With only one of them did I see anything but blackness or the familiar lacteal opacity, and that time I saw, to my pleasure and amazement, a variegated constellation of flects, specks, and dots. These I hastily drew. The instructor, noting my activity, came back from an adjoining desk, a smile on his lips and his eyebrows high in hope. He looked at my cell drawing. "What's that?" he demanded, with a hint of a squeal in his voice. "That's what I saw," I said. "You didn't, you didn't, you *didn't!*" he screamed, losing control of his temper instantly, and he bent over and squinted into the microscope. His head snapped up. "That's your eye!" he shouted. "You've fixed the lens so that it reflects! You've drawn your eye!"

Another course that I didn't like, but somehow managed to pass, was economics. I went to that class straight from the botany class, which didn't help me any in understanding either subject. I used to get them mixed up. But not as mixed up as another student in my economics class who came there direct from a physics laboratory. He was a tackle on the football team, named Bolenciecwcz. At that time Ohio State University had one of the best football teams in the country, and Bolenciecwcz was one of its outstanding stars. In order to be eligible to play it was necessary for him to keep up in his studies, a very difficult matter, for while he was not dumber than an ox he was not any smarter. Most of his professors were lenient and helped him along. None gave him more hints, in answering questions, or asked him simpler ones than the economics professor, a thin, timid man named Bassum. One day when we were on the subject of transportation and distribution, it came Bolenciecwcz's turn to answer a question. "Name one means of transportation," the professor said to him. No light came into the big tackle's eyes. "Just any means of transportation," said the professor. Bolenciecwcz sat staring at him. "That is," pursued the professor, "any medium, agency, or method of going from one place to another." Bolenciecwcz had the look of a man who is being led into a trap. "You may choose among steam, horse-drawn, or electrically propelled vehicles," said the instructor. "I might suggest the one which we commonly take in making long journeys across land." There was a profound silence in which everybody stirred uneasily, including Bolenciecwcz and Mr. Bassum. Mr. Bassum abruptly broke this silence in an amazing manner. "Choo-choo-choo," he said, in a low voice, and turned instantly scarlet. He glanced appealingly around the room. All of us, of course, shared Mr. Bassum's desire that Bolenciecwcz should stay abreast of the class in economics, for the Illinois game, one of the hardest and most important of the season, was only a week off. "Toot, toot, too-toooooooot!" some student with a deep voice moaned; and we all looked encouragingly at Bolenciecwcz. Somebody else gave a fine imitation of a locomotive letting off steam. Mr. Bassum himself rounded off the little show. "Ding, dong, ding, dong," he said, hopefully. Bolenciecwcz was staring at the floor now, trying to think, his great brow furrowed, his huge hands rubbing together, his face red.

"How did you come to college this year, Mr. Bolenciecwcz?" asked the professor, "*Chuffa chuffa, chuffa* chuffa."

"M'father sent me," said the football player.

"What on?" asked Bassum.

"I git an 'lowance," said the tackle, in a low, husky voice, obviously embarrassed.

"No, no," said Bassum. "Name a means of transportation. What did you *ride* here on?"

"Train," said Bolenciecwcz.

"Quite right," said the professor. "Now, Mr. Nugent, will you tell us—"

If I went through anguish in botany and economics—for different reasons—gymnasium work was even worse. I don't even like to think about it. They wouldn't let you play games or join in the exercises with your glasses on and I couldn't see with mine off. I bumped into professors, horizontal bars, agricultural students, and swinging iron rings. Not being able to see, I could take it but I couldn't dish it out. Also, in order to pass gymnasium (and you had to pass it to graduate) you had to learn to swim if you didn't know how. I didn't like the swimming pool, I didn't like swimming, and I didn't like the swimming instructor, and after all these years I still don't. I never swam but I passed my gym work anyway, by having another student give my gymnasium number (978) and swim across the pool in my place. He was a quiet, amiable blonde youth, number 473, and he would have seen through a microscope for me if we could have got away with it, but we couldn't get away with it. Another thing I didn't like about gymnasium work was that they made you strip the day you registered. It is impossible for me to be happy when I am stripped and being asked a lot of questions. Still, I did better than a lanky agricultural student who was cross-examined just before I was. They asked each student what college he was in—that is, whether Arts, Engineering, Commerce, or Agriculture. "What college are you in?" the instructor snapped at the youth in front of me. "Ohio State University," he said promptly.

It wasn't that agricultural student but it was another a whole lot like him who decided to take up journalism, possibly on the ground that when farming went to hell he could fall back on newspaper work. He didn't realize, of course, that that would be very much like falling back full-length on a kit of carpenter's tools. Haskins didn't seem cut out for journalism, being too embarrassed to talk to anybody and unable to use a typewriter, but the editor of the college paper assigned him to the cow barns, the sheep house, the horse pavilion, and the animal husbandry department generally. This was a genuinely big "beat," for it took up five times as much ground and got ten times as great a legislative appropriation as the College of Liberal Arts. The agricultural student knew animals, but nevertheless his stories were dull and colorlessly written. He took all afternoon on each of them, because he had to hunt for each letter on the typewriter. Once in a while he had to ask somebody to help him hunt. "C" and "L," in particular, were hard letters for him to find. His editor finally got pretty much annoyed at the farmer-journalist because his pieces were so uninteresting. "See here, Haskins," he snapped at him one day, "why is it we never have anything hot from you on the horse pavilion? Here we have two hundred head of horses on this campus—more than any other university in the Western Conference except Purdue—and yet you never get any real low-down on them. Now shoot over to the horse barns and dig up something lively." Haskins shambled out and came back in about an hour; he said he had something. "Well, start it off snappily," said the editor. "Something people will read." Haskins set to work and in a couple of hours brought a sheet of typewritten paper to the desk; it was a two-hundred word story about some disease that had broken out among the horses. Its opening sentence was simple but arresting. It read: "Who has noticed the sores on the tops of the horses in the animal husbandry building?"

Ohio State was a land grant university and therefore two years of military drill was compulsory. We drilled with old Springfield rifles and studied the tactics of the Civil War even though the World War was going on at the time. At 11 o'clock each morning thousands of freshmen and sophomores used to deploy over the campus, moodily creeping up on the old chemistry building. It was good training for the kind of warfare that was waged at Shiloh but it had no connection with what was going on in Europe. Some people used to think there was German money behind it, but they didn't dare say so or they would have been thrown in jail as German spies. It was a period of muddy thought and marked, I believe, the decline of higher education in the Middle West.

As a soldier I was never any good at all. Most of the cadets were glumly indifferent soldiers, but I was no good at all. Once General Littlefield, who was commandant of the cadet corps, popped up in front of me during regimental drill and snapped, "You are the main trouble with this university!" I think he meant that my type was the main trouble with the university but he may have meant me individually. I was mediocre at drill, certainly—that is, until my senior year. By that time I had drilled longer than anybody else in the Western Conference, having failed at military at the end of each preceding year so that I had to do it all over again. I was the only senior still in uniform. The uniform which, when new, had made me look like an interurban railway conductor, now that it had become faded and too tight made me look like Bert Williams in his bell-boy act. This had a definitely bad effect on my morale. Even so, I had become by sheer practise little short of wonderful at squad manoeuvres.

One day General Littlefield picked our company out of the whole regiment and tried to get it mixed up by putting it through one movement after another as fast as we could execute them: squads right, squads left, squads on right into line, squads right about, squads left front into line, etc. In about three minutes one hundred and nine men were marching in one direction and I was marching away from them at an angle of forty degrees, all alone. "Company, halt!" shouted General Littlefield, "That man is the only man who has it right!" I was made a corporal for my achievement.

The next day General Littlefield summoned me to his office. He was swatting flies when I went in. I was silent and he was silent too, for a long time. I don't think he remembered me or why he had sent for me, but he didn't want to admit it. He swatted some more flies, keeping his eyes on them narrowly before he let go with the swatter. "Button up your coat!" he snapped. Looking back on it now I can see that he meant me although he was looking at a fly, but I just stood there. Another fly came to rest on a paper in front of the general and began rubbing its hind legs together. The general lifted the swatter cautiously. I moved restlessly and the fly flew away. "You startled him!" barked General Littlefield, looking at me severely. I said I was sorry. "That won't help the situation!" snapped the General, with cold military logic. I didn't see what I could do except offer to chase some more flies toward his desk, but I didn't say anything. He stared out the window at the faraway figures of co-eds crossing the campus toward the library. Finally, he told me I could go. So I went. He either didn't know which cadet I was or else he forgot what he wanted to see me about. It may have been that he wished to apologize for having called me the main trouble with the university; or maybe he had decided to compliment me on my brilliant drilling of the day before and then at the last minute decided not to. I don't know. I don't think about it much any more.

Appreciation of Style

1. Identify the following characteristics of "University Days":
   a. Style of writing
   b. Author's tone
   c. Method of developing contents
   d. Point of view

2. Select some examples of particularly effective use of detail.

Test Your Comprehension

1. Thurber expressed his attitude toward his experience with botany. He also related the experience of a football player he observed in an economics class. Through these incidents, he implied criticism of some college practices. Identify the practices Thurber criticized.

2. Identify the theme of the essay. Support your conclusion by citing from the essay.

Vocabulary for Study

nebulous	mediocre	variegated
opacity	scarlet	husbandry
amiable	appropriation	interwoven

Figure 18. Now, where does this go? By Schain.

The Essay:
Topical Development

Many subjects seem to fall naturally into a number of different topics which are merely subdivisions of the subject itself. Just what topics or subdivisions a writer selects is a matter of judgment or preference. For example, a subject such as "The Parts of A Book" could be divided into the following topics: Preface, Table of Contents, Chapter Divisions, and Index. Another subject, "Homecoming Day," could be divided into Historical Background, Present Purpose and Importance, and Activities. Finally, the large topics may, themselves, often be broken into subtopics.

The organization of a topically organized essay generally shows a pattern like the following:

1. The author introduces the subject by stating his central or controlling idea which often includes a brief statement of his planned topics.
2. He develops his topics separately, arranging them in order of importance or preference or paralleling their normal physical arrangement as in the subject "The Parts of A Book."

The unity and smooth development of the subject are maintained by a careful development of the topics to fulfill the author's stated central or controlling idea. In the following essay by Paul Merrill, the author arranged his ideas by topic. The *order* of the topics probably could have been different, but Merrill made the choices you see in his essay to suit his own purpose. Study the essay to observe how the central idea is stated first and how it is followed by the topics which develop it in specific detail. Finally, study the explanatory notes in the margin.

A point of caution is very important concerning this particular essay, however. The author is using a rhetorical device called *irony*. This means that he is saying, in effect, the *opposite of what he means*. You are certainly familiar with the use of sarcasm, a kind of bitter humor about a serious subject which isn't really funny at all. Irony is really a kind of sarcasm and it is often used by writers to appeal to the reader's interest.

THE PRINCIPLES OF POOR WRITING
Paul W. Merrill

Books and articles on good writing are numerous, but where can you find sound, practical advice on how to write | *The subject is identified as the principles of poor writing;*

poorly? Poor writing is so common that every educated person ought to know something about it. Many scientists actually do write poorly, but they probably perform by ear without perceiving clearly how their results are achieved. An article on the principles of poor writing might help. The author considers himself well qualified to prepare such an article; he can write poorly without half trying.

The average student finds it surprisingly easy to acquire the usual tricks of poor writing. To do a consistently poor job, however, one must grasp a few essential principles:

the subject is limited in the controlling idea to three principles which involve the reader, the wording, and the use of revision

    I. Ignore the reader.
   II. Be verbose, vague, and pompous.
  III. Do not revise.

IGNORE THE READER

The world is divided into two great camps: yourself and others. A little obscurity or indirection in writing will keep the others at a safe distance; if they get close, they may see too much.

The first topic is identified: ignore the reader

Write as if for a diary. Keep your mind on a direct course between yourself and the subject; don't think of the reader—he makes a bad triangle. This is fundamental. Constant and alert consideration of the probable reaction of the reader is a serious menace to poor writing; moreover, it requires mental effort. A logical argument is that if you write poorly enough, your readers will be too few to merit any attention whatever.

The topic is developed:

Don't try to be clear

Ignore the reader wherever possible. If the proposed title, for example, means something to you, stop right there; think no further. If the title baffles or misleads the reader, you have won the first round. Similarly, all the way through you must write for yourself, not for the reader. Practice a dead-pan technique, keeping your facts and ideas all on the same level of emphasis with no tell-tale hints of relative importance or logical sequence. Use long sentences containing many ideas loosely strung together. *And* is the connective most frequently employed in poor writing because it does not indicate cause and effect, nor does it distinguish major ideas from subordinate ones. *Because* seldom appears in poor writing, nor does the semicolon—both are replaced by *and*.

Don't use emphasis, string ideas loosely, avoid connectives and proper punctuation

Make confusing use of pronouns

Camouflage transitions in thought. Avoid such connectives as *moreover, nevertheless, on the other hand.* If unable to resist the temptation to give some signal for a change in thought, use *however.* A poor sentence may well begin with *however* because to the reader, with no idea what comes next, *however* is too vague to be useful. A good sentence begins with the subject or with a phrase that needs emphasis.

Omit terms or explanations the reader needs to know in order to understand fully

The "hidden antecedent" is a common trick of poor writing. Use a pronoun to refer to a noun a long way back, or to one decidedly subordinate in thought or syntax; or the pronoun may refer to something not directly expressed. If you wish to play a little game with the reader, offer him the wrong antecedent as bait; you may be astonished how easy it is to catch the poor fish.

In ignoring the reader avoid parallel constructions which give the thought away too easily. I need not elaborate, for you probably employ inversion frequently. It must have been a naive soul who said, "When the thought is parallel, let the phrases be parallel."

In every technical paper omit a few items that most readers need to know. You had to discover these things the hard way; why make it easy for the reader? Avoid defining symbols; never specify the units in which data are presented. Of course it will be beneath your dignity to give numerical values of constants in formulae. With these omissions, some papers may be too short; lengthen them by explaining things that do not need explaining. In describing tables, give special attention to self-explanatory headings; let the reader hunt for the meaning of P^1r_O.

BE VERBOSE, VAGUE, AND POMPOUS

The second topic is identified: use words badly

The cardinal sin of poor writing is to be concise and simple. Avoid being specific; it ties you down. Use plenty of deadwood: include many superfluous words and phrases. Wishful thinking suggests to a writer that verbosity somehow serves as a cloak or even a mystic halo by which an idea may be glorified. A cloud of words may conceal defects in observation or analysis, either by opacity or by diverting the reader's attention. Introduce abstract nouns at the drop of a hat—even in those *cases* where the *magnitude* of the *motion* in a downward *direction* is inconsiderable. Make frequent use of the words *case, character, condition, former* and *latter, nature, such, very.*

The second topic is developed through use of example:

Use too many words

Use big words

Poor writing, like good football, is strong on razzle-dazzle, weak on information. Adjectives are frequently used to bewilder the reader. It isn't much trouble to make them gaudy or hyperbolic; at least they can be flowery and inexact.

Use complicated instead of simple structure

DEADWOOD

Bible: Render to Caesar the things that are Caesar's.

Poor: In the case of Caesar it might well be considered appropriate from a moral or ethical point of view to render to that potentate all of those goods and materials of whatever character or quality which can be shown to have had their original source in any portion of the domain of the latter.

Use more words than necessary

Shakespeare: I am no orator as Brutus is.

Poor: The speaker is not what might be termed an adept in the profession of public speaking, as might properly be stated of Mr. Brutus. (Example from P.W. Swain. *Amer. J. Physics, 13, 318, 1945.*)

Concise: The dates of several observations are in doubt.

Poor: It should be mentioned that in the case of several observations there is room for considerable doubt concerning the correctness of the dates on which they were made.

Reasonable: Exceptionally rapid changes occur in the spectrum.
Poor: There occur in the spectrum changes which are quite exceptional in respect to the rapidity of their advent.

Reasonable: Formidable difficulties, both mathematical and observational, stand in the way.
Poor: There are formidable difficulties of both a mathematical and an observational nature that stand in the way.

CASE

Reasonable: Two sunspots changed rapidly.
Poor: There are two cases where sunspots changed with considerable rapidity.

Reasonable: Three stars are red.
Poor: In three cases the stars are red in color.

RAZZLE-DAZZLE

Immaculate precision of observation and extremely delicate calculations. . . .

It would prove at once a world imponderable, etherealized. Our actions would grow grandific.

Well for us that the pulsing energy of the great life-giving dynamo in the sky never ceases. Well, too, that we are at a safe distance from the flame-licked whirlpools into which our earth might drop like a pellet of waste fluff shaken into the live coals of a grate fire.

DO NOT REVISE

Write hurriedly, preferably when tired. Have no plan; write down items as they occur to you. The article will thus be spontaneous and poor. Hand in your manuscript the moment it is finished. Rereading a few days later might lead to revision—which seldom, if ever, makes the writing worse. If you submit your manuscript to colleagues (a bad practice), pay no attention to their criticisms or comments. Later resist firmly any editorial suggestions. Be strong and infallible; don't let anyone break down your personality. The critic may be trying to help you or he may have an ulterior motive, but the chance of his causing improvement in your writing is so great that you must be on guard.

The third topic is identified: don't revise your work

FINAL SUGGESTION FOR POOR WRITING

Do not read:

Allbutt, Clifford. *Notes on the Composition of Scientific Papers.* Macmillan, 1923.
Flesch, Rudolf. *The Art of Plain Talk.* Harper, 1946.
Graves and Hodge. *The Reader Over Your Shoulder.* Macmillan, 1943.
Quiller-Couch, Arthur. *On the Art of Writing.* [V]. Putnam, 1928.
Suggestions to Authors of Papers Submitted for Publication by the United States Geological Survey. U.S. Gov. Ptg. Off., 1935.

The last section is not really an announced topic, but merely a reference to additional materials

Appreciation of Style

1. Even though this essay is topical in organization, does it show unity? What is the unifying thread in the essay?
2. Prove that this essay shows the use of irony.
3. What is the author's purpose in this essay?

Test Your Comprehension

1. Explain the meaning of the following terms in your own words: transitions in thought, hidden antecedent for pronouns, parallel construction, definition of terms and symbols, pompous writing, deadwood.
2. What is the value of revision?
3. Why is it unsafe to "ignore your reader"?

Vocabulary for Study

    subordinate   superfluous   syntax   verbosity

QUESTIONS FOR REVIEW

1. When introducing a topically organized subject, the author first states his _____

   _____ .

2. The central or controlling idea of a topically organized subject generally includes brief mention

   of the _____ in the essay.

3. A subject which seems to fall into subdivisions is conveniently broken into _____ for development.

4. All of the topics in a subject must be clearly related to the _____ .

5. The following is a topically organized subject. Supply the topics; check this text if you wish.

   a. *Central Idea:* Most books seem broken into a number of parts, each part having a

      particular purpose. The parts include: _____

      _____

      _____

   b. *Topics:*

      1. _____

      2. _____

      3. _____

4. _____

5. _____

6. _____

ANSWERS: 1. central or controlling idea; 2. topics; 3. topics; 4. central or controlling idea; 5. review this text's organization on page 225, paragraph one

Now, read the following essay as an example
of topical arrangement of ideas.

OVER-GENERALIZING
FALLACY NUMBER ONE: <u>SECUNDUM QUID</u>
Stuart Chase

One swallow does not make a summer, nor can two or three cases often support a dependable generalization. Yet all of us, including the most polished eggheads, are constantly falling into this mental mantrap. It is the commonest, probably the most seductive, and potentially the most dangerous, of all the fallacies.

You drive through a town and see a drunken man on the sidewalk. A few blocks further on you see another. You turn to your companion: "Nothing but drunks in this town!" Soon you are out in the country, bowling along at fifty. A car passes you as if you were parked. On a curve a second whizzes by. Your companion turns to you: "All the drivers in this state are crazy!" Two thumping generalizations, each built on two cases. If we stop to think, we usually recognize the exaggeration and the unfairness of such generalizations. Trouble comes when we do not stop to think—or when we build them on a prejudice.

This kind of reasoning has been around for a long time. Aristotle was aware of its dangers and called it "reasoning by example," meaning too few examples. What it boils down to is failing to count your swallows before announcing that summer is here. Driving from my home to New Haven the other day, a distance of about forty miles, I caught myself saying: "Everytime I look around I see a new ranch-type house going up." So on the return trip I counted them; there were exactly five under construction. And how many times had I "looked around"? I suppose I had glanced to right and left—as one must at side roads and so forth in driving—several hundred times.

In this fallacy we do not make the error, developed in Chapter 4, of neglecting facts altogether and rushing immediately to the level of opinion. We start at the fact level properly enough but *we do not stay there*. A case or two and up we go to a rousing over-simplification about drunks, speeders, ranch-style houses—or, more seriously, about foreigners, Negroes, labor leaders, teen-agers.

Over-generalizing takes many forms. It crops out in personal thinking and conversations as above. It is indispensable to those who compose epigrams and wisecracks, and most critics and reviewers find it very handy. It is standard for columnists and commentators who try to compress the complicated news stories of the day "into a nutshell." Newspaper headlines are a continuing exhibit of over-generalizing, but more from typographical necessity than deliberate intent. Cartoonists are under continual temptation. Those persons who go about scenting plots and conspiracies in the most innocent happenings are confirmed addicts, and so are those who follow esoteric cults of all varieties.

Straw Men

One vigorous branch is the creation of straw men to represent a class. You take a few stray characteristics, build a dummy around them, and then briskly demolish it. Here, for instance, is a debate between Russell Kirk and Arthur Schlesinger, Jr., on "Conservative vs. Liberal."[1] Mr. Kirk leads off with a picture of a "liberal" which would hardly fit Mr. Schlesinger:

> The liberal, old style, or new style, swears by the evangels of Progress; he thinks of society as a machine for attaining material aggrandizement, and of happiness as the gratification of mundane desires.

Mr. Schlesinger rejoins by creating a highly stylized "conservative":

> The conservative, on balance, opposes efforts at purposeful change because he believes that things are about as good as they can reasonably be expected to be, and that any change is more likely than not to be for the worse.

This judgment Mr. Kirk specifically rejects when he says: "The intelligent conservative does not set his face against all reform. Prudent social change is the means for renewing a society's vitality. . ." The boys have a zestful time, however, laying about them with wooden swords.

Much of the quarreling between rival ideologies takes this general form. The socialist erects a horrid verbal image of a bloated capitalist and knocks it over with a bang, while the rugged individualist gleefully annihilates a stuffed and bearded figure which has practically nothing in common with, say, Mr. Norman Thomas.

Another form, common among strong-minded characters, is to generalize that what is good for oneself is good for everybody. My father, for instance, liked his soup excessively hot, and was positive that everybody followed his taste. He was severe with cooks who did not serve liquids at a scalding temperature, and refused to believe that plenty of us lacked his copper lining. Whatever holiday he planned was sure, he thought, to be extravagantly enjoyed by the rest of the family—or indeed by any family—and he brushed aside as incomprehensible all alternate suggestions.

Finally, there are the prophets and predictors who use the thin-entering-wedge argument, known in scientific circles as extrapolation. You take a case or two, propound a universal pattern therefrom, and project the curve into the future. The next chapter will be devoted to this fallacy.

Our Old Cat and Another One

When I was about ten my grandfather once caught me indulging in a high, wide, and handsome generalization. He proceeded to tell me the story of our old cat, a story I have never forgotten.

A boy says: "Gee, there were a million cats in our back yard last night!"

"Did you count them?" asks his mother.

"No, but the place was full of cats."

"How many did you actually see?"

"Well, er, there was our old cat and another one."

My grandfather may not have cured me but he slowed me down.

A good deal of over-generalizing is harmless small talk. One weekend it rains, and the next weekend it rains again. So the suburban golfplayers and gardeners assure each other that it "always rains on weekends."

It is only a step, however, to something much more dangerous. In Arizona I met a woman who said, "I've had to let Maria go, and I'll never hire another Mexican. You can't trust any of them, not one!" I tried to reason with her but she was too angry to listen. She was building up, you see, a formidable case of race prejudice based on one or two examples. Because a certain Mexican maid had disappointed her, she was condemning all Mexicans in one sweeping conclusion.

---

1. *New York Times Magazine*, March 4, 1956.

How much of the prejudice against Negroes, Yankees, Jews, Japanese, Britishers, Puerto Ricans, is similarly built up? One or two unfortunate experiences are developed into an ironclad rule rejecting a whole race, culture, or religious group. To make it worse, the rejector himself is often to blame for the unfortunate experiences through his failure to understand people of a different culture. How much of the conflict and misery and persecution in the world today arises from this kind of over-generalizing?

Here is Mr. Smith, of Middletown, Nebraska, who spends three days in Greece on a package tour. On his return, he gives a talk at the Thursday Club to tell his friends all about Greece. The modern Greeks, he says, are very backward people—they have no decent traffic lights, they spend all day drinking coffee in sidewalk cafes, and don't properly repair the Parthenon. Meanwhile Mr. Parnassos of Athens spends three days in Chicago on a package tour and returns to inform his friends in the sidewalk cafe that Americans spend their time killing each other with sawed-off shotguns when they are not being annihilated on the highways.

"When I am told," said Dean Acheson, "that Americans are idealistic, or that Frenchmen are logical, or Germans emotionally unstable, or Asians inscrutable, I always listen to the ensuing observation with skepticism. Not that such generalizations may not have some basis in fact, but they can rarely carry the superstructure erected on them."[2] After Pearl Harbor, the superstructure erected by Americans to describe the Japanese people was largely unprintable, with "little yellow monkeys" among the milder epithets. Today, the superstructure has shifted back approximately to where it was before the war. The Japanese people have probably not changed much, but American generalizations about them have undergone two violent shifts in a dozen years.

Chester Bowles in *Ambassador's Report* observes that after three months in India it would have been easy to write the book, for he had learned all the pat answers by that time. After eighteen months it was much harder, for by then he knew that most of the pat answers were wrong. The longer he stayed, the more complicated India became. Messrs. Cohn and Schine, lieutenants of Senator McCarthy, were bothered by no such problem when they breezed through Europe in a few days, uncovering Communist conspiracies or evidence of "disloyalty" in various cities.

I Know a Man Who

Here is a group discussing social security after dinner. Mr. A. says: "I know a man who had eighteen thousand dollars in currency under his mattress, yet he went right ahead drawing benefits. That's social security for you!" A brisk battle then takes place on free enterprise versus the welfare state, with each contestant generalizing from a few hand-picked cases. "Would you hand the manufacture of atomic bombs over to Wall Street?" is countered by: "Would you hand the steel industry over to those bureaucrats in Washington?" Actually, of course, the U.S. Government must control certain activities in the public interest, such as atomic energy, while others are much better handled by private business. A meaningful discussion would attempt to find out where the line should be drawn.

At another dinner party I heard a woman say: "I had to take Leonard out of high school. Public schools are just impossible!" A man snaps back: "I'll never let John leave our high school. Private schools make children snobbish and they have no place in a democracy." Off they go for twenty minutes, while your author, sitting between the gunplay, has no chance to point out that it depends on the boy, the school, the teachers, the community, and quite a number of other things.

A politician in Rhode Island denounces compulsory automobile insurance. "It hasn't worked in Massachusetts," he thunders, "and it'll never work anywhere!"

At a public hearing in our town on two-acre zoning, a citizen arose and said he had heard that an acre of land had just been sold for two thousand dollars. "Now if this regulation goes

2. In *Harper's Magazine*, November, 1955.

through, and a young couple wants to build a house here, they will have to pay four thousand dollars for their land, and they simply can't afford it. What kind of democracy do you call that?" He sits down amid loud applause from the opposition. But there is still land in town to be had for two hundred dollars an acre. So an equally logical case could be made for a young couple starting life on a plot costing only four hundred dollars. Neither figure, of course, makes sense, for they are at the extreme ends of the cost spectrum. The real issue is a land cost somewhere in the middle, and, far more important for the young people's budget, the ratio of the land cost to the cost of the house.

Over the radio comes a news story of an escaped convict holding up a man and his wife in their home. He gets in the door on the plea that his car has broken down and he needs help. "That just goes to show," says a radio listener, "you don't dare help anyone in trouble any more!" If the whole community subscribed to this generalization, nobody would trust anybody, nobody would help anybody, and society would dissolve into anarchy. (Yes, this is a thumping generalization, too, but I believe that the assumption warrants the deduction.)

"Are you going to buy some of that new Ford stock, Mrs. Rowe?"

"No, I wouldn't touch it. Stocks are too risky!"

"What makes you think that?"

"Richard and I got caught in that Radio Common. It went down and down. It taught us a lesson, I can tell you!"

A valuable lesson, no doubt, but hardly enough to warrant avoiding the market all one's life. *What stocks, when, under what conditions, and recommended by whom?* Careful answers to these questions have returned some investors to the market after the debacle of the 1930's, to their considerable advantage.

In a Nutshell

Headline writers are forced to over-simplify ideas as well as pick the shortest words. WORST DEFEAT SINCE CHINA turns out to be a gain by Communists in the Indonesian elections. Many of us are pretty well conditioned to discount the headlines. Before making up our minds we read the news story under them. In this case the story says that the Indonesian elections might, under certain circumstances, some day, prove to be a serious defeat for the West. People who read only headlines must receive a fantastically twisted picture of the current world.

The distortion is made worse by the readers' appetite for violence and conflict. An ugly strike is always news, but a peaceful settlement is something for the bottom of page 42. Newspaper readers, if they believe what is printed, tend to generalize a society abounding in murderers, kidnapers, rapists, abortionists, stick-ups, arson, riots, and car crashes.

It is a pleasure to announce, accordingly, that nine radio and television stations in Chicago have agreed on a joint program for reporting race disturbances in the lowest possible key, without inflammatory statements.[3] These stations promise not to use superlatives or adjectives which might "incite or enlarge a conflict." They will avoid the use of the word "riot" until the trouble has become serious enough to warrant it. They will carefully verify first reports and get the true facts before breaking a story. "Stories must be written in calm, matter-of-fact sentences, and in such a tone that they will not be inflammatory."

Commentators and columnists who daily interpret the news are under almost as much compulsion as headline writers. When trouble broke out in the Formosa Straits in 1954, its causes were very far from simple. Not only the two Chinas and the U.S. were involved, but Russia, Japan, Britain, France, India, and indeed all of Asia. But at 7 p.m., Eastern Standard Time, Walter Newcomb,[4] the globe-trotting expert, is forced to say: "Let's get this Formosa business down to brass tacks"—and does so in ninety seconds flat. Marquand gives us a commentary on some commentators as they operated in World War II:

3. *New York Times*, September 24, 1955.
4. Borrowing the name of a character in *So Little Time* by J.P. Marquand.

Well, there you had it in a nutshell, or in a thumbnail sketch, if you want to put it that way. . . . The main thing is to remember that Hitler's timetable has been upset, and time was of the essence of gangster nations. . . . Jeffrey knew that the picture which Walter gave of the war and soldiers was distorted. It was not fair to select such simplicity to illustrate something which was immense and tragic. . . . It would have been better if people like Walter would stay at home where they belonged instead of trying to round out pictures in a nutshell.

As an occasional writer for popular magazines I am aware of this nutshell trouble. Editors prefer a package neatly wrapped, with no ifs, ands, or buts. Qualifications slow the story and annoy readers, who want clean-cut dramatic unity and easy answers. But one cannot write honest-ly about modern political or social questions—say, the farm problem—without considerable quali-fication. Simplification can easily turn into distortion. Better not to write the article at all.

Somebody Always Gets Hurt

Arguments about a proposed law—a new tariff act, for instance—are nearly always corrupted by over-generalizing. Any major enactment is bound to hurt somebody, and the real issue is to strike a balance between gains and losses. Lower tariffs may hurt the wool business, but does the consumer gain enough to compensate? Such accounting takes time and thought. How much simpler for the wool manufacturers to cry havoc, the nation is ruined; and for importers of woolens to cry prosperity will now advance to new peaks! What's good for General Motors may or may not be good for the country; the CIO publicity department is smarter with their slogan that what's good for the country is good for the CIO—but this might not always follow either.

Questions like these require thought and analysis, and many of them turn out like the story of the man who went down the street smashing windows. He said it was "good for trade." It might be good for the glass trade, but not for the storekeepers, while the waste made the whole community poorer.

In Summary

Why do we over-generalize so often and sometimes so disastrously? One reason is that the human mind is a generalizing machine. We would not be men without this power. The old academic crack: "All generalizations are false, including this one," is only a play on words. We *must* generalize to communicate and to live. But we should beware of beating the gun; of not waiting until enough facts are in to say something useful. Meanwhile it is a plain waste of time to listen to arguments based on a few hand-picked examples.

The generalizations we make are built up from cases the way a house is built out of stones, bricks, and lumber. If we see masons fitting large stones into a foundation, we are not likely to say: "This is going to be a stone house." If we see bricklayers starting a chimney we will hardly generalize: "This will be a brick house." In watching such physical operations, we have learned to wait until enough material is in place to warrant a reasonable inference about the kind of house it is going to be.

Chester Bowles did this about India. He waited until a great many facts were in place before telling us about that complicated country. But Chester Bowles, like the rest of us, if not on guard, could doubtless make two cats into a world of cats; two drunks into a reeling town, one swallow into a summer.

Generalizing is at the head of the reasoning process, and appears in many homely practices. Comparing, classifying, sorting, making bundles of similar objects and ideas, take up a substantial part of every normal person's day. The learning of children is largely generalizing—about doors, cars, dogs, slippery sidewalks; about spelling, arithmetic, and table manners. We also start new generalizations when we begin a collection of any kind—hi-fi records, stamps, autographs, prints. Much of this book is an exercise in generalizing about logical fallacies.

Generalizing is indeed central in the study of logic and the syllogism. Say the Liebers:[5]

A proposition may be *universal* (if it applies to all members of a class, like "All metals are elements"), or it may be *particular* (if it applies only to *some* members of a class, like "Some men are untrustworthy").

A person well grounded in logic is likely to be pretty shy of over-generalizing.

The story runs that a foreman took an intensive course in human relations given by one of the universities and paid for by his company. It included careful fact finding and delayed decisions. "What are we going to do for exercise," he demanded, "now that we've stopped jumping to conclusions?"

In serious discussion and problem solving, I am afraid we shall have to give up that particular form of exercise, exhilarating as it may be. George Eliot phrases it well in *Middlemarch:* "This power of generalizing, which gives man so much the superiority in mistake over dumb animals."

Appreciation of Style

1. Identify Stuart Chase's purpose in "Over-Generalizing."
2. Identify the controlling idea of the essay.
3. List the topics developed in this essay.
4. Did Chase write this essay for experts or the general reader? Support your opinion.
5. Cite a few examples of transition between paragraphs.

Test Your Comprehension

1. Explain reasoning from too few examples. Give an example from the essay.
2. What is a straw man?
3. Why did Chester Bowles say that he would have found it easier to write a book about India after being there for three months than he actually did after eighteen months? Explain in your own words.
4. What is the difference between "particular" and "universal" propositions (generalizations)?
5. Why are generalizations sometimes dangerous?

Vocabulary for Study

fallacies	conservative	inference	annihilated
anarchy	formidable	syllogism	esoteric
warrant	mundane	evangel	

---

5. *Mits, Wits, and Logic.*

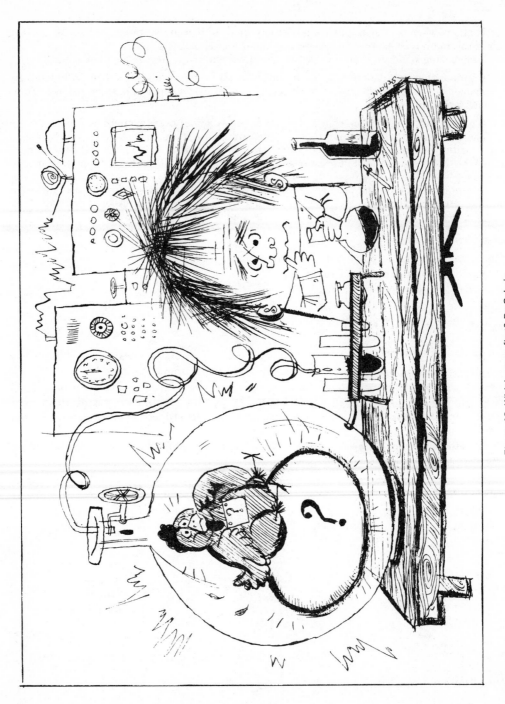

Figure 19. Which came first? By Schain.

The Essay:
Rational or Logical Development

A rationally or logically organized essay is the writer's way of using evidence and reasons to argue for or against an idea or belief. Generally, the writer states his idea and then supports it through evidence and clear reasoning to appeal to the reader's mind, not the reader's emotions. In essence, the most appropriate use of rational or logical development shows the presentation of facts and/or reasons which support the writer's central or controlling idea, and which, then, enable the reader to judge for himself whether he agrees with the writer.

Presenting Evidence to Support Central Idea

The author's most effective means of rational development is evidence, facts which support his central idea. A fact, whether pleasant or unpleasant, is simply so; furthermore, it can be checked by the reader himself. Let us observe how a brief central idea may be supported.

EXAMPLE

Central Idea: The progress of science today depends upon the foundation of past achievement.

Evidence: Isaac Newton said, "If I have seen further than other men, it is because I have stood on the shoulders of giants."

The Chinese invention of the rocket hundreds of years ago led gradually to our recent progress in space travel.

The discovery that germs cause disease led to our present ability to control most diseases caused by germs.

QUESTIONS ABOUT THE EXAMPLE

1. Do all of the statements presented in support of the central idea offer appropriate evidence?

_____

2. The use of Isaac Newton is the author's way of citing authority as evidence. Why is it

respectable to cite authority as evidence?_____

_____

3. Why does the statement about germs function to support the central idea?

_____

_____

4. Why would the following statement seem to provide further support for the central idea? "Men of science learn from past mistakes as well as past successes in performing their own work."

_____

_____

_____

5. The central idea of an argument is a general statement. Evidence in support of a central idea is

   an example of a_____case or instance.

ANSWERS: 1. yes, in an effective argument; 2. authority is expert; who should know better?; 3. It is a specific example of the general central idea; 4. It is a specific illustration that the past is a foundation for the future; 5. specific

Using Reasoning to Support Central Idea

The two most important types of reasoning are induction and deduction. They are the reverse of each other.

Induction

Induction shows the use of specific "bits" of evidence to arrive at a conclusion. Thus, to phrase it another way, *induction leads from the specific to the general.*

Example of Induction

Evidence
1. Monday, I cut myself with a knife.
2. Tuesday, I cut myself with a knife.
3. Wednesday, I cut myself with a knife.

Inductive (General) Conclusion

Knives are dangerous because they can penetrate the skin. I better be careful when I use one.

Deduction

Deduction shows the use of past knowledge, evidence or conclusions, to form new conclusions or judgments about specific things or experiences. To rephrase it, *deduction leads from the general to the specific.*

Example of Deduction

Past knowledge or conclusion

In the past, I learned that knives are dangerous because they can penetrate the skin and that I should be careful when I use one.

Specific Experience

Someone just gave me something which is clearly a knife.

Deductive Conclusion

I'm going to be careful with the knife that someone just gave me because I have learned that knives can be dangerous.

QUESTIONS ABOUT INDUCTION AND DEDUCTION

6. Inductive reasoning goes from _____ statements or facts to _____ conclusions.

7. Deductive reasoning goes from _____ statements or facts to _____ conclusions.

8. "I don't like ice cream. This (handed to you) is ice cream. Therefore, I won't like it." is an

    example of _____ reasoning.

9. "I went to two baseball games and I liked them. I saw three football games and I liked them too. The swimming and hockey tournaments I saw were exciting and fun. Therefore, I like

    sports activities and I plan to go to more of them." is an example of _____ reasoning.

10. Draw a conclusion from the following:
    a. I like candy.
    b. I enjoy cake.
    c. Ice cream excites me.

    _____

    _____

11. In question 10, you used _____ reasoning to draw a conclusion.

12. Draw a conclusion from the following:
    a. Baseball is a boring game.
    b. Someone gave me two tickets to a baseball game.

    _____

    _____

13. In question 12, you used _____ reasoning to draw a conclusion.

ANSWERS: 6. specific, general; 7. general, specific; 8. deductive; 9. inductive; 10. I like sweets in general, *or* I like desserts; 11. inductive, going from specific "bits" to a general conclusion; 12. The two tickets, if I use them, will lead to a boring experience; 13. deductive, going from a general conclusion in (a) to a specific conclusion about (b)

Avoid Emotional Appeal in Rational Development

An appeal to the mind presents something for the reader to think about. He is led, first, to understand and, second, to draw his own conclusions. On the other hand, an appeal to emotion, draws upon the reader's feelings and presents him with no rational choice at all; he is being, in essence, *forced* to accept the writer's beliefs.

EXAMPLE

All the criminals in prison would never have committed crimes if they had looked to God for guidance.

Analysis: This statement relies upon the reader's belief in God to persuade him. Do you believe that all crime and all criminals can be explained with a single idea?

QUESTIONS

Examine the following statements and identify the emotional appeal contained in each.

14. The starving people in foreign lands would solve their problems by adopting the American way.

_____

_____

15. Protest against the government is a form of disloyalty.

_____

_____

16. People on welfare are lazy.

_____

_____

17. Student protestors don't know what they're doing because they're immature.

_____

_____

18. Vote Republicrat or you're disloyal!

_____

_____

See answers to 14 through 18 at top of next page.

ANSWERS: 14. Appeals to the reader's affection for the American way; 15. Appeals to the reader's bad feelings about disloyalty and makes protest equal to disloyalty; 16. Appeals to the disreputable quality of laziness as an explanation of welfare; 17. Makes protest equal to immaturity; 18. Makes voting for the opposition equal to disloyalty

A Brief Review of Rational Essay Development

Rational or logical essay organization shows use of evidence and/or clear reasoning. It stresses specific supporting evidence for the author's central or controlling idea. It shows use of inductive and/or deductive reasoning in the formation of conclusions. Finally, rational organization shows avoidance of irrelevant emotional appeal.

Any essay in which the author wishes to argue for or against an idea or belief may be organized rationally. Finally, any controversial issue lends itself to rational treatment. For example, such subjects as "The Case for Aid to Underdeveloped Countries," "The Injustice of Censorship," and "Police Brutality, Does It Exist?" lend themselves to rational treatment because, strongly suggested by the titles, each suggests the likely development of one or more possible viewpoints which would require clear support.

In the following essay by Isaac Asimov, the author arranged his ideas rationally. He did not exhaust the subject in this particular essay in the sense that he could have presented much more supportive evidence for his central idea than he did. However, study the essay to see how he presented his central idea first and then supported it with evidence. Study the marginal notes as you read the text.

"INTRODUCTION" FROM <u>ADDING A DIMENSION</u>

Isaac Asimov

A number of years ago, when I was a freshly appointed instructor, I met, for the first time, a certain eminent historian of science. At the time I could only regard him with tolerant condescension.

I was sorry for a man who, it seemed to me, was forced to hover about the edges of science. He was compelled to shiver endlessly in the outskirts, getting only feeble warmth from the distant sun of science-in-progress; while I, just beginning my research, was bathed in the heady liquid heat at the very center of the glow.

In a lifetime of being wrong at many a point, I was never more wrong. It was I, not he, who was wandering in the periphery. It was he, not I, who lived in the blaze.

I had fallen victim to the fallacy of the "growing edge"; the belief that only the very frontier of scientific advance counted; that everything that had been left behind by that advance was faded and dead.

Asimov gives subject, relationship between science—past and progress today; his controlling idea is that he was wrong not to see the importance of this earlier in his life

But is that true? Because a tree in spring buds and comes greenly into leaf, are those leaves therefore the tree? If the new-born twigs and their leaves were all that existed, they would form a vague halo of green suspended in midair, but surely that is not the tree. The leaves, by themselves, are not more than trivial fluttering decoration. It is the trunk and limbs that give the tree its grandeur and the leaves themselves their meaning.

He compares all of science to a tree: analogy

There is not a discovery in science, however revolutionary, however sparkling with insight, that does not arise out of what went before. "If I have seen further than other men," said Isaac Newton, "it is because I have stood on the shoulders of giants."

Discovery arises from the past and gets meaning from it

And to learn that which goes before does not detract from the beauty of a scientific discovery but, rather, adds to it; just as the gradual unfolding of a flower, as seen by time-lapse photography, is more wonderful than the mature flower itself, caught in stasis.

In fact, an overly exclusive concern with the growing edge can kill the best of science, for it is not on the growing edge itself that growth can best be seen. If the growing edge only is studied, science begins to seem a revelation without a history of development. It is Athena, emerging adult and armed from the forehead of Zeus, shouting her fearful war cry with her first breath.

How dare one aspire to add to such a science? How can one ward off bitter disillusion when part of the structure turns out to be wrong. The perfection of the growing edge is meretricious while it exists, hideous when it cracks.

But add a dimension!

Take the halo of leaves and draw it together with branches that run into limbs that join to form a trunk that firmly enters the ground. It is the tree of science that you will then see, an object that is a living, growing, and permanent thing; not a flutter of leaves at the growing edge, insubstantial, untouchable, and dying with the frosts of fall.

Further support for his ideas:

Science gains reality when it is viewed not as an abstraction, but as the concrete sum of work of scientists, past and present, living and dead. Not a statement in science, not an observation, not a thought exists in itself. Each was ground out of the harsh effort of some man, and unless you know the man and the world in which he worked; the assumptions he accepted as truths; the concepts he considered untenable; you cannot fully understand the statement or observation or thought.

Science builds on past ideas

Consider some of what the history of science teaches.

First, since science originated as the product of men and not as a revelation, it may develop further as the continuing product of men. If a scientific law is not an eternal truth but merely a generalization which, to some man or group of men, conveniently described a set of observations, then to some other man or group of men, another generalization might seem even more convenient. Once it is grasped that scientific truth is limited

Men of science are human and learn from past mistakes as well as past success; this protects the student of science

and not absolute, scientific truth becomes capable of further refinement. Until that is understood, scientific research has no meaning.

Second, it reveals some important truths about the humanity of scientists. Of all the stereotypes that have plagued men of science, surely one above all has wrought harm. Scientists can be pictured as "evil," "mad," "cold," "self-centered," "absentminded," even "square" and yet survive easily. Unfortunately, they are usually pictured as "right" and that can distort the picture of science past redemption.

Scientists share with all human beings the great and inalienable privilege of being, on occasion, wrong; of being egregiously wrong sometimes, even monumentally wrong. What is worse still, they are sometimes perversely and persistently wrong-headed. And since that is true, science itself can be wrong in this aspect or that.

Even mistakes can lead to progress in methods and knowledge

With the possible wrongness of science firmly in mind, the student of science today is protected against disaster. When an individual theory collapses, it need not carry with it one's faith and hope and innocent joy. Once we learn to expect theories to collapse and to be supplanted by more useful generalizations, the collapsing theory becomes not the gray remnant of a broken today, but the herald of a new and brighter tomorrow.

Third, by following the development of certain themes in science, we can experience the joy and excitement of the grand battle against the unknown. The wrong turnings, the false clues, the elusive truth nearly captured half a century before its time, the unsung prophet, the false authority, the hidden assumption and cardboard syllogism, all add to the suspense of the struggle and make what we slowly gain through the study of the history of science worth more than what we might quickly gain by a narrow glance at the growing edge alone.

Conclusion: knowing science past highlights and gives pleasure to the men of science today because it gives their work meaning

To be sure, the practical thought might arise: But would it not be better if we learned the truth at once? Would we not save time and effort?

Yes, we might, but it is not as important to save time and effort as to enjoy the time and effort spent. Why else should a man rise before dawn and go out in the damp to fish, waiting happily all day for the occasional twitch of his line when, without getting out of bed, he might have telephoned the market and ordered all the fish he wanted?

It is for this reason, then, that I present this new collection of essays. It is my hope that, every once in a while, some vignette of Science Past may illuminate some corner of Science Present.

Appreciation of Style

1. In this logically organized essay, Asimov makes heavy use of comparison. What comparison(s) does he make? What figure(s) of speech does he use? *Be specific* in answering this question.

2. This essay is deductive; that is, Asimov makes a general statement of belief and then supports it by giving particular reasons. Prove this statement by referring to the text.

Test Your Comprehension

1. What is "the growing edge" of science?
2. What is the theme of this essay? State it and support your statement by making specific reference to the text.
3. Identify the author's purpose for writing this essay.

Vocabulary for Study

eminent	tenable	stasis
heady	persist	revelation
periphery	vignette	disillusion
halo	condescension	meretricious
emerging	trivial	redemption
hideous	insight	egregious
perverse		

Now, read the following correlated reading as
another example of rational organization.

NOBEL PEACE PRIZE ACCEPTANCE SPEECH

Martin Luther King, Jr.

I accept the Nobel prize for peace at a moment when 22 million Negroes of the United States of America are engaged in a creative battle to end the long night of racial injustice. I accept this award in behalf of a civil rights movement which is moving with determination and a majestic scorn for risk and danger to establish a reign of freedom and a rule of justice.

I am mindful that only yesterday in Birmingham, Alabama, our children, crying out for brotherhood, were answered with fire hoses, snarling dogs and even death. I am mindful that only yesterday in Philadelphia, Mississippi, young people seeking to secure the right to vote were brutalized and murdered.

I am mindful that debilitating and grinding poverty afflicts my people and chains them to the lowest rung of the economic ladder.

Therefore, I must ask why this prize is awarded to a movement which is beleaguered and committed to unrelenting struggle: to a movement which has not won the very peace and brotherhood which is the essence of the Nobel prize.

After contemplation, I conclude that this award which I received on behalf of that movement is profound recognition that nonviolence is the answer to the crucial political and moral question of our time—the need for man to overcome oppression and violence without resorting to violence and oppression.

Civilization and violence are antithetical concepts. Negroes of the United States, following the people of India, have demonstrated that nonviolence is not sterile passivity, but a powerful moral force which makes for social transformation. Sooner or later, all the people of the world will have to discover a way to live together in peace, and thereby transform this pending cosmic elegy into a creative psalm of brotherhood.

If this is to be achieved, man must evolve for all human conflict a method which rejects revenge, aggression and retaliation. The foundation of such a method is love.

The tortuous road which has led from Montgomery, Alabama, to Oslo bears witness to this truth. This is a road over which millions of Negroes are traveling to find a new sense of dignity.

This same road has opened for all Americans a new era of progress and hope. It has led to a new civil rights bill, and it will, I am convinced, be widened and lengthened into a superhighway of justice as Negro and white men in increasing numbers create alliances to overcome their common problems.

I accept the award today with an abiding faith in America and an audacious faith in the future of mankind. I refuse to accept the idea that the "isness" of man's present nature makes him morally incapable of reaching up for the eternal "oughtness" that forever confronts him.

I refuse to accept the idea that man is mere flotsam and jetsam in the river of life which surrounds him. I refuse to accept the view that mankind is so tragically bound to the starless midnight of racism and war that the bright daybreak of peace and brotherhood can never become a reality.

I refuse to accept the cynical notion that nation after nation must spiral down a militaristic stairway into the hell of thermonuclear destruction. I believe that unarmed truth and unconditional love will have the final word in reality. This is why right temporarily defeated is stronger than evil triumphant.

I believe that even amid today's mortar bursts and whining bullets, there is still hope for a brighter tomorrow. I believe that wounded justice, lying prostrate on the blood-flowing streets of our nations, can be lifted from this dust of shame to reign supreme among the children of men.

I have the audacity to believe that peoples everywhere can have three meals a day for their bodies, education and culture for their minds, and dignity, equality and freedom for their spirits. I believe that what self-centered men have torn down men other-centered can build up. I still believe that one day mankind will bow before the altars of God and be crowned triumphant over war and bloodshed, and nonviolent redemptive goodwill will proclaim the rule of the land. "And the lion and the lamb shall lie down together and every man shall sit under his own vine and fig tree, and none shall be afraid." I still believe that we shall overcome.

This faith can give us courage to face the uncertainties of the future. It will give our tired feet new strength as we continue our forward stride toward the city of freedom. When our days become dreary with low-hovering clouds and our nights become darker than a thousand midnights, we will know that we are living in the creative turmoil of a genuine civilization struggling to be born.

Today I come to Oslo as a trustee, inspired and with renewed dedication to humanity. I accept this prize on behalf of all men who love peace and brotherhood. I say I come as a trustee, for in the depths of my heart I am aware that this prize is much more than an honor to me personally.

Every time I take a flight I am always mindful of the many people who make a successful journey possible, the known pilots and the unknown ground crew.

So you honor the dedicated pilots of our struggle who have sat at the controls as the freedom movement soared into orbit. You honor, once again, Chief (Albert) Luthuli of South Africa, whose struggles with and for his people, are still met with the most brutal expression of man's inhumanity to man.

You honor the ground crew without whose labor and sacrifices the jetflights to freedom could never have left the earth.

Most of these people will never make the headlines and their names will not appear in Who's Who. Yet the years have rolled past and when the blazing light of truth is focused on this marvelous age in which we live—men and women will know and children will be taught that we have a finer land, a better people, a more noble civilization—because these humble children of God were willing to suffer for righteousness' sake.

I think Alfred Nobel would know what I mean when I say that I accept this award in the spirit of a curator of some precious heirloom which he holds in trust for its true owners—all those to whom beauty is truth and truth beauty—and in whose eyes the beauty of genuine brotherhood and peace is more precious than diamonds or silver or gold.

Appreciation of Style

1. Identify the point of view. Is it appropriate? Who is the "you" in the earlier paragraphs?
2. What tone does King show?
3. Find examples of metaphor.
4. Look for examples of effective use of comparison and/or contrast.
5. Prove that this essay is rationally organized.

Test Your Comprehension

1. Cite several reasons King gives in support of nonviolence versus violence.
2. Find the theme and prove your conclusion by referring to the speech.
3. Interpret: "I believe that what self-centered men have torn down men other-centered can build up."

Vocabulary for Study

curator	elegy	antithetical
cynical	tortuous	audacious
passivity	debilitating	prostrate
cosmic	beleaguered	sterile

Writing Sample Eleven: Write a criticism of one of the essays or stories in this textbook. You may deal with any aspect of the selection you like, but use a carefully structured logical organization in your paper. Refer to the instructions, the student model critical paper and the Assignment-Evaluation sheet which follow.

WRITING SAMPLE ELEVEN

ASSIGNMENT: Write a critical opinion about some aspect of a poem, a story or essay in this textbook.

Student Sample: *Interpreting two moods of a character*

One of the most common types of student essays is the critical paper. In such a paper, you are asked to select an idea from something you have read and to evaluate it from your own point of view. The idea you select may be as important as an author's theme or something of lesser importance. In essence, you are given freedom of choice to react to something which has interested you.

When writing a critical paper, you are *measuring the worth* of an idea, judging its importance, correctness and/or incorrectness; and your object is to express your own views about it. Therefore, you are obliged to be rational and/or factual in your comments. *You should not expect anyone to accept your unsupported opinion!*

Finally, in criticism, you should be *clear* in showing your agreement, disagreement, or both, with the ideas to which you react and in distinguishing your ideas from those of others.

DIRECTIONS: Write a brief criticism of an idea from an essay, story or poem. Confine your writing to a clear statement of the idea and its source, followed by your own opinions. Present facts and/or reasons to support your opinions and be as specific as possible.

1. Read the selection carefully.
2. Be certain you fully understand the idea which has interested you.
3. List your opinions carefully after phrasing the idea which has interested you in your own words.
4. List the facts and/or reasons which are needed to support your opinions, including, if necessary, brief quotations from the original.
5. Study the sample critical paper which follows.
6. Review the Assignment-Evaluation sheet which follows the critical paper to be certain you understand the criteria for contents.
7. Arrange your opinions and facts carefully.
8. Write a rough draft of your paper.
9. Compare your rough draft with the criteria for contents.
10. Rewrite or revise your paper as many times as necessary before handing it in.

SAMPLE STUDENT CRITICAL OPINION

The following sample paper is based upon the excerpt from the novel, *The Sensitives*, which appears in Chapter 10 on page 141 of this textbook.

THE OUTCAST

In the excerpt from the novel, The Sensitives, by Louis Charbonneau, one can see the character, Adam Cooper, undergo a change in mood. At the beginning of the selection, Cooper was somewhat bitter about his position in the Central Intelligence Agency, where his skill as a mind reader was used to interrogate suspects. However, Cooper was restricted in his contacts within the organization and was thought to be too much of a security risk: his superiors felt his mind-reading ability posed as much of a threat to the United States as to its enemies. However, the happy life Cooper enjoyed at home with his wife, Tina, compensated him for his rejection at work.

It was not until Cooper discovered that Tina had been unfaithful to him, and then lost her in an automobile accident, that the change in his mood took place. The knowledge of her betrayal removed the comforting influence which a happy home life had had upon his feelings about his rejection within the CIA.

Student's own title

Student describes the work he is critizing and gives his controlling idea

Student gives just enough information about the story to make his opinion clear

Cooper's first mood is given to set up the later contrast with the changed mood

Cooper's second mood and the reasons for it are identified and contrasted with the first mood

Now, unable to find happiness either at home or at work, he became deeply resentful of himself and others.

In comparing Cooper's two moods, one can see that during the time he was loved by his wife, he was content despite his rejection at work. However, when he discovered Tina's disloyalty to their marriage, his attitude toward himself was that he was a total failure and an outcast from society.

Student terminates essay by making final contrast between the two moods and concluding the resulting psychological state of the character

Study the Assignment-Evaluation sheet on the next page before you proceed further in your work.

EVALUATION SHEET FOR CRITICAL OPINION (SAMPLE 11)

Write a critical opinion of some aspect of an essay or story of your own choice.
Length: optional but be as brief as possible

Required in Contents	Full	Earned	For Study
1. Make a brief introductory description, including author, title, type of writing	20		
2. Identify clearly and specifically the aspect of the story you intend to criticize	20		
3. Give enough information about the work so your reader can understand your comments	20		
4. Develop your controlling idea (the aspect you selected to criticize) in concrete words and specific detail	20		
5. Support your ideas with facts and/or reasons	20		
PROOFREAD YOUR WORK CAREFULLY!	0		
TOTAL	100		

Instructor's Comments:

ENGLISH MECHANICS: Instructor Assigns Values for Criteria

Content Areas	Full	Earned	For Study
ORGANIZATION: Introduction Chronological Organization Topical Organization Rational Organization Smooth Development Termination	_____ _____ _____ _____ _____ _____		Chapter 13 Chapter 15 Chapter 16 Chapter 17 Chapter 14 Chapter 18
PARAGRAPHING: Introduction Development (unity) Development (coherence)	_____ _____ _____		Page 163 Page 165 Page 168
SENTENCES: completeness; variety; economy; use of modifiers; pronouns; agreement; use of verbs, phrases, clauses	_____		
USE OF LANGUAGE: Level of usage Idiomatic usage Vividness	_____		Chapter 8
PUNCTUATION AND CAPITALIZATION and related graphics: Quotation marks	_____		Chapter 7
SPELLING:			
TOTAL	100		

Mechanics not in this text are assigned in supplementary text.

Figure 20. Now, how do I finish? By Schain.

The Essay:
Combined Methods of Development
and Techniques of Termination

The problem of choice inherent in the written development of some subjects serves to support one of the most important ideas in this entire course of study: *whatever a writer does with any particular subject depends upon his understanding of its nature and his purpose for dealing with it.*

Often the three methods of essay development, chronological, topical, and rational, are combined. For example, consider the subject, "The Development of The Supermarket in The United States." Such a subject, the development of an institution, could be handled chronologically as a historical problem. On the other hand, it could be broken down into topics such as the following:

1. Definition and importance of the subject
2. The small, limited specialty store
3. The general store
4. The chain of specialty stores
5. Diversity and volume of products
6. Problems of distribution and marketing
7. The advantage of central purchasing
8. The first modern supermarkets
9. Economy and service to the customer

With topics such as those listed above, the author could combine chronology by offering historical data, in sequence, *within some of the topics.* Finally, even a third possibility exists: the author could use all of his data to argue in favor of the supermarket's contribution to the growth of the nation. How, then, would we describe the organization of an essay which combined methods of development? A simple answer is not possible, but we could say that one method predominated while the others were used to a lesser degree.

Finally, one remaining idea concerning essay development deserves mention: a writer must be honest in his handling of an essay. He is obligated not to allow his personal preferences *to distort* a subject. He should not eliminate essential facts or ideas, for example, nor should he knowingly apply false reasoning in order to mislead his reader.

REVIEW QUESTIONS ON ESSAY DEVELOPMENT

1. Define *topical* organization in an essay. _____

_____

_____

2. Define *rational* or logical organization in an essay. _____

_____

_____

3. Define *chronological* organization in an essay. _____

_____

_____

4. An essay has three general parts: _____, _____and _____.

5. An introduction states the _____ and the _____.

6. The controlling idea of an essay states _____

_____

7. The three types of essay development are _____

_____

8. The way in which a writer organizes an essay is a function of his_____.

ANSWERS: 1. arrangement by subdivisions of a subject; 2. use of evidence and reason to support a central idea; 3. arrange in a sequence by time; 4. introduction, development, termination; 5. subject and controlling or central idea; 6. the limitation of the subject; 7. chronological, topical, rational or logical; 8. purpose

To answer the following questions about essay organization, you will have to refer once again to some of the essays you read earlier as examples of chronological, topical, and rational methods of development.

EXAMPLE

Question: Claude Bernard's essay, "Carbon Monoxide Poisoning," on page 215, was given as an example of chronological organization. What other element of development appears in the essay?

Answer: Although Bernard's essay shows chronological organization predominantly because he shows the process of experimentation in sequence, he uses the evidence which he gathered inductively to come to a conclusion about his findings. Using evidence to come to a conclusion is a rational process.

9. Robert Benchley's article, "Do Insects Think?" on page 218, was given as an example of chronological organization. What other element of development appears in the essay?

_____

_____

_____

_____

10. A "statement of theme with support from the original work," was one of the essay assignments, on page 209, you were asked to write. What kind of essay organization is such an assignment?

_____

_____

_____

11. A "critical opinion" paper, on page 178, was one of the essay assignments you were asked to write. What kind of essay organization would such an assignment generally show?

_____

_____

_____

_____

_____

12. How is Chapter 12, "The Paragraph," in this textbook, organized? See page 163.

_____

_____

_____

13. How is the paragraph from "Ishi in Two Worlds," on page 175 organized?

_____

_____

14. What kind of organization is shown in "The True Believer" on page 176?

_____

_____

_____

15. How is "Crime and Barbaric Punishment" on page 185 organized?

_____

_____

ANSWERS: 9. Rational development is shown because Benchley uses inductive evidence to reach a conclusion; 10. Rational: theme statement is conclusion; textual support is evidence; 11. Criticism is expression of opinion and is a rational process if proper support for the opinion is given; 12. topically; 13. chronologically; 14. rational; 15. rational

Termination of an Essay

"Everything comes to an end," the philosopher once said, "but the problem of man is to see that the end, whatever it is, suits his purpose." Similarly, the writer's job in an essay is to terminate it in a way that suits his purpose. Beyond that, his termination should show an *obvious relationship* to the introduction and development of his ideas.

There are three principal methods of completing an essay:

1. *Summarizing* the highlights of development
2. *Drawing a conclusion* from facts and reasons previously presented
3. *Recommending* changes or action

Sometimes a combination of two or more of these methods of termination is used. Finally, the particular method of terminating depends upon the type of essay written.

Summarizing as an Ending

Suppose an essay were for the basic purpose of informing a reader objectively about some subject. To that end, the writer had presented an extensive amount of information; and, at the end of the essay, he wished *to reinforce* the reader's memory. The most effective way he could accomplish this is to summarize his data briefly so that the reader's last memory of the work consists of what the author wants him most to retain.

EXAMPLE: On the subject, "The Purposes for Writing an Essay"

> Ending: "As we have seen, a writer may have many different purposes for writing. These include definition, description, analysis, showing a process and argumentation."

Drawing A Conclusion as an Ending

Drawing a conclusion is appropriate to terminate a chain of reasoning. It is the "fruit" of the writer's analysis of a subject which could be either an objective analysis or an argument.

EXAMPLE: On the subject, "Why Everyone Should Not Vote"

> Ending: "No one can deny that the process of voting is essential in a democratic system. As we have seen, however, the voter who understands neither the issues nor the candidates may, through his ignorance, use his ballot to cancel out the intelligent choices of a knowledgeable citizen. Only those who are fully informed should cast ballots!"

Making A Recommendation as an Ending

A recommendation is a call to action, a demand or plea for *change* in existing practices or conditions. It should follow from adequate supportive data so that the reader is convinced of the *need for change*. Furthermore, the recommendation should be an appropriate solution to the problem.

EXAMPLE: On the subject, "Emergency Telephones Are Needed on the Highways!"

> Ending: "It is no longer debatable that the motorist in trouble on the highway needs some effective means of calling for help. What's more, the least expensive, most efficient means is the telephone. For these and all the other reasons I have given, I propose the immediate installation of free emergency telephones every 500 feet on all major highways.

QUESTIONS ABOUT TERMINATING AN ESSAY

To answer the following questions about essay termination, you will have to refer once again to some of the essays you read earlier as examples in the text.

16. Review the termination of "Do Insects Think?" on page 219. How is the essay terminated?

_____

_____

17. How is "The Principles of Poor Writing," terminated? See page 228.

_____

_____

18. How is "Over-Generalizing" terminated? See pages 234 and 235.

_____

_____

19. How is "Introduction" from *Adding A Dimension* terminated? See page 243.

_____

_____

20. How is "Nobel Peace Prize Acceptance Speech" terminated? See page 245.

_____

_____

ANSWERS: 16. conclusion from argument; 17. recommendation for additional study; 18. summary of highlights; 19. and 20. are conclusions from an argument

The Outline:
The Framework for the Essay

An outline is a kind of skeleton which shows ideas in sharp contrast without the structure of words which surround and sometimes "bury" ideas in ordinary writing. The outline has two general forms, the sentence or fragment, and it shows a consistency of structure within its parts. It is, furthermore, particularly useful in planning an essay because it helps the writer to classify and arrange his ideas into groups so that data which belong together are placed together.

Sample Outline Form

THIS IS AN OUTLINE

Title

CONTROLLING IDEA: State the controlling idea before beginning the outline itself.

I. All *main headings* take the same form.

    A. Subheadings with capital letters under I

    B. Second subheading under Roman numeral I

        1. item related to B

        2. second item related to B

II. Second *main heading* is a sentence also.

    A. Subheading under II in fragments also (See I.A.)

        1. item related to A in fragment also (See I.B.1.)

        2. second item related to A

            a. *minor item* under 2 usually a fragment

            b. second minor item under 2

            c. third minor item, *all lower case*

                (1) breakdown under c

                (2) breakdown under c

                    (a) related to (2)

                    (b) related to (2) also

                    (c) related to (2) also

    B. Second subheading under Roman numeral II

        1. item related to B

        2. item related to B

        3. item related to B

Sentence or *fragment*

Note: Breakdown in groups of two at least

Note: indenting required for each new breakdown to a lower category

Rules for Outlining

Refer to the sample outline as you review the rules for outlining which follow.

1. State the controlling idea before the outline.
2. Use Roman numerals for all main headings.
3. Be consistent in using the same structure for all main headings, either sentences or fragments for all. In the sample form, the main headings are both sentences.
4. Use capital letters to symbolize all subheadings.
5. Be consistent in structuring all subheadings, either sentences or fragments for all. In the sample form, the subheadings are fragments.
6. Use Arabic numbers for items related to subheadings.
7. Be consistent in structuring all items related to subheadings, either sentences or fragments for all, usually fragments. In the sample, the items related to subheadings are fragments.
8. Use lower case letters to symbolize minor items (see II A. 2. a.).
9. Be consistent in structuring all minor items, either sentences or fragments for all, usually fragments. In the sample, the minor items are fragments.
10. Use Arabic numbers with parentheses *(1)* for further breakdowns and lower case letters with parentheses *(a)* for items related to the Arabic numbers with parentheses (see II. A. 2. c. (2) (a)).
11. Be consistent in structuring all breakdowns with parentheses. They are nearly always in fragments as shown in the sample outline form.
12. Break down in groups of two *at least* whenever going from a higher to a lower category. If only one possible breakdown appears to exist, include it within the higher category immediately above.

Principles of Outlining

As explained in the introduction, the outline is useful in classifying ideas and in arranging them appropriately. This means that when a writer places his ideas in an outline, he should bear in mind their relative importance and that ideas of similar importance should be placed in the same *level* of category. Thus, if in a given essay there were approximately four major topics, each of these topics would become a main heading symbolized by a Roman numeral. Then, within each main heading, the lesser ideas would be appropriately arranged. For example, an essay on smog could be broken down as follows:

  I. Causes
 II. Effects at Present
III. Effects in The Future if Uncontrolled
IV. Remedies

How would the following ideas be arranged under the four main headings listed above?

1. engine research
2. plant damage
3. gas masks
4. average temperature rise
5. trees
6. food crops
7. respiratory diseases
8. factory smoke
9. plastic domes
10. heavy fines
11. heart attacks
12. exercise
13. oxygen
14. hydrocarbons
15. open fires
16. end of man
17. stinging eyes
18. cancer
19. fuels
20. animal life

Assuming that an outline were being constructed only in rough form at first, the following initial grouping of the ideas could be made under the main headings:

I. Causes: factory smoke, hydrocarbons, open fires, fuels

II. Effects at Present: plant damage, respiratory diseases, heart attacks, stinging eyes, cancer, food crops, animal life, trees

III. Effects in The Future if Uncontrolled: end of man, average temperature rise, exercise, oxygen, plastic domes,

IV. Remedies: engine research, heavy fines,

Does it become apparent that the arrangement of the ideas noted above could be refined further? For example, couldn't "animal life" and "food crops" as well as others be included within "Effects in The Future" as well as "Effects at Present"? Does it become equally apparent that some of the ideas *as stated* are not clear enough? Finally, are all of the ideas within the main headings, as stated above, of comparable importance? Consider this sample:

I. Causes
   A. Fuels
      1. hydrocarbons
      2. ?
   B. Factory Smoke
      1. hydrocarbons
      2. ?
   C. Open Fires
      1. hydrocarbons
      2. ?

Could "Causes" be modified as follows?

I. Causes

   A. Sources of Smog
      1. fuels
      2. factory smoke

      3. open fires
      4. ?
      5. ?
   B. Chemical Components of Smog
      1. hydrocarbons
      2. ?
      3. ?

Perhaps an examination of how to consider "Effects at Present" would be worthwhile.

II. Effects at Present

   A. Plant Damage
   B. Respiratory Diseases
   C. Heart Attacks
   D. Stinging Eyes
   E. Cancer
   F. Food Crops
   G. Animal Life
   H. Trees

Does inspection of these subheadings reveal something interesting, that some of them are really smaller "related items" and belong under some of the others? Consider the following rearrangement as a *possibility*.

II. Effects at Present

   A. Plant Damage
      1. food crops
      2. trees
      3. ?
      4. ?
   B. Respiratory Diseases
      1. cancer
      2. ?
      3. ?
      4. ?
   C. Heart Attacks
   D. Stinging Eyes
   E. Animal Life

Does this rearrangement look correct or do some of *these* subtopics appear to be "related items" under some of the others—particularly if a *new subtopic* is created?

II. Effects at Present

   A. Damage to Animal Life (new subheading)
      1. respiratory diseases
         a. cancer
         b. ?
         c. ?

      2. stinging eyes (Should this wording be changed?)
      3. heart attacks
      4. ?
  B. Plant Damage
      1. food crops
      2. trees
      3. ?
  C. ?

    Is it possible that still another rearrangement of main heading II would be desirable, or would it be enough to simply modify some of the wording and fill in additional details? It *does* seem that the problem of handling data, of classifying it, of arranging it, is considerable, doesn't it?

II. Effects at Present

  A. Damage to Animal Life
      1. respiratory diseases
          a. cancer
          b. emphysema   (new)
          c. nasal passages and sinuses   (new)
          d. ?
      2. diseases of the eyes   (new)
          a. ?
          b. ?
      3. diseases of the cardiovascular system   (new)
          a. heart attacks
          b. constriction of arteries and veins   (new)
          c. ?
          d. ?
      4. ?
      5. ?
  B. Damage to Plant Life
      1. food crops
          a. ?
          b. ?
      2. trees
          a. ?
          b. ?
  C. Damage to Marine Life   (new)
      1. ?
      2. ?
  D. Damage to Structures   (new)
      1. ?
      2. ?

    The handling of the original twenty ideas listed above may make clear how a writer's treatment of a subject can vary. He *does* have to understand his subject and how to classify its elements, doesn't he? He *does* have to formulate a clear purpose for writing, doesn't he? Simply, a writer must be *deliberate* in his handling of ideas, and he can make great use of the outline to arrange his ideas "naked" and without the interference which normal sentence and paragraph structure can give. As a *planning device*, there are few aids as useful as the outline.

QUESTIONS FOR REVIEW

1. An outline is like a _____ .

2. All main headings are symbolized by _____ .

3. Comparable elements of an outline should be structured _____
                                                              (three words)

_____ way.

4. Data in an outline are _____ .
                            (one word)

5. Breaking down from one category of an outline to another is in _____
                                                                    (three words)

_____ at least.

6. Outlines help the writer to see his ideas without the interference of surrounding words. (true

   or false) _____

ANSWERS: 1. skeleton; 2. Roman numerals; 3. in a similar; 4. classified; 5. groups of two; 6. true

---

Writing Sample Twelve: Make an outline of any one of the essays which you have read in this text. Remember to state a controlling idea as an introductory sentence before the outline itself. Review the Assignment-Evaluation sheet which follows before you start to work.

WRITING SAMPLE 12–EVALUATION

Write an outline of any one of the essays in this text which you have read.
Length: be as brief as possible

Required in Contents	Full	Earned	For Study

1. Use correct format
   a. main headings (Roman)
   b. subheadings (Capitals)
   c. related items (Arabic)
   d. minor items (Lower case)
   e. further breakdowns (Arabic and Lower case in parentheses)
	20		Chapter 19

2. Introductory controlling idea	20		Chapter 19
3. Place various headings and other elements in parallel structure *in groups of 2 or more*	20		Chapter 19
4. Select appropriate topics to outline the essay	20		Chapter 19
5. Set comparable ideas on the same *level* of importance	20		Chapter 19
PROOFREAD YOUR WORK CAREFULLY!	0		
TOTAL	100		

Instructor's Comments:

ENGLISH MECHANICS: Instructor Assigns Values for Criteria

Content Areas	Full	Earned	For Study

ORGANIZATION: Introduction
              Chronological Organization
              Topical Organization
              Rational Organization
              Smooth Development
              Termination
	———
	———
	———
	———
	———
	———
			Chapter 13
			Chapter 15
			Chapter 16
			Chapter 17
			Chapter 14
			Chapter 18

PARAGRAPHING: Introduction
              Development (unity)
              Development (coherence)
	———
	———
	———
			Note: ordinary mechanics not applicable if fragment outline is used, except spelling and punctuation

SENTENCES: completeness; variety; economy; use of modifiers; pronouns; agreement; use of verbs, phrases, clauses	———		

USE OF LANGUAGE: Level of usage
                      Idiomatic usage
                      Vividness
	———		

PUNCTUATION AND CAPITALIZATION and related graphics: Quotation marks	———		
SPELLING:			
TOTAL	100		

Mechanics not in this text are assigned in supplementary text.

Combining Skills

A Short Novel and
Final Writing Sample

In this final chapter, *The Answer*, a short novel by Philip Wylie, is presented. The work, although really a fantasy, was written in a realistic fashion. As you read, be conscious of the elements of writing you have studied in this textbook.

1. Author's purpose
2. Elements of structure: setting, plot and characterization
3. Significance or theme
4. Use of narrative and expository styles
5. Effective use of language: figures of speech, comparison and contrast, specific detail, interesting use of words
6. Use of characters, places and things as symbols

Ask yourself as you proceed: what important ideas did the author, Philip Wylie, wish to communicate? After you have finished reading the story, you will prepare your final writing sample. In it, you may practice, once again, the skills you practiced in your most recent writing: summary, theme identification, expression of critical opinion. All of these skills, furthermore, are demonstrated in a single, unified paper in which, hopefully, you will show understanding of the methods of essay development you have studied.

THE ANSWER
Philip Wylie

Fifteen minutes!"... The loudspeakers blared on the flight deck, boomed below, and murmured on the bridge where the brass was assembling. The length of the carrier was great. Consonants from distant horns came belatedly to every ear, and metal fabric set up echoes besides. So the phrase stuttered through the ship and over the sea. Fifteen minutes to the bomb test.

Major General Marcus Scott walked to the cable railing around the deck and looked at the very blue morning. The ship's engines had stopped and she lay still, aimed west toward the target island like an arrow in a drawn bow.

Men passing saluted. The general returned the salutes, bringing a weathered hand to a lofty forehead, to straight, coal-black hair above gray eyes and the hawk nose of an Indian.

His thoughts veered to the weather. The far surface of the Pacific was lavender; the nearby water, seen deeper, a lucent violet. White clouds passed gradually—clouds much of a size and shape—with cobalt avenues between. The general, to whom the sky was more familiar than the sea, marveled at that mechanized appearance. It was as if some cosmic weather engine—east, and below the Equator—puffed clouds from Brobdingnagian stacks and sent them rolling over the earth, as regular and even-spaced as the white snorts of a climbing locomotive.

He put away the image. Such fantasy belonged in another era, when he had been a young man at West Point, a brilliant young man, more literary than military, a young man fascinated by the "soldier poets" of the first World War. The second, which he had helped to command in the air, produced no romanticists. Here a third war was in the making, perhaps, a third that might put an end to poetry forever.

"Ten minutes! All personnel complete checks, take assigned stations for test!"

General Scott went across the iron deck on scissoring legs that seemed to hurry the tall man without themselves hurrying. Sailors had finished stringing the temporary cables which, should a freak buffet from the H-bomb reach the area, would prevent them from being tossed overboard. They were gathering, now, to watch. Marc Scott entered the carrier's island and hastened to the bridge on turning steps of metal, not using the shined brass rail.

Admiral Stanforth was there—anvil shoulders, marble hair, feldspar complexion. Pouring coffee for Senator Blaine with a good-host chuckle and that tiger look in the corners of his eyes. "Morning, Marc! Get any sleep at all?" He gave the general no time to answer. "This is General Scott, gentlemen. In charge of today's drop. Commands base on Sangre Islands. Senator Blaine—"

The senator had the trappings of office: the *embonpoint** and shrewd eyes, the pince-nez on a ribbon, the hat with the wide brim that meant a Western or Southern senator. He had the William Jennings Bryan voice. But these were for his constituents.

The man who used the voice said genuinely, "General, I'm honored. Your record in the Eighth Air Force is one we're almost too proud of to mention in front of you."

"Thank you, sir."

"You know Doctor Trumbul?"

Trumbul was thin and thirty, an all-brown scholar whose brown eyes were so vivid the rest seemed but a background for his eyes. His hand clasped Scott's. "All too well! I flew with Marc Scott when we dropped Thermonuclear Number Eleven—on a parachute!"

There was some laughter; they knew about that near-disastrous test.

"How's everybody at Los Alamos?" the general asked.

The physicist shrugged. "Same. They'll feel better later today—if this one comes up to expectations."

The admiral was introducing again. "Doctor Antheim, general. Antheim's from MIT. He's also the best amateur magician I ever saw perform. Too bad you came aboard so late last night."

Antheim was as quietly composed as a family physician—a big man in a gray suit.

"Five minutes!" the loud-speaker proclaimed.

You could see the lonely open ocean, the sky, the cumulus clouds. But the target island—five miles long and jungle-painted—lay over the horizon. An island created by volcanic cataclysm millions of years ago and destined this day to vanish in a man-patented calamity. Somewhere a hundred thousand feet above, Scott's own ship, a B-III, was moving at more than seven hundred miles an hour, closing on an imaginary point from which, along an imaginary line, a big bomb would curve earthward, never to hit, but utterly to devastate. You could not see his B-III and you would probably not even see the high, far-off tornadoes of smoke when, the bomb away, she let go with her rockets to hurtle off even faster from the expanding sphere of blast.

"Personally," Antheim, the MIT scientist, was saying to General Larsen, "it's my feeling that whether or not your cocker is a fawning type depends on your attitude as a dog owner. I agree, all cockers have Saint Bernard appetites. Nevertheless, I'm sold on spaniels. In all the field trials last autumn—"

Talking about dogs. Well, why not? Random talk was the best antidote for tension, for the electrically counted minutes that stretched unbearably because of their measurement. Scott had a

---

*Pointed

dog—his kids had one, rather: Pompey, the mutt, whose field trials took place in the yards and playgrounds of Baltimore, Maryland, in the vicinity of Millbrook Road. He wondered what would be happening at home—where Ellen would be at—he calculated time belts, the hour-wide, orange-peel-shaped sections into which man had carved his planet. Be evening on Millbrook Road—

John Farrier arrived—Farrier, of the great Farrier Corporation. His pale blue eyes looked out over the ship's flat deck toward the west, the target. But he was saying to somebody, in his crisp yet not uncourteous voice, "I consider myself something of a connoisseur in the matter of honey. We have our own apiary at Hobe Sound. Did you ever taste antidesma honey? Or the honey gathered from palmetto flowers?"

"Two minutes!"

The count-down was the hardest part of a weapons test. What went before was work—sheer work, detailed, exhausting. But what came after had excitements, real and potential, like hazardous exploring, the general thought; you never knew precisely what would ensue. Not precisely.

Tension, Scott repeated to himself. And he thought, *Why do I feel sad? Is it prescience of failure? Will we finally manage to produce a dud?*

Fatigue, he answered himself. Setting up this one had been a colossal chore. They called it Bugaboo—Operation Bugaboo in Test Series Avalanche. Suddenly he wished Bugaboo wouldn't go off.

"One minute! All goggles in place! Exposed personnel without goggles, sit down, turn backs toward west, cover eyes with hands!"

Before he blacked out the world, he took a last look at the sky, the sea—and the sailors, wheeling, sitting, covering their eyes. Then he put on the goggles. The obsidian lenses brought absolute dark. From habit, he cut his eyes back and forth to make certain there was no leak of light—light that could damage the retina.

"Ten seconds!"

The ship drew a last deep breath and held it. In an incredibly long silence, the general mused on thousands upon thousands of other men in other ships, ashore and in the air, who now were also holding back breathing.

"Five!"

An imbecile notion flickered in the general's brain and expired: He could leap up and cry "Stop!" He still could. A word from Stanforth. A button pressed. The whole shebang would chute on down, unexploded. And umpteen million dollars' worth of taxpayers' money would be wasted by that solitary syllable of his.

"Four!"

"Still," the general thought, his lips smiling, his heart frozen, "why should they—or anybody—*be doing this*?"

"Three seconds . . . two . . . one . . . zero!"

Slowly, the sky blew up.

On the horizon, a supersun grabbed up degrees of diameter and rose degrees. The sea, ship, praying sailors became as plain as they had been bare-eyed in full sun, then plainer still. Eyes, looking through the inky glass, saw the universe stark white. A hundred-times-sun-sized sun mottled itself with lesser whiteness, bulked up, became the perfect sphere, ascending hideously and setting forth on the Pacific a molten track from ship to livid self. Tumors of light more brilliant than the sun sprang up on the mathematical sphere; yet these, less blazing than the fireball, appeared as blacknesses.

The thing swelled and swelled and rose; nonetheless, instant miles of upthrust were diminished by the expansion. Abruptly, it exploded around itself a white lewd ring, a halo.

For a time there was no air beneath it, only the rays and neutrons in vacuum. The atmosphere beyond—incandescent, compressed harder than steel—moved toward the spectators. No sound.

The fireball burned within itself and around itself, burnt the sea away—a hole in it—and a hole in the planet. It melted part way, lopsided, threw out a cubic mile of fire this way—a scarlet asteroid, that.

To greet the birthing of a new, brief star, the regimental sky hung a bunting on every cloud. The mushroom formed quietly, immensely and in haste; it towered, spread, and the incandescent air hurtled at the watchers on the circumferences. In the mushroom new fire burst forth, cubic miles of phosphorpale flame. The general heard Antheim sigh. That would be the "igniter effect," the new thing, to set fire, infinitely, in the wake of the fire blown out by the miles-out blast. A hellish bit of physics.

Again, again, again the thorium-lithium pulse! Each time—had it been other than jungle and sea; had it been a city, Baltimore—the urban tinder, and the people, would have hair-fired in the debris.

The mushroom climbed on its stalk, the ten-mile circle of what had been part of earth. It split the atmospheric layers and reached for the purple dark, that the flying general knew, where the real sun was also unbearably bright.

Mouths agape, goggles now dangling, the men on the bridge of the Ticonderoga could look naked-eyed at the sky's exploded rainbows and seething prismatics.

"Stand by for the blast wave!"

It came like the shadow of eclipse. The carrier shuddered. Men sagged, spun on their bottoms. The general felt the familiar compression, a thousand boxing gloves, padded but hitting squarely every part of his body at once.

Then Antheim and Trumbul were shaking hands.

"Congratulations! That ought to be—about it!"

It for what? The enemy? A city? Humanity?

"Magnificent," said Senator Blaine. He added, "We seem O.K."

"Good thing too," a voice laughed. "A dozen of the best sets of brains in America, right in this one spot."

The general thought about that. Two of the world's leading nuclear physicists, the ablest member of the Joint Chiefs of Staff, a senator wise for all his vaudeville appearance, an unbelievably versatile industrialist, the Navy's best tactician. Good brains. But what an occupation for human brains!

Unobtrusively he moved to the iron stairs—the "ladder." Let the good brains and the sight-seers gape at the kaleidoscope aloft. He hurried to his assigned office.

An hour later he had received the important reports.

His B-III was back on the field, "hot," but not dangerous; damaged, but not severely; the crew in good shape. Celebrating, Major Stokely had bothered to add.

Two drones lost; three more landed in unapproachable condition. One photo recon plane had been hit by a flying chunk of something eighteen miles from ground zero and eight minutes—if the time was right—after the blast. Something that had been thrown mighty high or somehow remained aloft a long while. Wing damage and radioactivity; but, again, no personnel injured.

Phones rang. Messengers came—sailors—quick, quiet, polite. The Ticonderoga was moving, moving swiftly, in toward the place where nothing was, in under the colored bomb clouds.

He had a sensation that something was missing, that more was to be done, that news awaited—which he attributed again to tiredness. Tiredness: what a general was supposed never to feel—and the burden that settled on every pair of starred shoulders. He sighed and picked up the book he had read in empty spaces of the preceding night: Thoreau's "Walden Pond."

Why had he taken Thoreau on this trip? He knew the answer. To be as far as possible, in one way, from the torrent of technology in mid-Pacific; to be as close as possible to a proper view of Atomic-Age Man, in a different way. But now he closed the book as if it had blank pages. After all, Thoreau couldn't take straight Nature, himself; a couple of years beside his pond and he went back to town and lived in Emerson's back yard. For the general that was an aggrieved and aggrieving thought.

Lieutenant Tobey hurried in from the next office. "Something special on TLS. Shall I switch it?"

His nerves tightened. He had expected "something special" on his most restricted wire, without a reason for the expectation. He picked up the instrument when the light went red. "Scott here."

"Rawson. Point L15."

"Right." That would be instrument site near the mission school on Tempest Island.

"Matter of Import Z." Which meant an emergency.

"I see." General Scott felt almost relieved. Something was wrong; to know even that was better than to have a merely mystifying sense of wrongness.

Rawson—Major Dudley Rawson, the general's cleverest Intelligence officer, simply said, "Import Z, and, I'd say, General, the Z Grade."

"Can't clarify?"

"No, sir."

General Scott marveled for a moment at the tone of Rawson's voice: it was high and the syllables shook. He said, "Right, Raw. Be over." He leaned back in his chair and spoke to the lieutenant, "Would you get me Captain Elverson? I'd like a whirlybird ride."

The helicopter deposited the general in the center of the playing field where the natives at the mission school learned American games. Rawson and two others were waiting. The general gave the customary grateful good-by to his naval escort; then waited for the racket of the departing helicopter to diminish.

He observed that Major Rawson, a lieutenant he did not know and a technical sergeant were soaked with perspiration. But that scarcely surprised him; the sun was now high and the island steamed formidably.

Rawson said, "I put it through Banjo, direct to you, sir. Took the liberty. There's been a casualty."

"Lord!" The general shook his head. "Who?"

"I'd rather show you, sir." The major's eyes traveled to the road that led from the field, through banyan trees, toward the mission. Corrugated-metal roofs sparkled behind the trees, and on the road in the shade a jeep waited.

The general started for the vehicle. "Just give me what particulars you can—"

"I'd rather you saw—it—for yourself."

General Scott climbed into the car, sat, looked closely at the major.

He'd seen funk, seen panic. This was that—and more. The three men sweated like horses, yet they were pallid. They shook—and made no pretense of hiding or controlling it. A "casualty"—and they were soldiers! No casualty could—

"You said 'it,'" the general said. "Just what—"

"For the love of God, don't ask me to explain! It's just behind the mission buildings." Major Rawson tapped the sergeant's shoulder, "Can you drive O.K., Sam?"

The man jerked his head and started the motor. The jeep moved.

The general had impressions of buildings, or brown boys working in a banana grove, and native girls flapping along in such clothes as missionaries consider moral. Then they entered a colonnade of tree trunks which upheld the jungle canopy.

He was afraid in some new way. He must not show it. He concentrated on seeming not to concentrate.

The jeep stopped. Panting slightly, Rawson stepped out, pushed aside the fronds of a large fern tree and hurried along a leafy tunnel. "Little glade up here. That's where the casualty dropped."

"Who found—it?"

"The missionary's youngest boy. Kid named Ted. His dad too. The padre—or whatever the Devoted Brethren call 'em."

The glade appeared—a clear pool of water bordered by terrestrial orchids. A man lay in their way, face down, his clerical collar unbuttoned, his arms extended, hands clasped, breath issuing in hoarse groans.

From maps, memoranda, somewhere, the general remembered the man's name. "You mean Reverend Simms is the victim?" he asked in amazement.

"No," said Rawson; "up ahead." He led the general around the bole of a jacaranda tree. "There."

For a speechless minute the general stood still. On the ground, almost at his feet, in the full sunshine, lay the casualty.

"Agnostic," the general had been called by many; "mystic," by more; "natural philosopher," by devoted chaplains who had served with him. But he was not a man of orthodox religion.

What lay on the fringe of purple flowers was recognizable. He could not, would not, identify it aloud.

Behind him, the major, the lieutenant and the sergeant were waiting shakily for him to name it. Near them, prostrate on the earth, was the missionary—who had already named it and commenced to worship.

It was motionless. The beautiful human face slept in death; the alabastrine body was relaxed in death; the unimaginable eyes were closed and the immense white wings were folded. It was an angel.

The general could bring himself to say, in a soft voice, only, "It looks like one."

The three faces behind him were distracted. "It's an angel," Rawson said in a frantic tone. "And everything we've done, and thought, and believed is nuts! Science is nuts! Who knows, now, what the next move will be?"

The sergeant had knelt and was crossing himself. A babble of repentance issued from his lips—as if he were at confessional. Seeing the general's eyes on him, he interrupted himself to murmur, "I was brought up Catholic." Then, turning back to the figure, with the utmost fright, he crossed himself and went on in a compulsive listing of his sad misdemeanors.

The lieutenant, a buck-toothed young man, was now laughing in a morbid way. A way that was the sure prelude to hysteria.

"Shut up!" the general said; then strode to the figure among the flowers and reached down for its pulse.

At that, Reverend Simms made a sound near to a scream and leaped to his feet. His garments were stained with the black humus in which he had lain; his clerical collar flapped loosely at his neck.

"Don't you even touch it! Heretic! You are not fit to be here! You—and your martial kind—your scientists! Do you not yet see what you have done? Your last infernal bomb has shot down Gabriel, angel of the Lord! This is the end of the world!" His voice tore his throat. "And you are responsible! You are the destroyers!"

The general could not say but that every word the missionary had spoken was true. The beautiful being might indeed be Gabriel. Certainly it was an unearthly creature. The general felt a tendency, if not to panic, at least to take seriously the idea that he was now dreaming or had gone mad. Human hysteria, however, was a known field, and one with which he was equipped to deal.

He spoke sharply, authoritatively, somehow keeping his thoughts a few syllables ahead of his ringing voice, "Reverend Simms, I am a soldier in charge here. If your surmise is correct, God will be my judge. But you have not examined this pathetic victim. That is neither human nor Christian. Suppose it is only hurt, and needs medical attention? What sort of Samaritans would we be, then, to let it perish here in the heat? You may also be mistaken, and that would be a greater cruelty. Suppose it is not what you so logically assume? Suppose it merely happens to be a creature like ourselves, from some real but different planet—thrown, say, from its space-voyaging vehicle by the violence of the morning test?"

The thought, rushing into the general's mind from nowhere, encouraged him. He was at that time willing to concede the likelihood that he stood in the presence of a miracle—and a miracle of the most horrifying sort, since the angel was seemingly dead. But to deal with men, with their minds, and even his own thought process, he needed a less appalling possibility to set alongside apparent fact. If he were to accept the miracle, he would be obliged first to alter his own deep and hard-won faith, along with its corollaries—and that would mean a change in the general's very personality. It would take pain, and time. Meanwhile there were men to deal with—men in mortal frenzy.

The missionary heard him vaguely, caught the suggestion that the general might doubt the being on the ground to be Gabriel, and burst into grotesque, astounding laughter. He rushed from the glade.

After his antic departure, the general said grimly, "That man has about lost his mind! A stupid way to behave, if what he believes is the case!" Then, in drill-sergeant tones, he barked, "Sergeant! Take a leg. . . . Lieutenant, the other. . . . Rawson, help me here."

He took gentle hold. The flesh, if it was flesh, felt cool, but not yet cold. When he lifted, the shoulder turned easily; it was less heavy than he had expected. The other men, slowly, dubiously, took stations and drew nerving breaths.

"See to it, men," the general ordered—as if it were mere routine and likely to be overlooked by second-rate soldiers—"that those wings don't drag on the ground! Let's go!"

He could observe and think a little more analytically as they carried the being toward the jeep. The single garment worn by the angel was snow-white and exquisitely pleated. The back and shoulder muscles were obviously of great power, and constructed to beat the great wings. They were, he gathered, operational wings, not vestigial. Perhaps the creature came from a small planet where gravity was so slight that these wings sufficed for flying about. That was at least thinkable.

A different theory which he entertained briefly—because he was a soldier—seemed impossible on close scrutiny. The creature they carried from the glade was not a fake—not some biological device of the enemy fabricated to startle the Free World. What they were carrying could not have been man-made, unless the Reds had moved centuries ahead of everyone else in the science of biology. This was no hybrid. The angel had lived, grown, moved its wings and been of one substance.

It filled the back seat of the jeep. The general said, "I'll drive. . . . Lieutenant . . . Sergeant, meet me at the field. . . . Raw, you get HQ again on a Z line and have them send a helicopter. Two extra passengers for the trip out, tell them. Have General Budford fly in now, if possible. Give no information except that these suggestions are from me."

"Yes, sir."

"Then black out all communications from this island."

"Yes, sir."

"If the Devoted Brethren Mission won't shut its radio off, see that it stops working."

The major nodded, waited a moment, and walked down the jungle track in haunted obedience.

"I'll drive it," the general repeated.

He felt long and carefully for a pulse. Nothing. The body was growing rigid. He started the jeep. Once he glanced back at his incredible companion. The face was perfectly serene; the lurching of the vehicle, for all his care in driving, had parted the lips.

He reached the shade at the edge of the playing field where the jeep had first been parked. He cut the motor. The school compound had been empty of persons when he passed this time. There had been no one on the road; not even any children. Presently the mission bell began to toll slowly. Reverend Simms, he thought, would be holding services. That probably explained the absence of people, the hush in the heat of midday, the jade quietude.

He pulled out a cigarette, hesitated to smoke it. He wondered if there were any further steps which he should take. For his own sake, he again carefully examined the angel, and he was certain afterward only that it was like nothing earthly, that it could be an angel and that it had died, without any external trace of the cause. Concussion, doubtless.

He went over his rationalizations. If men with wings like this did exist on some small, remote planet; if any of them had visited Earth in rocket ships in antiquity, it would explain a great deal about what he had thitherto called "superstitious" beliefs. Fiery chariots, old prophets being taken to heaven by angels, and much else.

If the Russians had "made" it and dropped it to confuse the Free World, then it was all over; they were already too far ahead scientifically.

He lighted the cigarette. Deep in the banyans, behind the screens of thick, aerial roots and oval leaves, a twig snapped. His head swung fearfully. He half expected another form—winged, clothed in light—to step forth and demand the body of its fallen colleague.

A boy emerged—a boy of about nine, suntanned, big-eyed and muscular in the stringy way of boys. He wore only a T-shirt and shorts; both bore marks of his green progress through the jungle.

"You have it," he said. Not accusatively. Not even very emotionally. "Where's father?"

"Are you—"

"I'm Ted Simms." The brown gaze was suddenly excited. "And you're a general!"

The man nodded. "General Scott." He smiled. "You've seen"—he moved his head gently toward the rear seat—"my passenger before?"

"I saw him fall. I was there, getting Aunt Cora a bunch of flowers."

The general remained casual, in tone of voice, "Tell me about it."

"Can I sit in the jeep? I never rode in one yet."

"Sure."

The boy climbed in, looked intently at the angel, and sat beside the general. He sighed. "Sure is handsome, an angel," said the boy. "I was just up there at the spring, picking flowers, because Aunt Cora likes flowers quite a lot, and she was mad because I didn't do my arithmetic well. We had seen the old test shot, earlier, and we're sick and tired of them, anyhow! They scare the natives and make them go back to their old, heathen customs. Well, I heard this whizzing up in the air, and down it came, wings out, trying to fly, but only spiraling, sort of. Like a bird with an arrow through it. You've seen that kind of wobbly flying?"

"Yes."

"It came down. It stood there a second and then it sat."

"Sat?" The general's lips felt dry. He licked them. "Did it—see you?"

"See me? I was right beside it."

The boy hesitated and the general was on the dubious verge of prodding when the larklike voice continued, "It sat there crying for a while."

"Crying!"

"Of course. The H-bomb must of hurt it something awful. It was crying. You could hear it sobbing and trying to get its breath even before it touched the ground. It cried, and then it looked at me and it stopped crying and it smiled. It had a real wonderful smile when it smiled."

The boy paused. He had begun to look with fascination at the dashboard instruments.

"Then what?" the general murmured.

"Can I switch on the lights?" He responded eagerly to the nod and talked as he switched the lights, tried the horn. "Then not much. It smiled and I didn't know what to do. I never saw an angel before. Father says he knows people who have, though. So I said 'Hello,' and it said 'Hello,' and it said, after a minute or so, 'I was a little too late,' and tears got in its eyes again and it leaned back and kind of tucked in its wings and, after a while, it died."

"You mean the—angel—spoke to you—in English?"

"Don't they know all languages?" the boy asked, smiling.

"I couldn't say," the general replied. "I suppose they do."

He framed another question, and heard a sharp "Look out!" There was a thwack in the foliage. Feet ran. A man grunted. He threw himself in front of the boy.

Reverend Simms had crept from the banyan, carrying a shotgun, intent, undoubtedly, on preventing the removal of the unearthly being from his island. The lieutenant and sergeant, rounding a turn in the road, had seen him, thrown a stone to divert him, and rushed him. There was almost no scuffle.

The general jumped down from the jeep, took the gun, looked into the missionary's eyes and saw no sanity there—just fury and bafflement.

"You've had a terrible shock, Dominie," he said, putting the gun in the front of the jeep. "We all have. But this is a thing for the whole world, if it's what you believe it to be. Not just for here and now and you. We shall have to take it away and ascertain—"

"Ye of little faith!" the missionary intoned.

The general pitied the man and suddenly envied him; it was comforting to be so sure about anything.

Comforting. But was such comfort valid or was it specious? He looked toward the jeep. Who could doubt now?

He could. It was his way of being—to doubt at first. It was also his duty, as he saw duty.

Rawson, looking old and deathly ill, came down the cart track in the green shadows. But he had regained something of his manner. "All set, Marc. No word will leave here. Plane's on the way; General Budford's flying in himself. Old Bloodshed said it better be Z priority." The major eyed the white, folded wings. "I judge he'll be satisfied."

General Scott grinned slightly. "Have a cigarette, Raw." He sat beside the praying missionary with some hope of trying to bring the man's mind from dread and ecstasy back to the human problems—the awesome, unpredictable human enigmas—which would be involved by this "casualty."

One thing was sure. The people who had felt for years that man didn't yet know enough to experiment with the elemental forces of Nature were going to feel entirely justified when this story rocked the planet.

If, the general thought on with a sudden, icy feeling, it wasn't labeled Top Secret and concealed forever.

That could be. The possibility appalled him. He looked up angrily at the hot sky. No bomb effects were visible here; only the clouds' cyclorama toiling across the blue firmament. Plenty of Top Secrets up there still, he thought.

The President of the United States was awakened after a conference. When they told him, he reached for his dressing gown, started to get up and then sat on the edge of his bed. "Say that again."

They said it again.

The President's white hair was awry, his eyes had the sleep-hung look of a man in need of more rest. His brain, however, came wide awake.

"Let me have that in the right sequence. The Bugaboo test brought down, on Tempest Island, above Salandra Strait, an angel—or something that looked human and had wings, anyhow. Who's outside and who brought that over?"

His aide, Smith, said, "Weatherby, Colton and Dwane."

The Secretary of State. The chairman of the Joint Chiefs of Staff. The chairman of the Atomic Energy Commission.

"Sure of communications? Could be a terrific propaganda gag. The Reds could monkey with our wave lengths—" The President gestured, put on the dressing gown.

"Quadruple-checked. Budford talked on the scrambler. Also Marc Scott, who made the first investigation of the—er—casualty." Smith's peaceful, professorish face was composed, still, but his eyes were wrong.

"Good men."

"None better. Admiral Stanforth sent independent verification. Green, of AEC, reported in on Navy and Air Force channels. Captain Wilmot, ranking Navy chaplain out there, swore it was a genuine angel. It must be—something, Mr. President! Something all right!"

"Where is it now?"

"On the way, naturally. Scott put it aboard a B-III. Due in here by three o'clock. Coffee waiting in the office."

"I'll go out, Clem. Get the rest of the Cabinet up and here. The rest of the JCS. Get Ames at CIA. This thing has got to stay absolutely restricted till we know more."

"Of course."

"Scott with it?"

"Budford." Smith smiled. "Ranked Scott. Some mission, hunh? An angel. Imagine!"

"All my life I've been a God-fearing man," the President replied. "But I can't imagine. We'll wait till it's here." He started toward the door where other men waited tensely. He paused. "Whatever it is, it's the end to—what has been, these last fifteen years. And that's a good thing." The President smiled.

It was, perhaps, the longest morning in the history of the capital. Arrangements had been made for the transportation of the cargo secretly but swiftly from the airfield to the White House. A select but celebrated group of men had been chosen to examine the cargo. They kept flying in to Washington and arriving in limousines all morning. But they did not know why they had been summoned. Reporters could not reach a single Cabinet member. No one available at State or the Pentagon, at AEC or CIA could give any information at all. So there were merely conjectures, which led to rumors:

Something had gone wrong with an H-bomb.

The President had been assassinated.

Russia had sent an ultimatum.

Hitler had reappeared.

Toward the end of that morning, a call came which the President took in person. About thirty men watched his face, and all of them became afraid.

When he hung up he said unsteadily, "Gentlemen, the B-III flying it in is overdue at San Francisco and presumed down at sea. All agencies have commenced a search. I have asked, meantime, that those officers and scientists who saw, examined or had any contact with the— strange being be flown here immediately. Unless they find the plane and recover what it carried, that's all we can do."

"The whole business," Dwane said, after a long silence, "could be a hoax. If the entire work party engaged in Test Series Avalanche formed a conspiracy—"

"Why should they?" asked Weatherby.

"Because, Mr. Secretary," Dwane answered, "a good many people on this globe think mankind has carried this atomic-weapons business too far."

General Colton smiled. "I can see a few frightened men conspiring against the world and their own government, with some half-baked idealistic motive. But not a fleet and an army. Not, for that matter, Stanforth or Scott. Not Scott. Not a hoax."

"They'll report here tonight, gentlemen, in any case." The President walked to a window and looked out at the spring green of a lawn and the budding trees above. "We'll know then what they learned, at least. Luncheon?"

On the evening of the third day afterward, Marc Scott greeted the President formally in his office. At the President's suggestion they went out together, in the warm April twilight, to a low-walled terrace.

"The reason I asked you to come to the White House again," the President began, "was to talk to you entirely alone. I gathered, not from your words, but from your manner at recent meetings, General, that you had some feelings about this matter."

"Feelings, Mr. President?" He had feelings. But would the statesman understand or regard them as naïve, as childish?

The President chuckled and ran his fingers through his thick white hair in a hesitant way that suggested he was uncertain of himself. "I have a fearful decision to make." He sighed and was silent for several seconds as he watched the toy silhouettes of three jet planes move across the lemon-yellow sky. "There are several courses I can take. I can order complete silence about the whole affair. Perhaps a hundred people know. If I put it on a Top Secret basis, rumors may creep out. But they could be scotched. The world would then be deprived of any real knowledge of your—angel.

"Next, I could take up the matter with the other heads of state. The friendly ones." He paused and then nodded his head unsurely. "Yes. Even the Russians. And the satellite governments. With heaven knows what useful effect! Finally, I could simply announce to the world that you and a handful of others found the body of what appears to have been an angel, and that it was irretrievably lost while being flown to Washington."

Since the President stopped with those words, Marc said, "Yes, sir."

"Three equally poor possibilities. If it was an angel—a divine messenger—and our test destroyed it, I have, I feel, no moral right whatever to keep the world from knowing. Irrespective of any consequences."

"The consequences!" Marc Scott murmured.

"You can imagine them!" The President uncrossed his legs, stretched, felt for a cigarette, took a light from the general. "Tremendous, incalculable, dangerous consequences! All truly and decently religious people would be given a tremendous surge of hope, along with an equal despair over the angel's death and the subsequent loss of the—body. Fanatics would literally go mad. The news could produce panic, civil unrest, bloodshed. And we have nothing to show. No proof. Nothing tangible. The enemy could use the whole story for propaganda in a thousand evil ways. Being atheistic, they would proclaim it an American madness—what you will. Even clergymen, among themselves, are utterly unagreed, when they are told the situation."

"I can imagine."

The President smiled a little and went on, "I called half a dozen leaders to Washington. Cardinal Thrace. Bishop Neuermann. Father Bolder. Reverend Matthews. Every solitary man had a different reaction. When they became assured that I meant precisely what I said, they began a theological battle"—the President chuckled ruefully at the memory—"that went on until they left, and looked good for a thousand years. Whole denominations would split! Most of the clergy, however, agreed on one point: it was not an angel."

The general was startled. "Not an angel? Then, what—"

"Because it died. Because it was killed or destroyed. Angels, General, are immortal. They are not human flesh and blood. No. I think you can say that, by and large, the churches would never assent to the idea that the being you saw was Gabriel or any other angel."

"I hadn't thought of that."

"I had," the President replied. "You are not, General, among the orthodox believers, I take it."

"No, Mr. President."

"So I judged. Well, let me get to my reason for asking you to confer privately with me. The churchmen debated hotly—to use the politest possible phrase—over the subject. But the scientists—whom I also consulted"—he drew a breath and swallowed, like a man whose memory of hard-controlled temper is still painful—"the scientists were at scandalous loggerheads. Two of them actually came to blows! I've heard every theory you can conceive of, and a lot I couldn't. Every idea from the one that you, General, and all the rest of you out in the Pacific, were victims of mass hypnosis and the whole thing's an illusion, to a hundred versions of the 'little men from outer space' angle. In the meeting day before yesterday, however, I noticed you were rather quiet and reserved about expressing any opinion. I've since looked up your record. It's magnificent." The President hesitated.

Marc said nothing.

"You're a brave, brilliant, level-headed, sensitive person, and a man's man. Your record makes a great deal too plain for you to deny out of modesty. You are an exceptional man. In short, you're the very sort of person I'd pick to look into a mere report of an incident of that sort. So what I want—why I asked you here—is your impression. Your feelings. Your reactions at the time. Your reflections since. Your man-to-man, down-to-earth, openhearted emotions about it all—and not more theory, whether theological or allegedly scientific! Do you see?"

The appeal was forceful. Marc felt as if he were all the members of some audiences the President had swayed—all of them in one person, one American citizen—now asked—now all but commanded—to bare his soul. He felt the great, inner power of the President and understood why the people of the nation had chosen him for office.

"I'll tell you," he answered quietly. "For what it's worth. I'm afraid that it is mighty little." He pondered a moment. "First, when I suddenly saw it, I was shocked. Not frightened, Mr. President—though the rest were. Just—startled. When I really looked at the—casualty, I thought, first of all, that it was beautiful. I thought it had, in its dead face, great intelligence and other qualities."

The President rested his hand on the uniformed knee. "That's it, man! The 'other qualities'! What were they?"

Marc exhaled unevenly. "This is risky. It's all—remembered impression. I thought it looked kind. Noble too. Almost, but not exactly, sweet. I thought it had tremendous courage. The kind that—well, I thought of it as roaring through space and danger and unimagined risks to get here. Daring H-bombs. And I thought, Mr. President, one more thing: I thought it had determination—as if there was a gigantic feel about it of—mission."

There was a long silence. Then the President said in a low voice, "That all, Marc?"

"Yes. Yes, sir."

"So I thought." He stood up suddenly, not a man of reflection and unresolved responsibility, but an executive with work ahead. "Mission! We don't know what it was. If only there was something tangible!" He held out his hand and gripped the general with great strength. "I needed that word to decide. We'll wait. Keep it absolutely restricted. There might be another. The message to us, from them, whoever they are, might come in some different way or by more of these messengers! After all, I cannot represent them to the world—expose this incredible incident—without knowing what the mission was. But to know there was a mission—" He sighed and went on firmly, "When I finally get to bed tonight, I'll sleep, Marc, as I haven't slept since I took office!"

"It's only my guess," the general responded. "I haven't any evidence to explain those feelings."

"You've said enough for me! Thank you, General." Then, to Marc Scott's honor and embarrassment, the President drew himself straight, executed a salute, held it a moment, turned from the terrace and marched alone into the White House.

During the months-long, single day of Northern Siberia's summertime, on a night that had no darkness, a fireball burst suddenly above the arctic rim. As it rose, it turned the tundra blood-red. For a radius of miles the permafrost was hammered down and a vast, charred basin was formed. In the adjacent polar seas ice melted. A mushroom cloud broke through the atmospheric layers with a speed and to a height that would have perplexed, if not horrified, the Free World's nuclear physicists.

In due course, counters the world around would begin to click and the information would be whispered about that the Russians were ahead in the H-bomb field. That information would be thereupon restricted so that the American public would never learn the truth.

In Siberia the next morning awed Soviet technicians—and the most detached nuclear physicists have been awed, even stupefied, by their creations—measured the effects of their new bomb carefully: area of absolute incineration, area of absolute destruction by blast, putative scope of fire storm, radius of penetrative radiation, kinds and concentrations of radioactive fallout, half-lives, dispersion of same, kilos of pressure per square centimeter. Then, on maps of the United States of America, these technicians superimposed tinted circles of colored plastics, so that a glance would show exactly what such a bomb would destroy of Buffalo and environs, St. Paul, Seattle, Dallas, as well as New York, Chicago, Philadelphia, Los Angeles, and so on—the better targets. These maps, indicating the imaginary annihilation of millions, were identical with certain American maps, save for the fact that the latter bore such city names as Moscow, Leningrad, Stalingrad, Vladivostok, Ordzhonikidze, Dnepropertrovsk, and the like.

It was while the technicians were correlating their bomb data—and the sky over the test base was still lava—that coded word came in to the commanding officer of the base concerning a "casualty." The casualty had been found in dying condition by a peasant who had been ordered to evacuate his sod hut in that region weeks before. After the casualty, he had been summarily shot for disobedience.

The general went to the scene forthwith—and returned a silent, shaken man. Using communication channels intended only for war emergency, he got in touch with Moscow. The premier was not in his offices in the new, forty-six-story skyscraper; but his aides were persuaded to disturb him at one of his suburban villas. They were reluctant; he had retired to the country with Lamenula, the communist Italian actress.

The premier listened to the faint, agitated news from Siberia and said, "The garrison must be drunk."

"I assure you, Comrade—"

"Put Vorshiv on."

Vorshiv said, uneasily, the same thing. Yes, he had seen it. . . . Yes, it had wings. . . . No, it could not be an enemy trick. . . . No, there were no interplanetary vehicles about; nothing on the radar in the nature of an unidentified flying object. . . . Certainly, they had been meticulous in the sky watch; this had been a new type of bomb, incorporating a new principle, and it would never have done to let an enemy reconnaissance plane observe the effects.

"I will come," said the premier.

He ordered a new Khalov-239 prepared for the flight. He was very angry. Lamenula had been coy—and the premier had enjoyed the novelty of that, until the call from Siberia had interrupted. Now he would have to make a long, uncomfortable journey in a jet—which always frightened him a little—and he would be obliged to postpone the furthering of his friendship with the talented, beautiful, honeyhaired young Italian.

Night came to the Siberian flatlands and the sky clouded so that there was a semblance of darkness. A frigid wind swept from the Pole, freezing the vast area of mud created by the H-bomb. In the morning the premier came in at the base airfield, twelve jets streaming in the icy atmosphere, forward rockets blasting to brake the race of the great ship over the hard-packed terrain. It stopped only a few score rods short of the place where the "inadequate workers" lay buried—the more than ten thousand slaves who had died to make the field.

Curiously enough, it was an American jeep which took the premier out to the scrubby patch of firs. The angel lay untouched, but covered with a tarpaulin and prodigiously guarded round about by men and war machines.

"Take it off."

He stood a long time, simply looking, his silent generals and aides beside him.

Not a tall man, this Soviet premier, but broad, overweight, bearlike in fur clothing—a man with a Mongol face and eyes as dark, as inexpressive and unfeeling as prunes. A man whose face was always shiny, as if he exuded minutely a thin oil. A man highly educated by the standards of his land; a man ruthless by any standard in history.

What went through his head as he regarded the dazzling figure, he would not afterward have catalogued. Not in its entirety. He was afraid, of course. He was always afraid. But he had achieved that level of awareness which acknowledges, and uses, fear. In the angel he saw immediately a possible finish to the dreams of Engels, Marx, the rest. He saw a potential end of communism, and even of the human race. This milk-white cadaver, this impossible reality, this beauty Praxiteles* could never have achieved even symbolically, could mean—anything.

*A Greek sculptor.

Aloud, he said—his first remark—"Michelangelo would have appreciated this."

Some of the men around him, scared, breathing steam in the gray, purgatorial morning, smiled or chuckled at their chief's erudition and self-possession. Others agreed solemnly: Michelangelo—whoever he was or had been—would have appreciated this incredible carcass.

He then went up and kicked the foot of the angel with his own felted boot. It alarmed him to do so, but he felt, as premier, the duty. First, the noble comment; next, the boot.

He was aware of the fact that the men around him kept glancing from the frozen angel up toward the barely discernible gray clouds. They were wondering, of course, if it could be God-sent. Sounds came to him—bells of churches, litanies recited, chants—Gregorian music in Caucasian bass. To his nostrils came the smell of incense. He thought, as atheists must: What if they were right?

Against that thought he ranged another speedily enough; it was his custom. He wrenched the ears and eyes of his mind from the church pageantry of recollected boyhood, in the Czar's time, to other parts of his expanding domain. He made himself hear temple bells, watch sacred elephants parade, behold the imbecile sacrifices and rituals of the heathen. They, too, were believers, and they had no angels. Angels, he therefore reasoned, were myths.

It occurred to him—it had already been suggested to him by General Mornsk, of Intelligence—that some such being as this, come on a brief visit from an unknown small planet, had given rise to the whole notion of angels. He chuckled.

Vorshiv had the temerity to ask, "You have formed an opinion, comrade?"

The premier stared at the stringy, leathern man with his watery eyes and his record: eighteen million unworthy citizens "subdued." "Certainly." He looked once more at the casualty. "Autopsy it. Then destroy the remains."

"No," a voice murmured.

The premier whirled about. "Who said that?"

It was a young man, the youngest general, one born after 1917, one who had seen no world but the Soviet. Now, pale with horror and shame, the young man said, "I merely thought, sir, to preserve this for study."

"I detected sentiment. Credulity. Superstition. Your protest was a whimper."

The young officer showed a further brief flicker of dissent. "Perhaps—this being cannot be destroyed by our means."

The premier nodded at the body, and his thin, long lips became longer, thinner. A smile, perhaps. "Is not our second test planned for the very near future?"

"Tomorrow," Mornsk said. "But we are prepared to postpone it if you think the situation—"

"Postpone it?" The premier smiled. "On the contrary. Follow plans. Autopsy this animal. Attach what remains to the bomb. That should destroy it effectively." He glanced icily at the young general, made a daub at a salute and tramped over the ice-crisped tundra toward the jeeps.

On the way back to the base, Mornsk, of Intelligence, decided to mention his theory. Mornsk turned in his front seat. "One thing, Comrade. Our American information is not, as you know, what it was. However, we had word this spring of what the British call a 'flap.' Many sudden, very secret conferences. Rumors. We never were able to determine the cause—and the brief state of near-panic among the leadership has abated. Could it be—the 'flap' followed one of their tests—that they, too, had a 'casualty'?"

"It could be," the premier replied. "What of it?"

"Nothing. I merely would have thought, Comrade, that they would have announced it to the world."

The thin lips drew thinner again. "They are afraid. They would, today, keep secret a thousand things that, yesterday, they would have told one another freely. Freedom. Where is it now? We are driving it into limbo—their kind. To limbo." He shut his prune eyes, opened them, turned to the officer on his left. "Gromov, I hope the food's good here. I'm famished."

An old Russian proverb ran through his mind: "Where hangs the smoke of hate burns a fiercer fire called fear."

The trick, he reflected, was to keep that fire of fear alive, but to know at the same time it might consume you also. Then the trick was to make the fear invisible in the smokes of hatred. Having accomplished that, you would own men's souls and your power would be absolute, so long as you never allowed men to see how their hate was but fear, and so long as you, afraid, knowing it, hence more shrewd and cautious than the rest, did not become a corpse at the hands of the hating fearful.

There, in a nutshell, was the recipe for dictatorship. Over the proletariat. Over the godly believers. Over the heathen. Over all men, even those who imagined they were free and yet could be made to hate:

Frighten; then furnish the whipping boys. Then seize. Like governing children.

If more of these angels showed up, he reflected, it would simply be necessary to pretend they were demons, Lucifers, outer-space men bent on assassinating humanity. So simple.

The slate-hued buildings of the base rose over the tundra. From the frigid outdoors he entered rooms heated to a tropical temperature by the nearby reactors. There, too, the Soviets had somewhat surpassed the free peoples.

His secretary, Maximov, had thoughtfully forwarded Lamenula, to temper the hardships of the premier's Siberian hegira. He was amused, even somewhat stirred, to learn the young lady had objected to the trip, had fought, was even now in a state of alternate hysteria and coma—or simulated coma. A little communist discipline was evidently needed, and being applied; and he would take pleasure in administering the finishing touches.

Late that night he woke up with a feeling of uneasiness. A feeling, he decided, of fear. The room was quiet, the guards were in place, nothing menaced him to the immediate moment, and Lamenula was asleep. Her bruises were beginning to show, but she had learned how to avoid them in the future, which was the use of bruises.

What frightened him was the angel. Church music, which he had remembered, but refused to listen to in his mind, now came back to him. It did not cause him to believe that the visitor had given a new validity to an Old Testament. It had already caused him to speculate that what he, and a billion others, had thitherto regarded as pure myth might actually be founded on scientific fact.

What therefore frightened the premier as he lay on the great bed in the huge, gaudily decorated bedchamber, was an intuition of ignorance. Neither he nor his physicists, he nor his political philosophers—nor any men in the world that still, ludicrously, blindly, referred to itself as "free"—really knew anything fundamental about the universe. Nobody really knew, and could demonstrate scientifically, the "why" of time and space and energy—or matter. The angel—the very beautiful angel that had lain on the cold tundra—might possibly mean and be something that not he nor any living man, skeptic or believer, could even comprehend.

That idea wakened him thoroughly. Here was a brand-new dimension of the unknown to be faced. He sat up, switched on the light and put a cigarette in his thin mouth.

How, he asked himself, could this fear of the unknown be translated into a hatred of something known, and so employed to enhance power? His power. That was, invariably, the formulation; once made, it generally supplied its own answer.

You could not, however, set the people in the Soviets and the people in the rest of the world to hating angels. Not when, especially, their reality—or real counterpart—could never be exhibited and had become a military secret.

Mornsk's theory bemused him. Had the Americans also shot one down with an H-bomb? If so, they'd followed a procedure like his own, apparently. Saying nothing. Examining the victim, doubtless.

He realized he should go to sleep. He was to be roused early for the test of the next super-H-bomb, but he kept ruminating, as he smoked, on the people of the United States. *Whom,* he reflected, *we shall destroy in millions* in—The number of months and days remaining before the blitz of the U.S.A. was so immense a secret that he did not let himself reckon it exactly. *Whom we shall slaughter in sudden millions, soon.*

But suppose something intervened? Angels?

He smiled again. Even if such creatures had visited the earth once before, it was long ago. They might be here again now. They would presumably go away again, for millenniums. Ample time to plant the Red flag everywhere in the world.

Still, he could not know, and not to know was alarming.

There was a phone beside his bed. He could astound telephone operators halfway around the world, and yet, doubtless, in ten minutes, fifteen—perhaps an hour—he could converse with the President of the United States.

"Seen any angels, Mr. President? . . . What do you make of it? . . . Perhaps we aren't as knowing as we imagine. . . . Possibly we should meet and talk things over—postpone any—plans we might have for the near future? At least, until this matter of invading angels is settled."

It wouldn't be that simple or that quick, but it might be done. And it might be that that was the only possible way to save the Soviet, because it might be the one way left to save man and his planet.

He thought about the abandonment of the Communist philosophy, the scrapping of decades of horror and sacrifice, the relaxing of the steely discipline; he thought of the dreams of world domination gone glimmering—of "freedom" being equated with communism. There welled in him the avalanche of hatred which was his essence and the essence of his world. He ground out his cigarette and tried to sleep. . . .

In the morning, after the test shot—which was also very successful and, the premier thought, frightening—he requested the report on the autopsy of the casualty. He had to ask repeatedly, since it became clear that none of the nearby persons—generals, commissars, aides, technicians— wanted to answer. He commanded Mornsk.

The general sweated in the cold air, under a sky again clear and as palely blue as turquoise. "We have no report, Comrade. The autopsy was undertaken last night by Smidz. An ideal man, we felt—the great biologist, who happened to be here, working on radiation effects on pigs. He labored alone all night, and then—your orders, Comrade—the—remains were fixed to the bomb." Mornsk's glance at the towering mushroom disposed of that matter. "It was then discovered that Smidz made no notes of whatever he learned."

"Get Smidz."

"This morning early, Comrade, he killed himself."

General Scott did not return to the Pacific until nearly Christmastime. He had hoped not to go back at all, particularly since he had spent the autumn with his family in Baltimore, commuting weekdays to the Pentagon. In December, however, he received secret information of still another series of springtime nuclear-weapons tests and orders to fly again to the Sangre Islands, where he would prepare another of the group for total sacrifice. The death of islands was becoming commonplace to the weaponeers. In the unfinished span of his own military career, a suitable target had grown from a square of canvas stretched over a wooden frame to a building, and then to a city block, next a city's heart, and now, an island the size of Manhattan. This, moreover, was not holed, wrecked or merely set afire, but wiped off the earth's face, its roots burned away deep into the sea, its substance thrown, poisonous, across the skies.

He went reluctantly, but as a soldier must, aware that by now he had the broadest experience—among general officers—for the task at hand.

Work went ahead with no more than the usual quota of "bugs"—or what his orderly would have called "snafus." It was a matter of "multiple snafu," however, which finally led the general to order a light plane to fly him to Tempest Island. There had arisen an argument with the natives about property rights; there was some trouble with the placement of instruments; a problem about electric power had come up; and a continuing report of bad chow was being turned in from the island mess hall. Time for a high-echelon look-see.

As he flew in, General Scott noticed the changes which he had helped to devise. The mission playing field had been bulldozed big enough to accommodate fair-sized cargo planes on two

X-angled strips. Here and there the green rug of jungle had been macheted open to contain new measuring devices of the scientists. The harbor had been deepened; dredged-up coral made a mole against the purple Pacific as well as the foundation for a sizable pier. Otherwise, Tempest was the same.

His mind, naturally, returned to his previous trip and to what had been found on the island. The general had observed a growing tendency, even in Admiral Stanforth and Rawson, now a colonel, to recall the angel more as a figure of a dream than as reality. Just before the landing gear came down he looked for, and saw, the very glade in which the angel had fallen. Its clear spring was an emerald eye and the Bletias were in violet bloom all around.

Then he was on the ground, busy with other officers, busy with the plans and problems of a great nation, scared, arming, ready these days for war at the notice of a moment or at no notice whatever. Even here, thousands upon thousands of miles from the nervous target areas of civilization, the fear and the desperate urgency of man had rolled up, parting the jungle and erecting grim engines associated with ruin.

He was on his way to the headquarters tent when he noticed, and recognized, the young boy.

Teddy Simms, he thought, was about ten now, the age of his own son. But Teddy looked older than ten, and very sad.

The general stepped away from his accompanying officers. "You go on," he said. "I'll soon catch up. This is an old friend of mine." He waved then. "Hi, Ted! Why you all dressed up? Remember me?"

The youngster stopped and did recognize the general, with a look of anxiousness. He nodded and glanced down at his clothes. "I'm gonna leave! Tonight. It'll be"—his face brightened slightly—"my very first airplane ride!"

"That's swell!" The general had been puzzled by signs of apprehension in the boy. "How's your father? And your aunt? Cora, wasn't it?"

"She's O.K. But father—" His lip shook.

Marc Scott no longer smiled. "Your father—"

The boy answered stonily, "Went nuts."

"After—" the general asked, knew the answer and was unsurprised by the boy's increased anxiousness.

"I'm not allowed to say. I'd go to prison forever."

A jeepful of soldiers passed. The general moved to the boy's side and said, "With me, you are, Ted. Because I know all about it, too. I'm—I'm mighty sorry your father—is ill. Maybe he'll recover, though."

"The board doesn't think so. They're giving up the mission. That's why I'm going away. To school, Stateside. Father"—he fell in step with the general, leaping slightly with each stride—"Father never got any better—after that old day you were here."

"What say, we go back where—it happened? I'd like to see it once more, Ted."

"No." Teddy amended it, "No, sir. I'm not even allowed to talk about it. I don't ever go there!"

"It's too bad. I thought it was the most beautiful thing that ever happened to me in my life."

The boy stared at the man incredulously. "You did? Father thought it was the worst thing ever happened."

"I felt as if you, Ted—and I—all of us—were seeing something completely wonderful!"

The boy's face showed an agreement which changed, slowly, to a pitiable emotion—regret, or fear, perhaps shame. It was the general's intuition which bridged the moment: Teddy knew more than he had ever said about the angel; he had lied originally or omitted something.

"What is it, son?" The general's tone was fatherly.

Eyes darted toward the jungle, back to the general and rested measuringly, then hopelessly. It was as if the youngster had considered aloud running away and had decided his adversary was too powerful to evade.

He stood silent a moment longer; then said almost incoherently, "I never meant to keep it! But it is gold! And we were always so mighty poor! I thought, for a while, if Father sold it—But he couldn't even think of things like selling gold books. He had lost his reason."

If the general's heart surged, if his mind was stunned, he did not show it. "Gold books?" His eyes forgave in advance.

"Just one book, but heavy." The dismal boy looked at the ground. "I didn't steal it, really! That angel—dropped it."

The general's effort was tremendous. Not in battle had composure cost him as dear. "You—read it?"

"Huh!" the boy said. "It was in all kinds of other languages. 'Wisdom,' that angel said it was. 'Gathered from our whole galaxy—for Earth.' Did you ever know—" His voice intensified with the question, as if by asking it he might divert attention from his guilt. "Did you know there are other people on other planets of other suns, all around? Maybe Vega, or the North Star, or Rigel, or more likely old Sirius? That angel mentioned a few names. I forget which."

"No. I didn't realize it. And, you say, this book had a message for the people on Earth, written in all languages. Not English, though?"

"I didn't see any English. I saw—like Japanese and Arabian—and a lot of kinds of alphabets you never heard of—some just dots."

"And you—threw it away?" He asked it easily too.

"Naw. You couldn't do that! It's gold—at least, it looks like gold. All metal pages. It's got hinges, kind of, for every page. I guess it's fireproof and even space-proof, at the least. I didn't throw it away. I hid it under an old rock. Come on. I'll show you."

They returned to the glade. The book lay beneath a flat stone. There had been another the general was never to know about—a book buried beneath a sod hut in Siberia by a peasant who also had intended to sell it, for he, too, had been poor. But the other book, identical, along with the hovel above it, had been reduced to fractions of its atoms by a certain test weapon which had destroyed the body of its bearer.

This one the general picked up with shaking hands, opened and gazed upon with ashen face.

The hot sun of noon illumined the violet orchids around his tailored legs. The boy stood looking up at him, awaiting judgment, accustomed to harshness; and about them was the black and white filigree of tropical forest. With inexpressible amazement, Marc searched page after page of inscriptions in languages unknown, unsuspected until then. It became apparent that there was one message only, very short, said again and again and again, but he did not know what it was until, toward the last pages, he found the tongues of Earth.

A sound was made by the man as he read them—a sound that began with murmurous despair and ended, as comprehension entered his brain, with a note of exultation. For the message of icy space and flaring stars was this: "Love one another."

Appreciation of Style

1. Which is the strongest element of this story, setting, plot, theme, or characterization?
2. The style of the story seems quite realistic, but the story is really a fantasy. Explain.
3. Identify examples of effective use of language.

Test Your Comprehension

1. With whose characterizations are you made to feel more sympathetic, the Americans' or the Russians'? In what ways does the author reveal character?
2. What was the reaction of American religious leaders toward the unusual discovery?
3. What was the reaction of the Russians toward the unusual discovery?
4. Explain the use of angels as symbols in "The Answer." What do they mean?

5. The American angel was lost. The Russian angel's autopsy results were never reported because the doctor who examined the angel committed suicide. Wylie arranged this for a reason. Why?

6. The story makes a possible statement about the effect of the uncontrolled or unwise use of scientific knowledge. Develop this idea in your own words.

7. Give Wylie's purpose for writing the story.

Vocabulary for Study

consonants	prescience	misdemeanor
veered	mottled	vestigial
lucent	incandescent	enigma
kaleidoscope	ultimatum	Brobdignagian
cataclysm	diminish	fanatic
devastate	agnostic	tundra

SUGGESTED WRITING SAMPLE: Write a report on *The Answer*. Include summary of plot, setting, theme, characterization, and your critical opinion. Study the sample student papers in Chapters 12, 13, 14, and 17 once again.

WRITING SAMPLE–CRITICAL REPORT

Write a critical report on *The Answer*. Include summary of plot, setting, theme, characterization, and your opinion.

Length: optional but be as brief as you can

Required in Contents	Full	Earned	For Study
1. Give clear introduction to identify the author, the work and your central idea	20		
2. Summarize plot so the reader understands what the book is about	20		
3. Identify the theme and prove your conclusion	20		
4. Analyze characterization	20		
5. Express a critical opinion which is well-supported by facts and/or reasons	20		
NOTE: You do not need to arrange your paper in the same order as the criteria. Be as original as you wish but deal with all of the elements listed.			

TOTAL   100

Instructor's Comments:

ENGLISH MECHANICS: Instructor Assigns Values for Criteria

Content Areas	Full	Earned	For Study
ORGANIZATION: Introduction	———		Chapter 13
Chronological Organization	———		Chapter 15
Topical Organization	———		Chapter 16
Rational Organization	———		Chapter 17
Smooth Development	———		Chapter 14
Termination	———		Chapter 18
PARAGRAPHING: Introduction	———		Page 163
Development (unity)	———		Page 165
Development (coherence)	———		Page 168
SENTENCES: completeness; variety; economy; use of modifers; pronouns; agreement; use of verbs, phrases, clauses	———		
USE OF LANGUAGE: Level of usage / Idiomatic usage / Vividness	———		Chapter 8
PUNCTUATION AND CAPITALIZATION and related graphics: Quotation marks	———		Chapter 7
SPELLING:			

TOTAL   100

Mechanics not in this text are assigned in supplementary text.

Addendum
**Duplicate Evaluation Forms
for Writing Samples**

WRITING SAMPLE 1–EVALUATION

Write a unified composition which gives your reaction to your experiences in learning about your English class. Deal with the ideas listed in "required contents."

Length: approximately 125 words

Required in Contents	Full	Earned	For Study
1. What were your feelings about this class before the interviews and speeches began?	34		
2. What is your attitude toward class now that you know its members better?	33		
3. What are your feelings about the procedures used to introduce the members of the class to each other?	33		
TOTAL	100		

Instructor's Comments: (Note—proofread your work carefully or you may be given a study assignment in mechanics for the errors you make.)

ENGLISH MECHANICS: Instructor Assigns Values for Criteria

Content Areas	Full	Earned	For Study
ORGANIZATION: Introduction Chronological Organization Topical Organization Rational Organization Smooth Development Termination	_____ _____ _____ _____ _____ _____		Chapter 13 Chapter 15 Chapter 16 Chapter 17 Chapter 14 Chapter 18
PARAGRAPHING: Introduction Development (unity) Development (coherence)	_____		Page 163 Page 165 Page 168
SENTENCES: completeness; variety; economy; use of modifiers; pronouns; agreement; use of verbs, phrases, clauses	_____		
USE OF LANGUAGE: Level of usage Idiomatic usage Vividness	_____		Chapter 8
PUNCTUATION AND CAPITALIZATION and related graphics: Quotation marks	_____		Chapter 7
SPELLING:			
TOTAL	100		

Mechanics not in this text are assigned in supplementary text.

WRITING SAMPLE 1—EVALUATION

Write a unified composition which gives your reaction to your experiences in learning about your English class. Deal with the ideas listed in "required contents."

Length: approximately 125 words

Required in Contents	Full	Earned	For Study
1. What were your feelings about this class before the interviews and speeches began?	34		
2. What is your attitude toward class now that you know its members better?	33		
3. What are your feelings about the procedures used to introduce the members of the class to each other?	33		
TOTAL	100		

Instructor's Comments: (Note—proofread your work carefully or you may be given a study assignment in mechanics for the errors you make.)

ENGLISH MECHANICS: Instructor Assigns Values for Criteria

Content Areas	Full	Earned	For Study
ORGANIZATION: Introduction Chronological Organization Topical Organization Rational Organization Smooth Development Termination	____ ____ ____ ____ ____ ____		Chapter 13 Chapter 15 Chapter 16 Chapter 17 Chapter 14 Chapter 18
PARAGRAPHING: Introduction Development (unity) Development (coherence)	____		Page 163 Page 165 Page 168
SENTENCES: completeness; variety; economy; use of modifiers; pronouns; agreement; use of verbs, phrases, clauses	____		
USE OF LANGUAGE: Level of usage Idiomatic usage Vividness	____		Chapter 8
PUNCTUATION AND CAPITALIZATION and related graphics: Quotation marks	____		Chapter 7
SPELLING:			
TOTAL	100		

Mechanics not in this text are assigned in supplementary text.

WRITING SAMPLE 2—EVALUATION

Write a statement of your personal goals for this course. Relate your ideas to those you discovered in "Young Man Axelbrod."

Length: approximately 125 words

Required in Contents	Full	Earned	For Study
1. Based upon the objectives in the Orientation to this course, can you state goals you hope to accomplish?	34		
2. Can you relate your goals to the *importance* of having goals which you found in "Young Man Axelbrod"?	33		
3. Can you make your contents clear to a general reader, one who is not familiar with this lesson?	33		
PROOFREAD YOUR WORK CAREFULLY!	0		
TOTAL	100		

Instructor's Comments:

ENGLISH MECHANICS: Instructor Assigns Values for Criteria

Content Areas	Full	Earned	For Study
ORGANIZATION: Introduction Chronological Organization Topical Organization Rational Organization Smooth Development Termination	——— ——— ——— ——— ——— ———		Chapter 13 Chapter 15 Chapter 16 Chapter 17 Chapter 14 Chapter 18
PARAGRAPHING: Introduction Development (unity) Development (coherence)	——— ———		Page 163 Page 165 Page 168
SENTENCES: completeness; variety; economy; use of modifiers; pronouns; agreement; use of verbs, phrases, clauses	———		
USE OF LANGUAGE: Level of usage Idiomatic usage Vividness	———		Chapter 8
PUNCTUATION AND CAPITALIZATION and related graphics: Quotation marks	———		Chapter 7
SPELLING			
TOTAL	100		

Mechanics not in this text are assigned in supplementary text.

WRITING SAMPLE 2–EVALUATION

Write a statement of your personal goals for this course. Relate your ideas to those you discovered in "Young Man Axelbrod."

Length: approximately 125 words

Required in Contents	Full	Earned	For Study
1. Based upon the objectives in the Orientation to this course, can you state goals you hope to accomplish?	34		
2. Can you relate your goals to the *importance* of having goals which you found in "Young Man Axelbrod"?	33		
3. Can you make your contents clear to a general reader, one who is not familiar with this lesson?	33		
PROOFREAD YOUR WORK CAREFULLY!	0		
TOTAL	100		

Instructor's Comments:

ENGLISH MECHANICS: Instructor Assigns Values for Criteria

Content Areas	Full	Earned	For Study
ORGANIZATION: Introduction Chronological Organization Topical Organization Rational Organization Smooth Development Termination	_____ _____ _____ _____ _____ _____		Chapter 13 Chapter 15 Chapter 16 Chapter 17 Chapter 14 Chapter 18
PARAGRAPHING: Introduction Development (unity) Development (coherence)	_____ _____		Page 163 Page 165 Page 168
SENTENCES: completeness; variety; economy; use of modifiers; pronouns; agreement; use of verbs, phrases, clauses	_____		
USE OF LANGUAGE: Level of usage Idiomatic usage Vividness	_____		Chapter 8
PUNCTUATION AND CAPITALIZATION and related graphics: Quotation marks	_____		Chapter 7
SPELLING			
TOTAL	100		

Mechanics not in this text are assigned in supplementary text.

WRITING SAMPLE 3–EVALUATION

Write to re-create a moment of experience in narrative style.
Length: approximately 200 words

Required in Contents	Full	Earned	For Study
1. Use narrative hook as introduction to awaken reader's interest	25		
2. Use imagism (carefully chosen detail) to build a mental picture of the experience	25		
3. Provide emotional revelation to show how the character or "I" felt during the experience	25		
4. Make the significance (meaning) of the experience clear to the reader by showing what it meant to you (the character or the "I")	25		
PROOFREAD YOUR WORK CAREFULLY!	0		
TOTAL	100		

Instructor's Comments:

ENGLISH MECHANICS: Instructor Assigns Values for Criteria

Content Areas	Full	Earned	For Study
ORGANIZATION: Introduction	_____		Chapter 13
Chronological Organization	_____		Chapter 15
Topical Organization	_____		Chapter 16
Rational Organization	_____		Chapter 17
Smooth Development	_____		Chapter 14
Termination	_____		Chapter 18
PARAGRAPHING: Introduction			Page 163
Development (unity)	_____		Page 165
Development (coherence)	_____		Page 168
SENTENCES: completeness; variety; economy; use of modifiers; pronouns; agreement; use of verbs, phrases, clauses	_____		
USE OF LANGUAGE: Level of usage Idiomatic usage Vividness	_____		Chapter 8
PUNCTUATION AND CAPITALIZATION and related graphics: Quotation marks	_____		Chapter 7
SPELLING			
TOTAL	100		

Mechanics not in this text are assigned in supplementary text.

WRITING SAMPLE 3—EVALUATION

Write to re-create a moment of experience in narrative style.

Length: approximately 200 words

Required in Contents	Full	Earned	For Study
1. Use narrative hook as introduction to awaken reader's interest	25		
2. Use imagism (carefully chosen detail) to build a mental picture of the experience	25		
3. Provide emotional revelation to show how the character or "I" felt during the experience	25		
4. Make the significance (meaning) of the experience clear to the reader by showing what it meant to you (the character or the "I")	25		
PROOFREAD YOUR WORK CAREFULLY!	0		
TOTAL	100		

Instructor's Comments:

ENGLISH MECHANICS: Instructor Assigns Values for Criteria

Content Areas	Full	Earned	For Study
ORGANIZATION: Introduction Chronological Organization Topical Organization Rational Organization Smooth Development Termination	_____ _____ _____ _____ _____ _____		Chapter 13 Chapter 15 Chapter 16 Chapter 17 Chapter 14 Chapter 18
PARAGRAPHING: Introduction Development (unity) Development (coherence)	_____ _____		Page 163 Page 165 Page 168
SENTENCES: completeness; variety; economy; use of modifiers; pronouns; agreement; use of verbs, phrases, clauses	_____		
USE OF LANGUAGE: Level of usage Idiomatic usage Vividness	_____		Chapter 8
PUNCTUATION AND CAPITALIZATION and related graphics: Quotation marks	_____		Chapter 7
SPELLING			
TOTAL	100		

Mechanics not in this text are assigned in supplementary text.

WRITING SAMPLE 4—EVALUATION

Write to re-create a moment of experience in narrative style, but use a point of view *other than* first person.
Length: approximately 200 words

Required in Contents	Full	Earned	For Study
1. Use narrative hook	20		
2. Use imagism	20		
3. Show emotional revelation	20		
4. Make significance clear to reader as well as to character in narrative	20		
5. Show a single point of view but not first person	20		
PROOFREAD YOUR WORK CAREFULLY!	0		
TOTAL	100		

Instructor's Comments:

ENGLISH MECHANICS: Instructor Assigns Values for Criteria

Content Areas	Full	Earned	For Study
ORGANIZATION: Introduction	————		Chapter 13
Chronological Organization	————		Chapter 15
Topical Organization	————		Chapter 16
Rational Organization	————		Chapter 17
Smooth Development	————		Chapter 14
Termination	————		Chapter 18
PARAGRAPHING: Introduction	————		Page 163
Development (unity)	————		Page 165
Development (coherence)	————		Page 168
SENTENCES: completeness; variety; economy; use of modifiers; pronouns; agreement; use of verbs, phrases, clauses	————		
USE OF LANGUAGE: Level of usage / Idiomatic usage / Vividness	————		Chapter 8
PUNCTUATION AND CAPITALIZATION and related graphics: Quotation marks	————		Chapter 7
SPELLING:			
TOTAL	100		

Mechanics not in this text are assigned in supplementary text.

WRITING SAMPLE 4—EVALUATION

Write to re-create a moment of experience in narrative style, but use a point of view *other than* first person. Length: approximately 200 words

Required in Contents	Full	Earned	For Study
1. Use narrative hook	20		
2. Use imagism	20		
3. Show emotional revelation	20		
4. Make significance clear to reader as well as to character in narrative	20		
5. Show a single point of view but not first person	20		
PROOFREAD YOUR WORK CAREFULLY!	0		
TOTAL	100		

Instructor's Comments:

ENGLISH MECHANICS: Instructor Assigns Values for Criteria

Content Areas	Full	Earned	For Study
ORGANIZATION: Introduction	———		Chapter 13
Chronological Organization	———		Chapter 15
Topical Organization	———		Chapter 16
Rational Organization	———		Chapter 17
Smooth Development	———		Chapter 14
Termination	———		Chapter 18
PARAGRAPHING: Introduction	———		Page 163
Development (unity)	———		Page 165
Development (coherence)	———		Page 168
SENTENCES: completeness; variety; economy; use of modifiers; pronouns; agreement; use of verbs, phrases, clauses	———		
USE OF LANGUAGE: Level of usage Idiomatic usage Vividness	———		Chapter 8
PUNCTUATION AND CAPITALIZATION and related graphics: Quotation marks	———		Chapter 7
SPELLING:			
TOTAL	100		

Mechanics not in this text are assigned in supplementary text.

WRITING SAMPLE 5—EVALUATION

Write primarily dialogue in re-creating a moment of experience in narrative style.
Length: approximately 200 words

Required in Contents	Full	Earned	For Study
1. Use narrative hook (may be dialogue)	17		
2. Use imagism (emphasize speech)	17		
3. Show emotional revelation	17		
4. Make significance clear to reader	17		
5. Stress use of dialogue and choose verbs carefully to show *how* words are spoken; show development of *tension* between characters	17		
6. Use special mechanics: a. paragraph change of speaker b. quotation marks around words in dialogue c. punctuation within quotation marks as needed d. punctuate sentence stops of sentences containing speech	15		
TOTAL	100		

Instructor's Comments: REMEMBER TO PROOFREAD CAREFULLY!

ENGLISH MECHANICS: Instructor Assigns Values for Criteria

Content Areas	Full	Earned	For Study
ORGANIZATION: Introduction Chronological Organization Topical Organization Rational Organization Smooth Development Termination	——— ——— ——— ——— ——— ———		Chapter 13 Chapter 15 Chapter 16 Chapter 17 Chapter 14 Chapter 18
PARAGRAPHING: Introduction Development (unity) Development (coherence)	——— ——— ———		Page 163 Page 165 Page 168
SENTENCES: completeness; variety; economy; use of modifiers; pronouns; agreement; use of verbs, phrases, clauses	———		
USE OF LANGUAGE: Level of usage Idiomatic usage Vividness	———		Chapter 8
PUNCTUATION AND CAPITALIZATION and related graphics: Quotation marks	———		Chapter 7
SPELLING:			
TOTAL	100		

Mechanics not in this text are assigned in supplementary text.

WRITING SAMPLE 5—EVALUATION

Write primarily dialogue in re-creating a moment of experience in narrative style.
Length: approximately 200 words

Required in Contents	Full	Earned	For Study
1. Use narrative hook (may be dialogue)	17		
2. Use imagism (emphasize speech)	17		
3. Show emotional revelation	17		
4. Make significance clear to reader	17		
5. Stress use of dialogue and choose verbs carefully to show *how* words are spoken; show development of *tension* between characters	17		
6. Use special mechanics: a. paragraph change of speaker b. quotation marks around words in dialogue c. punctuation within quotation marks as needed d. punctuate sentence stops of sentences containing speech	15		
TOTAL	100		

Instructor's Comments: REMEMBER TO PROOFREAD CAREFULLY!

ENGLISH MECHANICS: Instructor Assigns Values for Criteria

Content Areas	Full	Earned	For Study
ORGANIZATION: Introduction	————		Chapter 13
Chronological Organization	————		Chapter 15
Topical Organization	————		Chapter 16
Rational Organization	————		Chapter 17
Smooth Development	————		Chapter 14
Termination	————		Chapter 18
PARAGRAPHING: Introduction	————		Page 163
Development (unity)	————		Page 165
Development (coherence)	————		Page 168
SENTENCES: completeness; variety; economy; use of modifiers; pronouns; agreement; use of verbs, phrases, clauses	————		
USE OF LANGUAGE: Level of usage Idiomatic usage Vividness	————		Chapter 8
PUNCTUATION AND CAPITALIZATION and related graphics: Quotation marks	————		Chapter 7
SPELLING:			
TOTAL	100		

Mechanics not in this text are assigned in supplementary text.

WRITING SAMPLE 6–EVALUATION

Write a narrative-mood sequence showing a third person character experiencing an emotion which builds gradually until he is compelled to act.
Length: approximately 200 words

Required in Contents	Full	Earned	For Study
1. Use narrative hook to show character's initial emotion	20		
2. Provide sense impressions in some believable sequence to stimulate the character	20		
3. Show character reacting gradually to sense impressions to reveal their influence on him	20		
4. Use character's reactions to sense impressions to show change in his emotional state	20		
5. Show character committing an obvious act which is consistent with his change of mood	20		
PROOFREAD YOUR WORK CAREFULLY!	0		
TOTAL	100		

Instructor's Comments:

ENGLISH MECHANICS: Instructor Assigns Values for Criteria

Content Areas	Full	Earned	For Study
ORGANIZATION: Introduction	————		Chapter 13
Chronological Organization	————		Chapter 15
Topical Organization	————		Chapter 16
Rational Organization	————		Chapter 17
Smooth Development	————		Chapter 14
Termination	————		Chapter 18
PARAGRAPHING: Introduction	————		Page 163
Development (unity)	————		Page 165
Development (coherence)	————		Page 168
SENTENCES: completeness; variety; economy; use of modifiers; pronouns; agreement; use of verbs, phrases, clauses	————		

USE OF LANGUAGE: Level of usage
    Idiomatic usage
    Vividness
	————		Chapter 8

PUNCTUATION AND CAPITALIZATION and related graphics: Quotation marks	————		Chapter 7
SPELLING:			
TOTAL	100		

Mechanics not in this text are assigned to supplementary text.

WRITING SAMPLE 6—EVALUATION

Write a narrative-mood sequence showing a third person character experiencing an emotion which builds gradually until he is compelled to act.

Length: approximately 200 words

Required in Contents	Full	Earned	For Study
1. Use narrative hook to show character's initial emotion	20		
2. Provide sense impressions in some believable sequence to stimulate the character	20		
3. Show character reacting gradually to sense impressions to reveal their influence on him	20		
4. Use character's reactions to sense impressions to show change in his emotional state	20		
5. Show character committing an obvious act which is consistent with his change of mood	20		
PROOFREAD YOUR WORK CAREFULLY!	0		
TOTAL	100		

Instructor's Comments:

ENGLISH MECHANICS: Instructor Assigns Values for Criteria

Content Areas	Full	Earned	For Study
ORGANIZATION: Introduction	————		Chapter 13
Chronological Organization	————		Chapter 15
Topical Organization	————		Chapter 16
Rational Organization	————		Chapter 17
Smooth Development	————		Chapter 14
Termination	————		Chapter 18
PARAGRAPHING: Introduction	————		Page 163
Development (unity)	————		Page 165
Development (coherence)	————		Page 168
SENTENCES: completeness; variety; economy; use of modifiers; pronouns; agreement; use of verbs, phrases, clauses	————		
USE OF LANGUAGE: Level of usage Idiomatic usage Vividness	————		Chapter 8
PUNCTUATION AND CAPITALIZATION and related graphics: Quotation marks	————		Chapter 7
SPELLING:			
TOTAL	100		

Mechanics not in this text are assigned to supplementary text.

WRITING SAMPLE 7—EVALUATION

Write: (Select own *limited* subject) _____

_____

Length: optional _____

Required in Contents	Full	Earned	For Study
1. Limit subject	20		
2. Identify purpose (define, describe, analyze, argue) _____ _____	20		
3. Select clear controlling or central idea _____ _____	20		
4. Assign point values only to the techniques you use: a. *concrete* vs abstract b. specific detail c. comparison d. contrast e. narrative style f. expository style g. other: _____	_____ _____ _____ _____ _____ _____ _____		
TOTAL	100		

Instructor's Comments:

ENGLISH MECHANICS: Instructor Assigns Values for Criteria

Content Areas	Full	Earned	For Study
ORGANIZATION: Introduction	_____		Chapter 13
Chronological Organization	_____		Chapter 15
Topical Organization	_____		Chapter 16
Rational Organization	_____		Chapter 17
Smooth Development	_____		Chapter 14
Termination	_____		Chapter 18
PARAGRAPHING: Introduction	_____		Page 163
Development (unity)	_____		Page 165
Development (coherence)	_____		Page 168
SENTENCES: completeness; variety; economy; use of modifiers; pronouns; agreement; use of verbs, phrases, clauses	_____		

USE OF LANGUAGE: Level of usage
     Idiomatic usage
     Vividness
	_____		Chapter 8

PUNCTUATION AND CAPITALIZATION and related graphics: Quotation marks	_____		Chapter 7
SPELLING:			
TOTAL	100		

Mechanics not in this text are assigned in supplementary text.

WRITING SAMPLE 7—EVALUATION

Write: (Select own *limited* subject) _____

_____

Length: optional _____

Required in Contents	Full	Earned	For Study
1. Limit subject	20		
2. Identify purpose (define, describe, analyze, argue) _____ _____	20		
3. Select clear controlling or central idea _____	20		
4. Assign point values only to the techniques you use: a. *concrete* vs abstract b. specific detail c. comparison d. contrast e. narrative style f. expository style g. other: _____	_____ _____ _____ _____ _____ _____ _____		
TOTAL	100		

Instructor's Comments:

ENGLISH MECHANICS: Instructor Assigns Values for Criteria

Content Areas	Full	Earned	For Study
ORGANIZATION: Introduction	_____		Chapter 13
Chronological Organization	_____		Chapter 15
Topical Organization	_____		Chapter 16
Rational Organization	_____		Chapter 17
Smooth Development	_____		Chapter 14
Termination	_____		Chapter 18
PARAGRAPHING: Introduction	_____		Page 163
Development (unity)	_____		Page 165
Development (coherence)	_____		Page 168
SENTENCES: completeness; variety; economy; use of modifiers; pronouns; agreement; use of verbs, phrases, clauses	_____		
USE OF LANGUAGE: Level of usage Idiomatic usage Vividness	_____		Chapter 8
PUNCTUATION AND CAPITALIZATION and related graphics: Quotation marks	_____		Chapter 7
SPELLING:			
TOTAL	100		

Mechanics not in this text are assigned in supplementary text.

WRITING SAMPLE 8—EVALUATION

Write a critical opinion of some aspect of James Baldwin's excerpt from *Another Country.*
Length: (select your own length)

Required in Contents	Full	Earned	For Study
1. Show a clear purpose for your criticism_____	25		
2. Make a clear statement of your controlling idea	25		
3. Give enough information about the selection so your reader can understand your comments	25		
4. Develop your controlling idea in concrete words and specific detail	25		
PROOFREAD YOUR WORK CAREFULLY!			

TOTAL   100

Instructor's Comments:

ENGLISH MECHANICS: Instructor Assigns Values for Criteria

Content Areas	Full	Earned	For Study
ORGANIZATION: Introduction	_____		Chapter 13
Chronological Organization	_____		Chapter 15
Topical Organization	_____		Chapter 16
Rational Organization	_____		Chapter 17
Smooth Development	_____		Chapter 14
Termination	_____		Chapter 18
PARAGRAPHING: Introduction	_____		Page 163
Development (unity)	_____		Page 165
Development (coherence)	_____		Page 168
SENTENCES: completeness; variety; economy; use of modifiers; pronouns; agreement; use of verbs, phrases, clauses	_____		
USE OF LANGUAGE: Level of usage Idiomatic usage Vividness	_____		Chapter 8
PUNCTUATION AND CAPITALIZATION and related graphics: Quotation marks	_____		Chapter 7
SPELLING:			

TOTAL   100

Mechanics not in this text are assigned in supplementary text.

WRITING SAMPLE 8—EVALUATION

Write a critical opinion of some aspect of James Baldwin's excerpt from *Another Country.*
Length: (select your own length)

Required in Contents	Full	Earned	For Study
1. Show a clear purpose for your criticism _____ _____	25		
2. Make a clear statement of your controlling idea	25		
3. Give enough information about the selection so your reader can understand your comments	25		
4. Develop your controlling idea in concrete words and specific detail	25		
PROOFREAD YOUR WORK CAREFULLY!			

TOTAL   100

Instructor's Comments:

ENGLISH MECHANICS: Instructor Assigns Values for Criteria

Content Areas	Full	Earned	For Study
ORGANIZATION: Introduction	_____		Chapter 13
Chronological Organization	_____		Chapter 15
Topical Organization	_____		Chapter 16
Rational Organization	_____		Chapter 17
Smooth Development	_____		Chapter 14
Termination	_____		Chapter 18
PARAGRAPHING: Introduction	_____		Page 163
Development (unity)	_____		Page 165
Development (coherence)	_____		Page 168
SENTENCES: completeness; variety; economy; use of modifiers; pronouns; agreement; use of verbs, phrases, clauses	_____		

USE OF LANGUAGE: Level of usage
      Idiomatic usage
      Vividness
	_____		Chapter 8

PUNCTUATION AND CAPITALIZATION and related graphics: Quotation marks	_____		Chapter 7
SPELLING:			

TOTAL   100

Mechanics not in this text are assigned in supplementary text.

EVALUATION SHEET FOR SUMMARY (SAMPLE 9)

Write a brief summary of an essay or story of your own choice.
Length: optional but related to the length of original

Required in Contents	Full	Earned	For Study
1. Make brief introductory description, including author, title, type of writing	15		
2. Give *typical* important details from the original	35		
3. Imitate organization of the original	15		
4. Adopt the same tone as the original	15		
5. Avoid expressing your own opinion	10		
6. Be as brief as possible	10		
PROOFREAD YOUR WORK CAREFULLY!	0		
TOTAL	100		

Instructor's Comments:

ENGLISH MECHANICS: Instructor Assigns Values for Criteria

Content Areas	Full	Earned	For Study
ORGANIZATION: Introduction	———		Chapter 13
Chronological Organization	———		Chapter 15
Topical Organization	———		Chapter 16
Rational Organization	———		Chapter 17
Smooth Development	———		Chapter 14
Termination	———		Chapter 18
PARAGRAPHING: Introduction	———		Page 163
Development (unity)	———		Page 165
Development (coherence)	———		Page 168
SENTENCES: completeness; variety; economy; use of modifiers; pronouns; agreement; use of verbs, phrases, clauses	———		
USE OF LANGUAGE: Level of usage Idiomatic usage Vividness	———		Chapter 8
PUNCTUATION AND CAPITALIZATION and related graphics: Quotation marks	———		Chapter 7
SPELLING:			
TOTAL	100		

Mechanics not in this text are assigned in supplementary text.

EVALUATION SHEET FOR SUMMARY (SAMPLE 9)

Write a brief summary of an essay or story of your own choice.
Length: optional but related to the length of original

Required in Contents	Full	Earned	For Study
1. Make brief introductory description, including author, title, type of writing	15		
2. Give *typical* important details from the original	35		
3. Imitate organization of the original	15		
4. Adopt the same tone as the original	15		
5. Avoid expressing your own opinion	10		
6. Be as brief as possible	10		
PROOFREAD YOUR WORK CAREFULLY!	0		
TOTAL	100		

Instructor's Comments:

ENGLISH MECHANICS: Instructor Assigns Values for Criteria

Content Areas	Full	Earned	For Study
ORGANIZATION: Introduction	_____		Chapter 13
Chronological Organization	_____		Chapter 15
Topical Organization	_____		Chapter 16
Rational Organization	_____		Chapter 17
Smooth Development	_____		Chapter 14
Termination	_____		Chapter 18
PARAGRAPHING: Introduction	_____		Page 163
Development (unity)	_____		Page 165
Development (coherence)	_____		Page 168
SENTENCES: completeness; variety; economy; use of modifiers; pronouns; agreement; use of verbs, phrases, clauses	_____		
USE OF LANGUAGE: Level of usage Idiomatic usage Vividness	_____		Chapter 8
PUNCTUATION AND CAPITALIZATION and related graphics: Quotation marks	_____		Chapter 7
SPELLING:			
TOTAL	100		

Mechanics not in this text are assigned in supplementary text.

EVALUATION SHEET FOR THEME (SAMPLE 10)

Write a statement of the theme of an essay or story of your own choice. Support your selection of theme by making reference to the original work.

Length: optional but be as brief as possible

Required in Contents	Full	Earned	For Study
1. Make a brief introductory description, including author, title, type of writing	30		
2. State the theme as clearly and specifically as possible	30		
3. Present specific evidence from the original to support your selection of the theme. Be certain you show a clear connection between the theme and the evidence you give.	30		
4. Avoid expressing your own opinion	10		
PROOFREAD YOUR WORK CAREFULLY!	0		
TOTAL	100		

Instructor's Comments:

ENGLISH MECHANICS: Instructor Assigns Values for Criteria

Content Areas	Full	Earned	For Study
ORGANIZATION: Introduction Chronological Organization Topical Organization Rational Organization Smooth Development Termination	—— —— —— —— —— ——		Chapter 13 Chapter 15 Chapter 16 Chapter 17 Chapter 14 Chapter 18
PARAGRAPHING: Introduction Development (unity) Development (coherence)	—— —— ——		Page 163 Page 165 Page 168
SENTENCES: completeness; variety; economy; use of modifiers; pronouns; agreement; use of verbs, phrases, clauses	——		
USE OF LANGUAGE: Level of usage Idiomatic usage Vividness	——		Chapter 8
PUNCTUATION AND CAPITALIZATION and related graphics: Quotation marks	——		Chapter 7
SPELLING:			
TOTAL	100		

Mechanics not in this text are assigned in supplementary text.

EVALUATION SHEET FOR THEME (SAMPLE 10)

Write a statement of the theme of an essay or story of your own choice. Support your selection of theme by making reference to the original work.

Length: optional but be as brief as possible

Required in Contents	Full	Earned	For Study
1. Make a brief introductory description, including author, title, type of writing	30		
2. State the theme as clearly and specifically as possible	30		
3. Present specific evidence from the original to support your selection of the theme. Be certain you show a clear connection between the theme and the evidence you give.	30		
4. Avoid expressing your own opinion	10		
PROOFREAD YOUR WORK CAREFULLY!	0		
TOTAL	100		

Instructor's Comments:

ENGLISH MECHANICS: Instructor Assigns Values for Criteria

Content Areas	Full	Earned	For Study
ORGANIZATION: Introduction Chronological Organization Topical Organization Rational Organization Smooth Development Termination	——— ——— ——— ——— ——— ———		Chapter 13 Chapter 15 Chapter 16 Chapter 17 Chapter 14 Chapter 18
PARAGRAPHING: Introduction Development (unity) Development (coherence)	——— ——— ———		Page 163 Page 165 Page 168
SENTENCES: completeness; variety; economy; use of modifiers; pronouns; agreement; use of verbs, phrases, clauses	———		
USE OF LANGUAGE: Level of usage Idiomatic usage Vividness	———		Chapter 8
PUNCTUATION AND CAPITALIZATION and related graphics: Quotation marks	———		Chapter 7
SPELLING:			
TOTAL	100		

Mechanics not in this text are assigned in supplementary text.

EVALUATION SHEET FOR CRITICAL OPINION (SAMPLE 11)

Write a critical opinion of some aspect of an essay or story of your own choice.
Length: optional but be as brief as possible

Required in Contents	Full	Earned	For Study
1. Make a brief introductory description, including author, title, type of writing	20		
2. Identify clearly and specifically the aspect of the story you intend to criticize	20		
3. Give enough information about the work so your reader can understand your comments	20		
4. Develop your controlling idea (the aspect you selected to criticize) in concrete words and specific detail	20		
5. Support your ideas with facts and/or reasons	20		
PROOFREAD YOUR WORK CAREFULLY!	0		
TOTAL	100		

Instructor's Comments:

ENGLISH MECHANICS: Instructor Assigns Values for Criteria

Content Areas	Full	Earned	For Study
ORGANIZATION: Introduction	———		Chapter 13
Chronological Organization	———		Chapter 15
Topical Organization	———		Chapter 16
Rational Organization	———		Chapter 17
Smooth Development	———		Chapter 14
Termination	———		Chapter 18
PARAGRAPHING: Introduction	———		Page 163
Development (unity)	———		Page 165
Development (coherence)	———		Page 168
SENTENCES: completeness; variety; economy; use of modifiers; pronouns; agreement; use of verbs, phrases, clauses	———		
USE OF LANGUAGE: Level of usage / Idiomatic usage / Vividness	———		Chapter 8
PUNCTUATION AND CAPITALIZATION and related graphics: Quotation marks	———		Chapter 7
SPELLING:			
TOTAL	100		

Mechanics not in this text are assigned in supplementary text.

EVALUATION SHEET FOR CRITICAL OPINION (SAMPLE 11)

Write a critical opinion of some aspect of an essay or story of your own choice.
Length: optional but be as brief as possible

Required in Contents	Full	Earned	For Study
1. Make a brief introductory description, including author, title, type of writing	20		
2. Identify clearly and specifically the aspect of the story you intend to criticize	20		
3. Give enough information about the work so your reader can understand your comments	20		
4. Develop your controlling idea (the aspect you selected to criticize) in concrete words and specific detail	20		
5. Support your ideas with facts and/or reasons	20		
PROOFREAD YOUR WORK CAREFULLY!	0		
TOTAL	100		

Instructor's Comments:

ENGLISH MECHANICS: Instructor Assigns Values for Criteria

Content Areas	Full	Earned	For Study
ORGANIZATION: Introduction	———		Chapter 13
Chronological Organization	———		Chapter 15
Topical Organization	———		Chapter 16
Rational Organization	———		Chapter 17
Smooth Development	———		Chapter 14
Termination	———		Chapter 18
PARAGRAPHING: Introduction	———		Page 163
Development (unity)	———		Page 165
Development (coherence)	———		Page 168
SENTENCES: completeness; variety; economy; use of modifiers; pronouns; agreement; use of verbs, phrases, clauses	———		
USE OF LANGUAGE: Level of usage / Idiomatic usage / Vividness	———		Chapter 8
PUNCTUATION AND CAPITALIZATION and related graphics: Quotation marks	———		Chapter 7
SPELLING:			
TOTAL	100		

Mechanics not in this text are assigned in supplementary text.

WRITING SAMPLE 12—EVALUATION

Write an outline of any one of the essays in this text which you have read.
Length: be as brief as possible

Required in Contents	Full	Earned	For Study

1. Use correct format
  a. main headings (Roman)
  b. subheadings (Capitals)
  c. related items (Arabic)
  d. minor items (Lower case)
  e. further breakdowns (Arabic and Lower case in parentheses)
	20		Chapter 19

2. Introductory controlling idea	20		Chapter 19
3. Place various headings and other elements in parallel structure *in groups of 2 or more*	20		Chapter 19
4. Select appropriate topics to outline the essay	20		Chapter 19
5. Set comparable ideas on the same *level* of importance	20		Chapter 19
PROOFREAD YOUR WORK CAREFULLY!	0		
TOTAL	100		

Instructor's Comments:

ENGLISH MECHANICS: Instructor Assigns Values for Criteria

Content Areas	Full	Earned	For Study
ORGANIZATION: Introduction Chronological Organization Topical Organization Rational Organization Smooth Development Termination	—— —— —— —— —— ——		Chapter 13 Chapter 15 Chapter 16 Chapter 17 Chapter 14 Chapter 18
PARAGRAPHING: Introduction Development (unity) Development (coherence)	—— —— ——		*Note: ordinary mechanics not applicable if fragment is used, except spelling and punctuation*
SENTENCES: completeness; variety; economy; use of modifiers; pronouns; agreement; use of verbs, phrases, clauses	——		
USE OF LANGUAGE: Level of usage Idiomatic usage Vividness	——		
PUNCTUATION AND CAPITALIZATION and related graphics: Quotation marks	——		
SPELLING:			
TOTAL	100		

Mechanics not in this text are assigned in supplementary text.

WRITING SAMPLE 12—EVALUATION

Write an outline of any one of the essays in this text which you have read.
Length: be as brief as possible

Required in Contents	Full	Earned	For Study

1. Use correct format
   a. main headings (Roman)
   b. subheadings (Capitals)
   c. related items (Arabic)
   d. minor items (Lower case)
   e. further breakdowns (Arabic and Lower case in parentheses)
	20		Chapter 19

2. Introductory controlling idea	20		Chapter 19
3. Place various headings and other elements in parallel structure *in groups of 2 or more*	20		Chapter 19
4. Select appropriate topics to outline the essay	20		Chapter 19
5. Set comparable ideas on the same *level* of importance	20		Chapter 19
PROOFREAD YOUR WORK CAREFULLY!	0		
TOTAL	100		

Instructor's Comments:

ENGLISH MECHANICS: Instructor Assigns Values for Criteria

Content Areas	Full	Earned	For Study

ORGANIZATION: Introduction
   Chronological Organization
   Topical Organization
   Rational Organization
   Smooth Development
   Termination
	_____
	_____
	_____
	_____
	_____
	_____
			Chapter 13
			Chapter 15
			Chapter 16
			Chapter 17
			Chapter 14
			Chapter 18

PARAGRAPHING: Introduction
   Development (unity)
   Development (coherence)
	_____
	_____
	_____
			Note: ordinary mechanics not applicable if fragment outline is used, except spelling and punctuation

SENTENCES: completeness; variety; economy; use of modifiers; pronouns; agreement; use of verbs, phrases, clauses	_____		

USE OF LANGUAGE: Level of usage
   Idiomatic usage
   Vividness
	_____		

PUNCTUATION AND CAPITALIZATION and related graphics: Quotation marks	_____		
SPELLING:			
TOTAL	100		

Mechanics not in this text are assigned in supplementary text.

WRITING SAMPLE—CRITICAL REPORT

Write a critical report on *The Answer.* Include summary of plot, setting, theme, characterization, and your opinion.

Length: optional but be as brief as you can

Required in Contents	Full	Earned	For Study
1. Give clear introduction to identify the author, the work and your central idea	20		
2. Summarize plot so the reader understands what the book is about	20		
3. Identify the theme and prove your conclusion	20		
4. Analyze characterization	20		
5. Express a critical opinion which is well-supported by facts and/or reasons	20		
NOTE: You do not need to arrange your paper in the same order as the criteria. Be as original as you wish but deal with all of the elements listed.			

TOTAL   100

Instructor's Comments:

ENGLISH MECHANICS: Instructor Assigns Values for Criteria

Content Areas	Full	Earned	For Study
ORGANIZATION: Introduction	———		Chapter 13
Chronological Organization	———		Chapter 15
Topical Organization	———		Chapter 16
Rational Organization	———		Chapter 17
Smooth Development	———		Chapter 14
Termination	———		Chapter 18
PARAGRAPHING: Introduction	———		Page 163
Development (unity)	———		Page 165
Development (coherence)	———		Page 168
SENTENCES: completeness; variety; economy; use of modifers; pronouns; agreement; use of verbs, phrases, clauses	———		
USE OF LANGUAGE: Level of usage Idiomatic usage Vividness	———		Chapter 8
PUNCTUATION AND CAPITALIZATION and related graphics: Quotation marks	———		Chapter 7
SPELLING:			

TOTAL   100

Mechanics not in this text are assigned in supplementary text.

WRITING SAMPLE—CRITICAL REPORT

Write a critical report on *The Answer.* Include summary of plot, setting, theme, characterization, and your opinion.

Length: optional but be as brief as you can

Required in Contents	Full	Earned	For Study
1. Give clear introduction to identify the author, the work and your central idea	20		
2. Summarize plot so the reader understands what the book is about	20		
3. Identify the theme and prove your conclusion	20		
4. Analyze characterization	20		
5. Express a critical opinion which is well-supported by facts and/or reasons	20		
NOTE: You do not need to arrange your paper in the same order as the criteria. Be as original as you wish but deal with all of the elements listed.			

TOTAL   100

Instructor's Comments:

ENGLISH MECHANICS: Instructor Assigns Values for Criteria

Content Areas	Full	Earned	For Study
ORGANIZATION: Introduction	_____		Chapter 13
Chronological Organization	_____		Chapter 15
Topical Organization	_____		Chapter 16
Rational Organization	_____		Chapter 17
Smooth Development	_____		Chapter 14
Termination	_____		Chapter 18
PARAGRAPHING: Introduction	_____		Page 163
Development (unity)	_____		Page 165
Development (coherence)	_____		Page 168
SENTENCES: completeness; variety; economy; use of modifers; pronouns; agreement; use of verbs, phrases, clauses	_____		
USE OF LANGUAGE: Level of usage Idiomatic usage Vividness	_____		Chapter 8
PUNCTUATION AND CAPITALIZATION and related graphics: Quotation marks	_____		Chapter 7
SPELLING:			

TOTAL   100

Mechanics not in this text are assigned in supplementary text.

INDEX